The Causes of Wealth

THE CAUSES

OF

WEALTH

By Jean Fourastié

Translated and Edited by
Theodore Caplow

The Free Press of Glencoe, Illinois

This book is the American edition, revised, adapted, and supplemented, of *Machinisme et Bien-Être,* published by Editions de Minuit, Paris, in the collection "L'homme et la Machine," directed by Georges Friedmann. Copyright by Editions de Minuit, Paris.

Contents

CHAPTER   PAGE

Editor's Introduction 7

Introduction 13

PART ONE: THE LEVEL OF LIVING

I   Wages and Purchasing Power in France . . . 25

II   General Indicators of the Level of Living . . . 59

III   The Level of Living in the World 100

IV   Level of Living and the Productivity of Work . . 118

PART TWO: STYLE OF LIFE

V   Occupational Factors,
Duration of Work, Education 159

VI   Individual and Family Factors 182

VII   Health and Life Expectancy 215

Appendix 233

Index 235

EDITOR'S INTRODUCTION

WHEN I first read this book, soon after its original publication in 1951, I was struck by the wealth of new fact and new theory in its pages. Today, after many readings, my admiration for Professor Fourastié's almost single-handed attempt to create a new specialty on the borderline between economics and sociology has not diminished but grown. I still find it difficult to believe, as I follow his forceful exposition of the relationship between price trends and the distribution of the labor force or his history of the place of bread in the budget of the average family, that topics of such overwhelming importance scarcely have been discussed by social scientists in this century so obsessed with social problems.

There are some other modern writers, of course, who have given poverty and wealth their due place in the social panorama. Fourastié himself acknowledges his debt to Colin Clark, whose *Conditions of Economic Progress* constitutes a parallel exploration of neglected territory. Such recent works as Josué De Castro's *Geography of Hunger* and Fred Cottrell's *Energy and Society* analyze the material progress that the more favored portion of humanity has made in the past few generations and the inequalities that this same progress has introduced into the world. Each of these four authors finds it difficult to explain or understand the indifference of other scholars to the ordinary living conditions of mankind. Fourastié, speaking of famine in former centuries, comments that "horrible episodes which brought the death of one out of five living beings are passed by in silence while every detail is given about the marriage of the Dauphin."

Years ago, F. Stuart Chapin established a course at the University of Minnesota on "Social Aspects of Housing and Standards of Living," which I took over from him towards his retirement. It was while seeking a textbook for this course that I first encountered *Machinisme et Bien-Être*. Anyone who examines the literature on this double-jointed subject will find himself confronted with an enormous mass of material on housing and only a handful of scattered works on the standard of living, which is certainly more significant. Incidentally, at the first class meeting of each term, the students were routinely asked a naïve question which ran as follows: "Who are happier, other things being equal, the rich or the poor?" Again and again the students answered in the same fashion. A majority of each class said that the poor were happier, a minority were undecided or thought the question illogical. A few deviants believed the rich to be more satisfied.

This attitude is not easy to explain, but it is very widespread. The problems associated with technical progress lead us to doubt its plainest manifestations. Our author puts this eloquently in his concluding chapter when he writes that "a man who, two centuries ago, would not even have learned to read—if he had survived to maturity—profits by his windows, the central heating of his apartment, and the 300,000 copies of the newspaper for which he writes, announcing that humanity has arrived at the last stage of barbarism." There was more to the reaction of my students than this, however. Unlike the French humanist, encouraged to a vigorous pessimism by every tradition of his milieu, these adolescents from prairie farms and suburbs in the American Midwest, were not disposed to question the concept of progress. What they expressed was rather a complex puritanism which insists that worldly goods are incapable of providing the satisfactions for which we seek them.

This is not the place to explore the tangled skein of symbols surrounding production and consumption. We do not really need to do so. The brute facts of hunger and plenty, comfort and want, wealth and poverty, convertibles and handcarts, are sufficiently salient to claim our attention regardless of the exact priority we place upon them. Yet it is curious how a stubborn faith in the moral superiority of low incomes over high still flourishes in the American environment which Fourastié so much admires, and which he repeatedly presents as a model to the French.

I would remind the American reader who cannot entirely accept Fourastié's idealization of our way of life, to remember that he is preaching to his countrymen and not to us, however much we may learn by overhearing the sermon. His works—in the best tradition of some of the great Frenchmen whom he quotes—Vauban, Voltaire, Villermé—are directed to the major problems of his own era. They are not intended to amuse scholars but to persuade a nation. Their scientific quality develops because the author has chosen, as his best means of persuasion, the weapons of the positivist tradition—empirical data and experimental induction.

The empirical data alone would assure this book a notable place in the social scientist's library. The author's far-ranging curiosity leads him to a wide variety of unusual facts that would be fascinating even if they did not serve to illustrate a theory. Thus, the reader is likely to remember the history of window glass based on the paintings of the old masters, the explanation of why silk stockings with runs are repaired in Paris but thrown away in New York, the pious and pathetic tale of little Francinet, the apprentice weaver, the statistics of sewer connections, the comparative history of barbershop prices, and the wonderful parable of the Maharaja and the 100,000 Hindus. I am sure that Fourastié is more interested in instruction than entertainment, but his technique of taking the commonplaces of daily life and showing them to be essential indexes of the progress of civilization has something very attractive about it.

In much the same way, it is a temptation to evaluate his theoretical contributions by their inherent interest rather than their theoretical importance. The closing of the fan of salaries, for example, and the inexorable equalization of working conditions between the cabinet minister and the office boy, has seldom been discussed and has not previously, so far as I know, been explained. The influence of scientific progress on productivity and the direct association of productivity with the distribution of the labor force has been hinted at elsewhere in general terms, but never before described with such precision and detail. Fourastié's method of converting money prices into hourly wage units of the same time and place is not new, but the use he makes of this measurement to discriminate among commodities unequally affected by technical progress is an

altogether remarkable accomplishment. The reader is likely
to find that once he has grasped this idea he can never let it
loose. There are very few devices in all of social science which
serve to explain as many different events and to solve as many
of the puzzles of common sense, as does this very simple trick
of expressing a price in terms of a laborer's local wages for
purposes of comparison with other prices. Whether the general
hypothesis that all price trends can be explained in terms of the
degree of technical progress in the production of particular
commodities has been verified here, a sociological critic can
hardly presume to say. There is much need for further analysis
on many of these matters. For example, I cannot fully accept
the idea that with a shift of the labor force toward tertiary
employments there is an end to the steady reduction in the
length of the work day and the work year. The accumulating
evidence seems to suggest instead that such activities as teaching and healing can also be modified by the division of labor.

Indeed, there are many specific points in which there is
room for further discussion. Fourastié's explanation of economic progress is essentially linear, if not monistic. Scientific
discovery leads to invention which leads to changing methods
of production, redistribution of the labor force, changes in
consumption, and, finally, modification of the style of life.
There remains, of course, the question as to why scientific
discoveries are unequally utilized in different countries. There
is also the determinism of energy resources, which Cottrell
has explained so well. There is the influence of the fiscal
machinery, to which many economists assign a central place
in technical progress. All of these questions remain to be
resolved and will undoubtedly be resolved in good time. But
we already owe to Fourastié, still in mid-career, the major
achievements of revolutionizing the study of poverty and
wealth and converting budget analysis from one of the dullest
specialties in the social sciences to one of the most promising.

Readers of the French edition were warned in a footnote
that the original work was based upon the stenographic tran-
script of a series of lectures and could "make no claim to
literary elegance." The same caveat must be repeated with increased emphasis for this translation. Readers of the original

edition were also urged to seek out the author's other books
and articles, in which many of the ideas introduced here became more fully developed. A list of these works will be found
in the Appendix.

A good many changes from the French edition have been
introduced, some by the author, some by the editor. As far
as possible, tables and statistics have been brought up to date,
and a number of new tables have been added. On the other
hand, documentation to local archives and to some other biblio-
graphical material not readily accessible to American students
has been omitted. In the interests of coherence, tables and
charts are renumbered. Chapter VI, on Style of Life, has been
extensively amended to make it more meaningful for the
reader unfamiliar with the details of the French household.
The author's afterthoughts and the editor's suggestions have
been incorporated into the text as convenience dictated.

The errors of transcription or of fact which the volume contains may be chargeable to either the author or the editor or
to both. Errors of translation, of course, are my responsibility
alone.

Thanks are due to Professor Georges Friedmann who spon-
sored the original work and whose wise comments facilitated
the translation; to Barbara Caplow, who spent long hours
translating notes and verifying such details as the definition
of *millet* and the value of the *livre tournois;* to Barbara Nel-
son and Patricia James for competent and painstaking assist-
ance with the several drafts of the manuscript; and to the
editors of The Free Press for their patience and laissez faire.

T. C.
Minneapolis

The Causes of Wealth

INTRODUCTION

MAN is beginning to understand the first consequences of the industrial revolution. In the course of the
nineteenth century, he was satisfied with very vague forecasts
of a predominantly emotional character: euphoric faith in a
science that was going to be able to resolve all problems; fear
of, or desire for, a social revolution; contempt for the previous
centuries of irrational obscurantism—such were the essential
elements of a summary and largely utopian philosophy.

It was by observing the conditions imposed upon the worker
at work that the scientific study of the influence of technical
progress upon human life began. This study was by no means
disinterested. Its object was to facilitate production and to
increase industrial profits. It was only after twenty years or so
that a more objective study of man at work began to establish
the bases of a new science, "A veritable conglomeration of
techniques," as Georges Friedmann calls it.[1]

However, the most important part of the problem presented
by the development of industrial techniques has for all practical purposes not yet been raised. It concerns the consequences
of *machinisme*,* not so much for man at work, but for man
outside of his work. Technical progress, indeed, does not only
modify the conditions of work. It transforms the results of
work, and therefore the facts of economic life. These, in turn,
transform human life.

Until now, the study of this problem, so important for humanity, has been the sole preserve of novelists. About 1925,
Toynbee and Spengler advanced the general idea that the decline of civilizations was incontestable and unavoidable.[2] Many

---

* The French word *machinisme* has no precise English equivalent, and
therefore has not been translated in many places throughout the book. *Machinisme* includes not only the technical fact of mechanization, but its sociological implications as well. T.C.

writers, novelists or philosophers, developed a romantic version
of this idea, above all in Europe. Paul Valéry wrote the sentence
which every French student knows by heart, "We know that
our civilizations are mortal." Georges Duhamel reinforced the
classic pessimism of the French bourgeois with his "Scènes de
la vie future." Aldous Huxley has treated certain tendencies to
automatism in his witty and spirited *Brave New World*.

Our object is to proceed to a first approach to the problem
on the scientific level, in other words, to take account of the
empirical data that have accumulated in the last hundred years
and of those facts that have both a serious importance for the
human equilibrium and unquestionable reality. We shall study
how *machinisme* modifies the traditional conditions of existence
directly through occupational life and indirectly through economic life. We shall also examine how *machinisme* may lead
to an occupational and economic development that deserves
to be called social progress.

Although our program may be ambitious, we are not ap-
proaching the human problem in its total complexity. The
object of study is limited to the material conditions of life in
society. That is to say, to the problems which are classically
economic problems—the relations of men with things.

The idea of human equilibrium involves many other factors
beside economic factors. To get an idea of the evolution of
civilization, it would be necessary to study organic equilibrium
(health), affective equilibrium (happiness), intellectual equilibrium (intelligence), moral and religious equilibrium, the
awareness of the future, the place of the immediate present in
the evolution of man and humanity, and above all, social and
political equilibrium (inter-human relations). Such an examination of the living conditions of "the total man" exceeds the
limits of this work. Nevertheless, it is certain that familiarity
with economic conditions is an indispensable part of the study
of the situation imposed upon man by the modern world. Economic conditions have an important influence on the total
equilibrium; for example, it is very difficult to speak of intellectual life in the case of a population whose level of living
does not permit intermediate education for any sizable fraction of the population. The moral life is meaningless for a
man pressed by hunger.

It would seem then that the study of the material conditions of human life in the contemporary world would be one of the essential foundations of the history of civilization. We hope that this sketch of the economic history of technical progress, in spite of its gaps and defects, will possibly be useful to the general historian for whom economics and technology are only aspects of a complex ensemble which is primarily social and political.

The effects of *machinisme* on the general conditions of economic life have been obvious. They have resulted, in the first place, in the growth of the volume of production, and in the second place, in the creation of products that did not exist before or that were formerly very rare. As a matter of fact, until the industrial revolution, practically all production consisted of food staples; eight-tenths of the labor force worked at production of this type. All other consumption goods, furniture, cloth, works of art, means of locomotion, arms, and so forth, were the privilege of the minority who controlled the means of production (that is to say, the land and, until the abolition of serfdom, labor). Such goods were produced in very limited quantity and they were extremely rare, and contrary to the usual notion, they were highly priced. The luxury which the possession of the most powerful model of automobile represents nowadays for an American, or even for a Frenchman, is very far from the equivalent of that involved in 1700 with the presence of a mirror two meters square over the mantelpiece of a reception room in a mansion of the Marais.

Technical progress permitted the liberation of a more and more important part of the labor force from agricultural labor, giving this labor force, on the one hand, the opportunity to produce other goods in growing quantity, and on the other hand, the means of lowering selling prices. Not only have famines—organic elements of the traditional cycle whose tragic reality is easily forgotten—practically disappeared in the countries which have benefitted from industrial progress, but also, for an increasing proportion of the population, expenses for food have ceased to be dominant, and have little by little made place for other needs. To illustrate this fact, a single example may suffice: Before 1800, agricultural production represented about 80 per cent of the total production of the richest nations of the globe. After 1940, however, in the United States, agricultural production represented less than 10 per cent of the total dollar value of production. It must be noted that this change in proportion was not obtained by a reduction in the absolute volume of agricultural production per capita of the population; on the contrary, the latter has grown constantly; it is by an even greater relative increase of non-agricultural production that the relative position of agriculture has thus diminished, and the structure of consumption has been correspondingly modified.

This profound modification of traditional economic structures did not come about without difficulty and even suffering. Painful gaps occurred between the real and the desirable; economic depressions were the most obvious expressions of this lack of harmony. The fact that we record economic progress following technical progress need not be viewed as an apologetic argument in favor of the economic, social, juridical, or political regimes. On the contrary, it must be observed that progress was made not because of, but in spite of, the preservation of certain institutions. This is why it has been more rapid in the United States than in Europe and more rapid in Europe than in Asia. Europe, and France particularly, provide a favorable vantage from which to observe the long-term developments. Traces of the past are more conspicuous than in the United States, and they are of a richer past, so that one sees better than in America how the new ways of life have displaced the old. The very slowness of progress is favorable for observation, and permits us to avoid certain errors of excessive enthusiasm.

The gap between the real and the possible, probably rather negligible before 1700, increases steadily before our very eyes.

Thus humanity, having lost the equilibrium of former centuries, pursues an equilibrium that becomes ever more remote, just because of previous gains. This period is profoundly demoralizing; it is easy for European people to draw pessimistic conclusions from the observation of present conditions. Because man is increasingly dissatisfied as he watches his opportunities increase, because he judges matters in terms of a past whose real conditions he has forgotten, he is tempted to misinterpret the progress already made and to misunderstand its conditions. It is these results and these conditions that we wish to analyze. It is for others to say if, from an intellectual or moral point of view, humanity has gained or lost. On a purely material basis, that of economics, let us try merely to prepare an exact accounting.

One more general remark is necessary to define the scope of our inquiries. M. Friedmann and I have given this work the title of *Machinisme et Bien-Être,* in order to emphasize the two most concrete elements of the economic problems presented by the industrial revolution. The word *machinisme* is taken here in its broadest sense to refer to the totality of technical procedures in production, consumption, and distribution. Among these procedures, the use of machines is the most striking; but it is more and more evident that the machine is only one of the possible means of advancement. Just as capital is not the cause of economic progress, so the machine is not the cause of technical progress. The true cause of technical progress is the scientific advance which furnishes the active possibility of producing an increasingly greater amount of goods and services in a given amount of working time. The machine is only one of the means of increasing this productivity. In fact, it becomes more apparent every day that other methods are claiming an increasing importance in economic life. These include the organization of work, the organization of markets, the design of the product, the technical control of material in process, psychology, applied psychology, sociometry, and all of the other applications of the new human sciences to work.

Thus, in the title of this work, the word *machinisme* could be legitimately replaced by such terms as technical progress, organization of labor, or productivity of work.

In the same way, the word "welfare"* is schematic, because the economic transformations of the modern world often involve problems that did not exist formerly, for example, in connection with housing. In sum, our object is to study the evolution of the material conditions imposed upon men by economic evolution, without regard to their favorableness.

The human consequences of contemporary economic evolution can be grouped into two orders of fact: *level of living* and *style of life.*

"Level of living" is a measure of the consumption of all

---

* *Bien-être.*

goods and services that can be valued in money, that is to say, those obtained with salaries and other money which constitutes "purchasing power."

Studies of the level of living involve the comparison of income with the price of a group of consumed goods. They lead to the examination of the structure of expenditure. The structure of expenditure is not at all the same in the working class and in the employer class. In the poorer classes, expenses for food have a predominant place. They absorb practically the entire income. For the comfortably situated consumers, the proportion of food expenses is much less. This same disproportion of budgets can be found from one period to another, as, for example, between the working class consumption for 1700 or 1800 and the budgets of today. The historical development and the contemporary variation are phenomena that must be studied together and that are mutually illuminating.

Taking account of the differential structure of budgets, the level of living can be measured, at least approximately, and with suitable precautions and reservations, by a single figure expressed in a given monetary unit and referring to a specific date. Thus the level of living is a "synthesizable" element.

In contrast, we group under the term "style of life" those areas of consumption where a monetary evaluation is difficult and rather futile, as, for example, when there is such a difference between the price of the service and its importance for the purchaser that the price loses all significance. The case of penicillin is relevant. It is obvious that penicillin has a price, but in certain cases a small dose of it can prevent the death of a human being. The price of penicillin is practically useless for evaluating the advantage conferred by its discovery.

The sphere of the style of life extends thus from hygiene and prosthetic devices all the way to leisure—the length of the working day. It includes a whole series of non-quantifiable elements like climate, housing, neighborhood and urban facilities, heating and air conditioning, what we call comfort, the domestic arts, the use of elevators; even intellectual equipment such as libraries, research centers, record and film collections. The style of life includes a very numerous and heterogeneous array of facts. It is impossible to combine them for analysis. To bring them into the picture at all, we must therefore rather arbitrarily select a certain number of factors for examination. The field being so vast and practically unexplored, our study will have—much more than for the level of living—the character of an outline. On some points we shall be reduced to simple inventories and hasty samplings.

The reader should then consider this book as an introduction to a body of fascinating but complex data. It is to be hoped that this essay will lead him to the study of other books and stimulate concrete research that will progressively renovate the social sciences and give to man a more and more solid grasp of the realities of the physical world.*

---

* The author would like to express his appreciation to at least a few of the English-speaking authors whose research has helped or stimulated his own: A. L. Bowley, Dorothy Brady, Yale Brozen, Colin Clark, Shepard B. Clough, Frederic Dewhurst, Allan B. Fisher, Siegfried Giedion, J. R. Hicks, Lewis Mumford, John U. Nef, J. E. Thurold Rogers, P. A. Sorokin, William F. Ogburn, Faith Williams, and Carle C. Zimmerman. He would also like to mention the very worthwhile Conference on Quantitative Description of Technical Change which he had the honor to attend in April, 1951, at Princeton.

Special acknowledgment is due to Allan B. Fisher for his book, *The Clash of Progress and Security,* published as early as 1935. Among the critical appraisals of the viewpoint which the present book embodies, are those of Pierre Jaccard of the University of Lausanne, *Politique de l'Emploi et de l'Education* (Paris: Payot, 1957), and Martin Wolfe, "The Concept of Economic Sectors," *Quarterly Journal of Economics,* August, 1955.

PART ONE

The Level of Living

THE THREE most conspicuous economic phenomena of the modern world are the depopulation of the countryside, the so-called crises of overproduction, and the profound differences in level of living from one country to another. Of these three phenomena, the third is doubtless the most important, because it summarizes the principal features of economic life for the individual.

In a secular society, the essential purpose of political action is the improvement of the level of living of the citizens. It is therefore astonishing that the central problem of modern collectivities has not been scientifically studied to a greater extent. In this area, as in many others, there is yet no scientific body of knowledge. It is just beginning to appear, and its continuity, dependent upon the efforts of a few isolated individuals, is by no means assured. Strikingly enough, the first efforts to create a science of the level of living go back more than two centuries to the *Dîme Royale* of Vauban. Continued by Arthur Young, Levasseur, and Villermé, the tradition of objective studies on the level of living has never completely disappeared from economic literature. Nevertheless, it has never been able to develop into a coherent and continuous whole. At the present time, the problem of the level of living still appears almost unexplored. Sporadic observations, picturesque anecdotes, some hasty generalizations, some radical errors, certain blind indifferences, political biases and class prejudices confuse and obscure problems which are already very complex in themselves.

The level of living is essentially the relationship between a money income and the cost of goods consumed. There are considerable uncertainties associated with both the numerator and the denominator of this ratio. First of all, it is very difficult to determine the income of a population. Disparities can be very important, not only from place to place in the same country, but also from one profession to another. Certain categories of income like profits, fees, rents, and interest are almost impossible to establish statistically. Wages themselves can vary appreciably, not only between occupational categories, but between enterprises. It is only for relatively recent years that we have any usable statistics of average wages, by occupation and by industry.

There are even more difficult problems involved in getting a true picture of consumption. The structure of consumption varies considerably with people, places, and above all, with time. The very notion of "minimum subsistence" varies from the simple to the complex, as we shall see further on.

The statistical study of the level of living implies, therefore, a careful objectivity and a minute attention to detail that has probably discouraged many economists. It is more agreeable for the intellect to work on such great principles as general equilibrium, or marginal utility, or the investment multiplier, than to note minutely the nature of consumption in the working class suburbs of the great cities.

Moreover, to sketch the history of the level of living of a people, the French for example, we have hardly more than fragments of data to be critically scrutinized. Most of our contemporaries, having read the accounts of banquets under Louis XIV, think that their ancestors were not willing to sit down to table unless they were presented with a six course meal. At the other extreme is the chronicler who declares the country deserted because he finds no carts on the national highway of the period.

The most important reason why we know so little about the level of living of our ancestors, even the closest of them, is that the level of living is merely the economic version of the most banal aspects of ordinary life. The natural tendency of the historian or the chronicler is to describe those events that escape the daily routine and which strike the observer, as they strike the mass of people, by their unusual character. This explains why so many books, wherein we would like to find simple information on the budget of workmen or bourgeois, on their furniture or their food, speak only of tragic events, of wars, murders and rapes, or at most, of sensational banquets, of fêtes or of princely marriages.*

Under these circumstances, and as has been previously said, the present study cannot be more than a sketch. It cannot be denied, however, that certain essential results have already been verified. Enough of the old chronicles and old texts have recently been published so that the general outline of the material situation of the average Frenchman in the course of the last three centuries can now be seen quite clearly. One can try, if not to resolve the essential problems of the level of living, at least to bring together a certain number of the elements indispensable to that task.

The essential problems of the level of living can be reduced to two: Can the disparity that is presently observed between the average levels of living in different countries be explained by an evolution through time? What are the causes of this evolution through time? An answer to these two questions would necessarily give some information about the feasibility of raising the level of living of any population.

This part of the study will be divided into four chapters. The first two chapters present a sketch of the history of the level of living of Western nations for the past two or three centuries. This sketch will be based on the presently available documents concerning a single great country, France, taken as a typical example of such evolution. The third chapter will

---

* It is for similar reasons that our contemporary science of the style of life begins with prehistory. Science is born of curiosity and an essentially naïve approach. It is only with the progress of time that it becomes self-conscious and aspires to utility, that is to say, to be applied.

discuss recent comparisons of average levels of living in different countries. The contemporary measurements have a clearly more ambitious character than the older studies. They tend, indeed, to go beyond *examples* of the average level of living, and to give directly the averages of the national level of living. They rest upon advanced statistical methods.

In the fourth chapter, we shall try to explain the facts recorded in the course of the three previous chapters. We shall search for the predominant causes of the evolution. We shall try to discover the relations that exist between the level of living and other major economic factors: the distribution of the labor force, the structure and volume of production, prices, rents and profits, economic crises, and so forth.

Chapter I

WAGES AND PURCHASING
POWER IN FRANCE

IF THE MOVIES had existed before the seventeenth century, economic science would long since have passed out of the pioneer stage. A film like *Farrebique** will give our grandchildren a better understanding of the life of contemporary farmers than a thousand classic treatises on the history of France. Photography registers not only what is exceptional, but everything that lies within the field of the lens. To all of these men, to all of those women whom painters have fixed on their canvases, and who tell us some of their thoughts, I should like to pose some simple questions that would have seemed devoid of interest to them, and that are for me the foundation of the study of historical causation: "What kind of furniture have you?" "Have you sheets on your bed?" "Have you mattresses of straw?" "Have you forks and spoons?" "How many knives have you?" "How many servants do you have?" "How many hours do you keep the lights on during the wintertime?" "Do you have glass in your windows?" But the painters and the chroniclers seldom give us answers to these questions, precisely because they would have seemed banal and obvious. The reason that these practises seem obvious is that they endured for long periods and were not very different for the grandson than they had been for the grandfather. That which constitutes their interest for us is just this—that they are *phenomena of slow evolution* which, as a result, appear to be

---

* *Farrebique* is the name of a film produced about 1947 which describes daily life in a backward rural village in France (in the Department of Aveyron).

largely independent of social action, or, in other words, determinate.

It is thus understandable why "historicizing" history (*histoire historisante* in Lucien Febvre's phrase) abounds and why it leads only rarely to scientific conclusions. Before becoming aware of what really constitutes historical determinism, man attaches himself very naturally to what strikes his imagination, which is precisely the unpredictable and the fortuitous. The effort of our generation is to find in the daily routine the necessary material for historical science.

This "historicizing" mentality explains why history has survived until our day almost entirely without reference to economic reality or with false ideas concerning that reality. Either the historian accepts as normal that which is really exceptional and was described by the chronicler because it was exceptional, or he overlooks the existence of a norm completely. This is why, for example, with reference to the level of living, the Frenchman of today imagines his ancestor dining normally like Louis XIV on the day of the inauguration of the Chateau of Vaux.

The available factual documents give an entirely different picture.

The celebrated text of La Bruyère has been buried under the dissertations of professors of literature and political historians. It has become established that La Bruyère never left the world of gilded salons and that he certainly knew much less than we do about the peasants of his district. But it was Vauban who wrote in 1698, in his *Projet de Dîme Royale*:

> The wandering life which I have led for 40 years or more, having often given me occasion to see and visit under many circumstances the greater part of the provinces of this kingdom. . . . I have often had occasion to give scope to my reflections, and to observe the good and the evil of the regions, to examine their condition and situation, and that of the peoples, whose poverty having often excited my compassion, led me to seek out its cause. . . . It is certain that misery is pushed to extremes and that if it is not remedied, the little people will fall into an extremity from which they will never rise; the great roads of the countryside and the streets of

cities and towns being full of beggers, whom hunger and nakedness drive from their homes.

By all the researches which I have been able to make, during the many years that I have applied myself to them, I have concluded with certainty that, in these recent times, close to a tenth part of the population is reduced to beggary, and actually begs. That of the nine other parts, there are at least five which are in no condition to give alms to these, because they themselves are very nearly reduced to this unfortunate condition. Of the four other tenths which remain, three are extremely uncomfortable, and embarrassed by debts and processes: and that in the tenth, where I put all of the gentry, clergy and laic, all of the high nobility, all of the lesser nobility, military and civil officers, the prosperous merchants and the propertied and comfortable middle class, one can hardly be sure of a hundred thousand families: and I do not believe it to be false, if I should say that there are not ten thousand small or great, whom one may say to be certainly well off. . . .[3]

The high price of salt makes it so rare, that it causes a kind of famine in the kingdom. The little people are not able to season meat for their use, for lack of salt. There is hardly a household which would not be able to raise a pig, which they do not do because they have nothing with which to salt it. They do not even salt their soup but half, and often not at all. . . .[4]

For the rest, everything that I say about this is not taken from hearsay and casual inspections of the country, but on visits and enumerations which were exact and carefully planned, on which I had worked for two or three years in succession.[5]

About 1730, the crude plow without wheels obliges the peasants "to work prone, almost like animals, they had only small donkeys to pull the plow and one sees them harness up their almost naked wives at the same time." They feed themselves "with rye bread from which the chaff has not been removed, which is heavy and black as lead. Their children eat this bread, and a four year old girl has as large a belly as a pregnant woman." Dupont de Nemours, who wrote these words, had no apparent interest in blackening the facts.

The problem of a historical evolution of the level of living is thus posed. Three kinds of studies enable us to verify it. In this chapter we shall study income and nominal wages and then, separately, the purchasing power of nominal wages. The statistics of per capita consumption will permit us later on to relate these two initial inquiries.

NOMINAL WAGES AND SALARIES

Of all the returns for goods and services, wages are the best known. The figures for income other than wages and salaries are practically unobtainable except in very special cases. Happily, the salaries of certain categories of high administrative employees furnish a good index of the income of the middle classes, because of the easy mobility between these positions and managerial positions in large scale private enterprise. The emoluments of councilors of state, of section chiefs in ministerial agencies, financial officers, and so forth, permit the recipients to live in bourgeois style.

To say that salaries and wages are among the best known prices does not at all imply that we have accurate knowledge of them. Here also, the spurious analogy of wage rates has led many historians to underestimate their importance. Nevertheless, the widespread nature of the phenomenon means that traces are left in a host of documents such as account books, itemized statements, and notarial acts. But these documents have been preserved at random. It requires considerable analysis to draw valid conclusions from such disparate elements. The oldest statistical series of average salaries goes back to 1806. It was prepared by the General Statistical Office of France and it refers to certain categories of skilled workers at Paris. Not a single statistical average of workers' wages in the provinces was calculated before 1844. At that date the oldest series of averages for a well defined group of provincial workers begins—for workmen employed in the coal mines. Francois Simiand has extended this series back as far as 1789, by means of data furnished to the inquiries of 1884 and 1901 by the Anzin and Aniche companies.

The salaries of officials, which were relatively stable in that era, have been estimated for several kinds of employment as far back as 1800. For the period of the *ancien régime,* a determination of this kind is impossible because of the variety of remunerations. Plurality of office was the rule and salaries were based on this plurality. The principal posts received different rewards according to the personality of the incumbent and the other functions that he exercised. In the present state of knowledge, it would take a considerable effort to give even a rough idea of the salaries of officials and officers before 1789.

In sum, we do not have any scientifically calculated statistical average of wages for any occupational group for the period before 1800. Nevertheless, it is possible to form a fairly exact idea of the *wages of workers of average skill.* D'Avenel has published a considerable mass of documents dealing with wages, unfortunately nearly unusable because of the systematic work that he accomplished in translating the money of the time into standard francs of 1900 or 1914. The conversion rates that he adopted were based on the silver content of the *livre tournois.** The twenty-five-year averages which he calculated are questionable. The remarkable work of Father Hanauer is similarly very difficult to use for the same reason. In order to find the value of the averages in the original currency, it is necessary to undo what the author has accomplished with so much toil. Nevertheless, the relative stability of wages in that era enables us to distinguish different orders of magnitude, so that some definite findings may be drawn from these studies and from a great number of other investigations and original documents.

Another interesting result of the statistics of d'Avenel and Hanauer is the picture they provide of the hierarchy of salaries and wages when occupational groups are compared. The great work of d'Avenel gives a table showing the wages of agricultural laborers with and without subsistence, and of certain other categories of wage earners from the year 1200 until 1888. It appears from this that agricultural laborers throughout the course of the centuries earned almost one-half less than skilled workers. Similarly, the wages of women were always at

---

* In 1795 the livre was legally converted into the franc at the rate of 81 livres to 80 francs. T.C.

least 30 per cent less than those of men. From 1476 to 1890, the wages of women remained less than the wages of men in the proportion of 60 to 100, except during the years 1626 to 1675 (rates of 71 and 68), and from 1726 to 1750 (rate of 66).

The wage level of the agricultural day laborer is fairly well known nowadays. First approximated by Jean Jaurès and later by Paul Louis, this series was studied by Ernest Labrousse and a number of other investigators.

The general results of these studies are summarized in the three following tables:

Table I gives the trends of the hourly wage of the unskilled laborer in cities other than Paris, from 1725 to 1959. This table, whose sources and methods of calculation are taken from the author's pamphlet on retail and wholesale prices,[6] can be regarded as valid within an error of 20 per cent. The figures for dates earlier than 1870 are maximum figures, that is to say that the observed values are, in 90 per cent of the cases, less than the values given in the table.

Table II shows the annual salaries of certain categories of officials for the period 1800-1951.[7]

The third table allows us to follow changes in the *fan of salaries* and to note that the relative standing of various salaries is in a perpetual state of flux. The salary of a councilor of state increased by a factor of at least 40 from 1800 to 1948; the salary of a professor at the Collège de France by 100; the average salary of an office boy in a government agency by 220; the hourly wages of laborers in provincial cities by more than 400. The wage rate of workers without special job training had increased to 80 per cent of the skilled-worker wage rate at the end of the period, compared to an average of about 50 per cent before 1800. The wage rate of women has also been raised in comparison to that of men and the present difference is only about 20 per cent.

Family allowances constitute nowadays an important equalizing factor between the incomes of different occupational groups, because of the fact that these allowances are not proportional to earnings, but are the same from the top to the bottom of the hierarchy. The Chief Justice of the Court of Accounts, assuming him to be the father of two dependent

*Table I—Hourly Wages for Unskilled Labor in France**

Dates	Hourly Wage	Index (1910 = 100)
1725	0.075	22
1735	0.075	22
1745	0.08	24
1755	0.08	24
1765	0.085	27
1770	0.09	26
1780	0.09	28
1785	0.095	29
1790	0.10†	30
1800	0.14	42
1810	0.18	54
1820	0.17	51
1830	0.17	52
1840	0.19	58
1850	0.195	58
1860	0.205	61
1870	0.22	67
1880	0.235	70
1890	0.255	76
1900	0.29	88
1910	0.33	100

	Direct Hourly Wage	Adjusted Hourly Wage‡	Index (Direct Hourly Wage)	Index (Adjusted Hourly Wage)
1920	1.67	—	500	—
1930	3.18	3.33	965	1,010
1935	2.87	3.15	870	950
1940	5.09	6.10	1,540	1,850
1941	5.87	7.33	1,780	2,225
1942	6.82	8.52	2,070	2,570
1943	7.48	9.35	2,270	2,835
1944§	13.01	16.25	3,940	4,925
1945	20.69	26.90	6,270	8,150
1946	27.16	35.30	8,230	10,700
1947	36.95	48.00	11,200	14,545
1948	55.55	72.21	16,900	21,880
1951	95.00	130.00	28,500	39,000
1954	110.00	148.00	33,000	44,500
1957	135.00	185.00	40,500	55,500
1959	160.00	217.00	48,500	66,000

* Average paid by the employer for one hour of work by a laborer in the provinces.
† The figures to this point represent *livres;* after this point they represent *francs.*
‡ The adjusted hourly wage includes family allocations, fringe benefits, and payments in kind.
§ Figures for 1944 and subsequent years refer to the month of October.

children, earned in 1948 not more than four and a half times
as much as his office boy *by hour of work,* although the difference between these two positions was of the order of 50 to 1
in 1800. At that time the annual earnings were 1000 francs
for the office boy and 35,000 francs for the Chief Justice.
Furthermore, the office boy was required to give about 3,000
hours of work per year, as against less than 2,000 for the high
official.

It is not at all doubtful that the fan of salaries was even
wider under the *ancien régime.* To give a general idea of the
earnings of the ruling classes in the seventeenth century, we
may look at three examples.

The first example concerns the salary and perquisites of
Colbert, the famous minister of King Louis XIV. As general
superintendent of buildings, he received only 24,000 pounds
a year, but at all times he received additional salary payments,
bonuses and *satisfecit* which raised his total income out of the
public treasury to about 100,000 pounds. In addition, he had
the freedom to undertake private ventures whose accounts
are unknown to us, but which were on a considerable scale.
Considering only the 100,000 pounds of public earnings, Colbert earned at least 500 times the average salary of an unskilled
laborer. In 1955, the hourly wage of a laborer was about 150
francs, and the coefficient of 500 would give 75,000 francs per
hour and 200 million per year. The reader may want to calculate for himself the amount of gross earnings that would be
necessary today to have this net income after taxes.*

A second example also shows the enormous inequalities of
income that existed in earlier eras. The fees of the surgeon
Félix, who operated on Louis XIV for a fistula in 1686, were
300,000 pounds, 1,500 times the wages of a laborer. The physi-
cian Daguin received a related fee of 100,000 pounds. There
were a number of auxiliary charges, so that the royal treasury
paid out a total of 572,000 pounds or close to 10 million hourly
wage units. It is true that Félix had to try out his procedure
on a large number of patients before operating on the king.
Quite aside from these royal fees, Félix enjoyed a European

---

* About 600 million francs or 2,000,000 dollars. (Furthermore, Colbert evidently had a very large income from private sources also.)

Table II—Annual Salaries of Certain Categories of Officials*

DATES	COUNCILOR OF STATE	DIRECTOR OF A MINISTRY		BUREAU CHIEF		EDITOR		OFFICE BOY		PROFESSOR AT THE COLLEGE DE FRANCE
		Maximum	Minimum	Maximum	Minimum	Maximum	Minimum	Maximum	Minimum	
1800	25,000	—	—	8,000	3,000	3,000	—	1,000	—	6,000
1810	—	—	—	8,000	3,000	3,000	—	900	—	6,000
1820	24,000	15,000	—	8,000	3,000	3,000	—	1,200	1,000	—
1830	12,000	—	—	—	—	—	—	—	—	6,000
1840	16,000	—	—	—	—	—	—	—	—	—
1850	12,000	—	—	—	—	2,800	—	—	—	—
1860	25,000	20,000	13,500	10,000	4,000	—	—	1,800	1,000	—
1870	18,000	20,000	13,500	9,000	5,000	3,600	1,800	—	—	7,500
1880	16,000	20,000	13,500	—	—	—	—	1,900	1,000	10,000
1890	16,000	20,000	13,500	—	—	—	—	—	—	10,000
1900	16,000	20,000	13,500	10,000	6,000	4,500	1,200	1,900	1,000	10,000
1910	16,000	20,000	13,500	12,000	6,000	6,000	1,500	2,400	1,200	10,000
1920	25,000	30,000	25,000	18,000	14,000	11,000	7,000	5,200	3,800	23,000
1930	100,000	125,000	100,000	60,000	45,000	30,000	14,000	11,500	9,000	64,000
1940	98,000	120,000	98,000	62,000	49,000	37,000	23,300	—	—	72,700
1945	318,000	358,000	318,000	206,000	170,000	110,000	82,000	66,400	58,500	255,000
1948	780,000	862,000	780,000	555,000	477,000	273,000	246,300	234,200	209,000	637,000
1958	3,831,000	4,059,000	3,375,000	2,349,000	1,745,000	—	1,010,000	587,000	492,000	3,375,000

* Assumed to be married, with two dependent children, and living in Paris. See French edition for detailed sources.

reputation. On the other hand, if the operation had not succeeded, a flogging might well have taken the place of his
honorarium.[8]

Finally, a third illustration of the spread of the fan of salaries under the *ancien régime* can be drawn from the conditions of employment cited by Vauban for the four inspectors
general of the army and the 140 military commissaries. Each
inspector general received 24,000 pounds, or about 450,000
hourly wage units of the period. Each commissary received
5,100 pounds or about 100,000 hourly wage units. The modern equivalent would be 180,000 dollars without taxes.

As far as the regularity of earnings is concerned, we must
not lose sight of the frequent occurrence of unemployment.
After 1830, cyclical phenomena in the modern sense of the
word were especially severe. Here is how Levasseur describes
the economic crises that occurred between 1830 and 1837 at
Sedan, a city where, according to all contemporary observers,
the situation of the working population was comparatively
favorable:

> At Sedan, according to a report submitted by the mayor to
> the ministry, before the crisis of 1831, the textile workers, to
> the number of 12,500, had earned an average of two and one-
> half francs a day. The crisis of 1830 to 1831 reduced their
> number to 5,000 and the wage to one and a half francs. These
> increased respectively to 11,000 and two and one-quarter
> francs from 1832 on, but there was again a depression in 1835.
> The working population fell to 9,000 and the wage to one and
> a half francs. Later, there was a slight recovery—10,000 em-
> ployed workers at two francs a day—but during the actual
> depression there were not more than 7,000 in the workshops.
> They were hired at the rate of two francs, but did not earn in
> reality more than one and a half francs because they had only
> three-quarters of a day's work. The women earned a bare
> 60 to 75 *centimes* per day. Local and private charity relieved
> the temporary indigence of the working population, but al-
> ways very incompletely.[10]

Table III—Comparative Indexes of Wages and Salaries in Certain Occupations Since 1800*

Dates	Skilled Worker, Paris	Carpenter, Paris	Laborer, Paris	Skilled Worker, Provinces	Laborer, Provinces	Miner	Councilor of State	Director of a Ministry —Max.	Director of a Ministry —Min.	Bureau Chief —Max.	Bureau Chief —Min.	Editor —Max.	Editor —Min.	Office Boy —Max.	Office Boy —Min.	Professor at the Collège de France
1800	48	43					156			66	50	50		42		60
1810	48						156	75		66	50	50		38	83	60
1820	48	45		52			150									
1830	57	54		54		42	75									50
1840	57	52		56		43	94					42				
1850	69	62		60		46	75									
1860	73	68		75		61	156	100	100	83	67			75	83	
1870		93		82		74	112	100	110	75	83	60	120			75
1880		115			91	83	100	100						79	83	100
1890	92	100		94	98	93	100	100	100	83	100	75	80			100
1900	99			99			100	100	100	100	100	100	100			100
1910	100		100	100	100	100	156	100						100	100	100
1920	380		450	478	475	383	625	150	185	105	233	180	165	215	315	230
1930	670	600	810	788	860	738	610	625	740	500	750	500	930	480	750	640
1940	1,125	1,000	1,900	1,320	1,510	1,260	1,980	600	725	520	825	620	1,540			727
1945	4,250		5,230	6,200	6,900	3,350	4,880	1,790	2,350	1,720	2,840	1,840	5,450	2,750	4,850	2,550
1948	11,650	11,000	14,400	16,600	19,500	16,100	11,650	4,300	5,800	4,650	7,960	4,575	16,400	9,800	17,200	6,370
1954	21,000		23,500	30,500	34,500			9,550	13,300	11,700	16,900	13,600	42,500	18,800	33,200	16,800

* See French Edition for detailed sources.

Strikes and fluctuations in employment were not peculiar to the nineteenth century. Before that they were just as common and more violent because of more widespread poverty. At the present time, the traveler who visits the underdeveloped countries of the world will find unemployed groups of men almost everywhere, demonstrating the shortage of work in the small towns as in the cities. These serious disturbances in the volume and continuity of employment have occurred continually.[11] They should never be lost from view when we consider the income of the whole of the working class. The major phenomenon of worker unemployment will be considered at length in a later chapter.

THE PURCHASING POWER OF WAGES

A study of monetary wage rates alone does not give any idea of the level of living of the wage earners. If, in fact, between the time of Louis XIV and 1959, the average hourly wage of the provincial unskilled laborer has been multiplied by about 2,000, increasing from one *sou* and six *deniers* to about 150 francs, the price of many goods has also risen greatly.

Purchasing power can be measured by the comparison of money wages with the price of the goods purchased with the wages. The term *real wages* is used to designate this relationship between the nominal salary and the price of the appropriate consumer goods.

Here, however, we encounter the central problem in the study of level of living, namely, that the very nature of consumption varies with the level of real earnings. For example, a wage earner who earns twice as much as another wage earner in the same place at the same time is not likely to buy twice as much bread, twice as many potatoes, and so forth. On the contrary, he spends more than twice as much for clothing, housing, and various non-alimentary goods. If the trends of all prices of consumer goods were parallel through time—if, for example, when the price of bread is multiplied by ten, the prices of potatoes, clothes, books, and all other merchandise and services are also increased by the same factor—the problem of the structure of consumption would not present itself. But it is the special characteristic of economic history continuously to present new disparities among price trends. In the short run, these are essentially due to maladjustment between production and consumption schedules. For example, if, for whatever reason over a period of several months, the supply of potatoes is greater than the demand without any corresponding surpluses of grain or of meat, the price of potatoes will decline by comparison with the prices of these other commodities. In the long run, however, it is the cost of production that controls the trends of selling prices and for that reason the *long-term price trends are determined by technical progress.*

Consequently, if we measure the purchasing power of a salary in relation to the consumption of a product or a service whose production has not been subject to any technical improvement, we observe a total lack of advancement in that sector of the level of living. With one *sou* and six *deniers,* the workman of 1680 was able to go to the barber as often as the contemporary workman with his 150 francs.

On the other hand, if we measure purchasing power in relation to a product that has been subject to intense technical advancement, we find a prodigious improvement in the level of living. For example, the price of a mirror four yards square has increased less than eight-fold in absolute price since 1702. It cost 2,750 pounds at that time, it now costs 21,000 francs. The purchasing power of a wage unit measured in relation to this product is therefore about 250 times as great in 1955 as it was in 1702.

These examples suggest that it is impossible to evaluate purchasing power without specifying at the same time the nature of the consumption involved.

The Four Great Types of Consumption

The consumption schedules that can be observed in the contemporary world are very diversified and undergo continuous change. We can group them in four major types by order of increasing income, as follows:

1) Consumption schedules with a predominance of millet.
2) Consumption schedules with a predominance of wheat bread.
3) Consumption schedules with a predominance of miscellaneous foods.
4) Consumption schedules with a predominance of non-alimentary goods.

Historically, the three earlier types of consumption schedule correspond to the average national situation in France of 1700, France of 1830, and France of 1955. The fourth type of situation has begun to be typical in such countries as the United States, Sweden, and the British dominions.

Consumption schedules with a preponderance of coarse cereals. Jean Jaurès[12] in his *History of Socialism* writes that the average daily wage of the unskilled worker under the *ancien régime* was nearly equivalent to 10 pounds of wheaten bread. The day laborer of 1750 earned no more than one franc per day on the average. Assuming that 240 pounds of wheat was then worth 25 francs—a figure which was taken as the classic average at that time—this represents less than 10 pounds of wheat, and therefore less than 10 pounds of bread a day.

But this laborer had an average of three children. He worked only about 290 days a year and the intermittent labor of his wife represented, at most, about 60 francs, entirely absorbed by expenses for clothing (not to mention kitchen utensils, taxes, and rent). The 290 francs of annual earnings of the head of the family made possible the purchase of an annual average of 2,800 pounds of wheat bread, about 560 pounds per person per year, or about one and one-half pounds per person per day. A kilogram of wheat bread furnished 2,380 calories, of which 2,040 were in the form of carbohydrates, and only 60 in the form of fats. A pound and a half of bread therefore represents 1,800 calories, of which 45 are in the form of fats. We are far from the 3,200 calories, of which 530 should be in the form of fats, which are nowadays estimated as necessary for the subsistence of the average category of manual workers. To reach the 2,900 calories necessary, on the average, to a member of this hypothetical family, it would be necessary to add to the 750 grams of bread a little more than a liter and a half of very good milk. However, the price of a liter of milk was, in general, higher than the price of a kilogram of bread, so that one might say that the average salary of 1750 was about one-third of the physiological subsistence minimum. (See Table IV).

Table IV—Daily Caloric Needs for a Family of Five People

	Proteins	Fats	Carbohydrates	Total
Needs of 2 children	440	680	2,680	3,800
Needs of 1 adolescent	400	680	2,320	3,400
Needs of 1 woman	300	540	1,960	2,800
Needs of 1 man	380	770	3,150	4,300
Total	1,520	2,670	10,110	14,300
Average per person	304	534	2,022	2,860
Amounts of these calories found in:				
1.5 pounds of bread	210	45	1,530	1,785
1.5 liters of milk	210	495	300	1,005
Total	420	540	1,830	2,790

Although the wage rate of .8 to 1 franc per day was very stable throughout the course of the eighteenth century, so that the total income of a working family could hardly exceed a maximum figure of 350 francs per year, by contrast the price of bread was extremely unstable. Table V, which follows, is taken from the first book of M. Labrousse, and shows what the variations were from one year to another in the price of this essential staple. Even more than the previous table, this one gives us a picture that is essential for any understanding of the fundamental character of the level of living of the average man before the recent surge of technical progress.* The very existence of humanity was bound up to the production of cereals. It was impossible to store up surpluses, partly for

---

* M. Meuvret (*Histoire des prix des céréales* . . . , *op. cit.*), points out that the averages, to be meaningful, must be based on the harvest year and not on the calendar year. Therefore, the difference in price between the years would appear still more extreme. The worker bought his bread on a precarious day-to-day basis.

technical reasons, but above all because there was no realization of the necessity of storage. Those who stored supplies, functioning as monopolists, were correctly held responsible for famines. Meteorological circumstances might transform a region from plenty to starvation without warning. Transportation from one region to another was not practical on a sufficient scale to equalize resources. In 1757, 240 pounds of wheat was worth 13.5 at Auch and 24 at Alençon, but in 1759, we find wheat more dear at Auch, 20.7, than at Alençon, 20.5. In 1764,

Table V—Current Price of Wheat in France from 1756 to 1790*

Year	At Alençon	In Alsace	At Amiens	At Auch
1756	16.15	13.00	13.80	12.40
1757	24.00	15.30	25.20	13.50
1758	18.35	14.75	14.85	16.75
1759	17.50	15.60	13.85	20.70
1760	16.85	17.95	15.20	18.25
1761	15.55	15.90	13.35	16.40
1762	18.60	16.25	16.15	15.30
1763	14.15	14.25	13.35	16.50
1764	12.35	13.40	13.20	18.50
1765	15.95	14.50	16.05	16.50
1766	17.85	16.20	16.35	22.30
1767	21.90	18.30	22.85	21.55
1768	27.80	19.90	29.20	20.65
1769	29.60	21.00	22.70	22.75
1770	34.40	29.85	23.55	26.25
1771	28.65	30.55	26.20	27.50
1772	26.10	22.10	33.75	23.65
1773	26.95	24.15	24.60	27.65
1774	22.80	18.40	20.95	23.45
1775	27.85	19.85	24.25	20.45
1776	23.45	15.50	18.45	19.50
1777	24.75	17.30	19.50	22.65
1778	21.40	20.55	17.90	28.75
1779	22.25	20.60	15.90	18.45
1780	21.80	18.65	15.15	18.10
1781	22.20	19.15	17.50	21.90
1782	21.80	20.15	16.45	30.90
1783	21.35	20.65	17.25	25.70
1784	27.20	21.75	23.35	20.65
1785	24.55	20.55	18.60	20.50
1786	23.05	17.10	16.60	23.55
1787	22.60	20.40	17.35	22.70
1788	23.90	25.45	21.00	26.10
1789	32.40	31.70	33.75	33.85
1790	27.90	35.35	21.40	29.75

* Based on the Parisian setier of 240 pounds.

Alençon showed the lowest price which occurred during a forty year period, 12.4, but six years later, it showed one of the highest, 34.4. The years 1768, 1769, 1770, and 1771, were hard years for the entire kingdom, but it was in 1772 that the people of Amiens reached the worst point of the crisis, 33.75, while for the other areas improvement was already underway. Seven years later, in 1780, wheat at Amiens had fallen to less than half this price, 15.15. It climbed again to reach 33.75 in 1789. If we note that these are annual averages and that the seasonal and daily movements have many more variations still, it is possible to form an idea of the instability of living conditions under the traditional system.[15]

The amplitude of these variations made the price of wheat the essential variable of the level of living of the people under that economic system. If real earnings had amounted to a pound and a half of bread per person per day, this would have been, in spite of its nutritional inadequacy, clearly less painful than a situation in which real earnings varied within a few years from close to three pounds to less than one. The periods in which the price of wheat was high were periods of frightful misery—a topic to which we will return later on.

The condition of the average man in the traditional era of humanity, that is to say before 1800, may then be summarized in the following way: The purchasing power of the working classes depended essentially upon the weather, and the level of living per capita and per day of a working class family varied between a maximum of about two and a half to three pounds of wheat during the best years and an extremely low minimum which, as late as the eighteenth century, often fell below a single pound of bread a day. To visualize this level of living, it should be recalled that, aside from all nicety about the distribution of calories into proteins, carbohydrates and so forth, two and a half pounds of bread is equal to 3,000 calories or exactly the average nutritional minimum when divided among a family of five persons. In one out of four years in the eighteenth century, and in one out of every five years in the seventeenth century, this minimum ration was attained. The average ration in the deficit years may be estimated as low as one-half or two-thirds of minimum subsistence.

Thus in economies of the type that prevailed in France and in virtually the entire world except for Great Britain and North America before 1750, the per capita consumption of food and consequently the per capita production of food were plainly less than the physiological minimum. It is essential to realize that under these conditions, *consumption and also production must have consisted almost entirely of cereals.* The large scale production of meat was precluded by the fact that it requires an agricultural area five or ten times as great to produce the same number of meat calories as cereal calories. In order to produce pork, beef, or milk, grain must be fed to the animal. Pork requires 6 kilograms of grain per kilogram of weight on the hoof. Beef requires 12 kilograms per kilogram, and milk requires 1.3 kilograms. One kilogram of these products contains from 800 to 2,000 calories. The same kilogram of wheat gives 2,400 calories if made into bread.

Let us assume, for example, that with given techniques and a given number of labor hours, a hectare* of given land produces ten quintals† of wheat. This was about the maximum output before 1800 for the best land in the best years. The harvest would furnish 2,400,000 calories. The same land used for dairy production would not give more than 550,000 calories. In the production of beef, it would give still less, perhaps 170,000 calories. The same land, then, is able to support 2.7 persons if it is used for cereals, 0.6 persons if it is used for milk, 0.2 persons if it is used to raise cattle, at a rate of 2,500 calories per person per day. These figures are obviously approximate, but their order of magnitude is certain. It is remarkable that historians have tried and still try to describe and explain contemporary economic development without having placed in evidence a causal factor as simple and important as this.[16]

These differences in the output of calories per hectare can be explained, in part, by differences in output or productivity per worker, although manpower is a more important factor for a hectare in cereal crops than for the same amount of land used for livestock. However, the dominant factor in primitive

---

* Two and one-half acres.

† 100 kilograms; ten quintals equal 1,000 kilograms.

economies is not the rarity of manpower, which is on the contrary superabundant, but the scarcity of land which follows from the density of population. With her 25 million inhabitants and her 35 million arable hectares, France of 1700 was not able to direct her production except to the cereals. To provide 600 pounds of wheat per head per year to a population of 20 million people, a harvest of six million tons of wheat was necessary. With an average output of six quintals to the hectare, this required ten million hectares. Since, with the farming methods of the time, an average piece of land had to be left fallow at least one year out of three and would produce only a meager harvest of spring wheat or vegetables the second year, it is evident that the area annually planted in grain could hardly exceed these ten million hectares. If there had been any effort to produce calories in richer forms like milk, meat, and fruits, on any large scale, the nutritional deficit would have been even greater than it was.

Likewise, it is clear why populations that are dense in relation to their technology (such as France in 1750, the Balkan countries, India, or China today) must be satisfied almost exclusively with cereals—wheat, corn, and rice.

When, as in the case of France of 1750, the nutritional poverty becomes sufficiently great, the principal effort of production is diverted to those cereals that we regard as secondary today (rye, barley, oats, buckwheat). As a matter of fact, these cereals give a slightly higher number of calories per hectare than does wheat.[17]

The Frenchman of that era did not have the slightest idea of the number of calories produced by a unit of wheat, of rice, of barley, or of oats, any more than the Indian or the Chinese does today. He had, nevertheless, adopted just those crops which permitted a maximum density of population. *This determinism was accomplished through the price mechanism.* The output in bushels per hectare is clearly higher for the secondary cereals than for wheat, especially on mediocre land. Thus the secondary cereals are normally less dear than wheat. This is the reason why bread made with the secondary cereals, although clearly less nourishing and much less tasty and digestible, appeared preferable to the consumer. The outputs per hectare

in rye were about the same on marginal land as the outputs
per hectare in wheat on the best land; concerning barley, the
average output compared to that of wheat in the proportion
of nine to six. This is why in the years of scarcity and high
wheat prices, the demand for barley, rye, and buckwheat becomes greater, as shown by Labrousse.[18] There results from this
an upset in production and the secondary grains tend to dis-
place wheat.

These facts make it clear that the level of living characteristic of 1700 involved not only the predominance of food expenses in the average budget, and not only the predominance
of expenditures for grain in comparison to other foods, but
also the predominance of coarse cereals—that is, "millet," a
mixture of wheat and other cereals, usually rye, in a variable
proportion somewhere in the neighborhood of one part of
wheat flour to one part of other cereals. Vauban, in *Dîme
Royale,* estimates the average budget of an agricultural laborer's
family of four persons as follows:

1/3 of a *minot* of salt	
(a barrel of 17 kilograms)	8 *livres*, 16 *sous*
10 *setiers* of mixed cereals	
(1,200 kilograms)	60 *livres*
Rent, maintenance and other food items	15 *livres*, 4 *sous*
Taxes	Maximum of 6 *livres*,
	minimum of 3 *livres*
TOTAL	Approximately 90 *livres*

In this type of budget, the ration of coarse cereal, being
2,400 pounds a year for four persons, gives less than two pounds
of millet per capita per day. This ration corresponds to 400
grams of wheat bread and 400 grams of rye bread, or about
1,500 calories. The expenditures for coarse cereal in this workman's budget amounted to about 68 per cent of the total.

The foregoing example illustrates the purchasing power
of a day laborer in 1750, the price of wheat being taken at 25
francs per *setier,* the average price during a large part of the
eighteenth century. Toward 1789, Levasseur described a practically identical situation: "I have reached the conclusion after
extensive calculation and on the basis of elaborate data obtained from country priests, that in the most indigent families,

each individual has an allowance of only 60 to 70 *livres* per year including men, women and children, and that families which live on bread and dairy products, having a cow grazed by their children along the roadside and hedges, spend even less than this."[19] Thus the situation hardly differed at all from that described by Vauban, since between 1698 and 1790 the average price of wheat had increased from 7 to 25 *livres*.

From black bread to the frigidaire. In studies of the working class level of living, coarse grain flour is not mentioned after 1825. After that date in France, white bread made of wheat flour always appears and is explicitly designated. Moreover, the percentage of the total budget used for the purchase of bread decreased steadily from 1825 to the present.

In the era before 1830, expenditures for bread were always greater than half of the total expenditures for food, and constituted something between a third and a half of the total budget of working class families. De Morogues[20] estimates the consumption of bread during the period 1825 to 1832 at 19 ounces per person per day (almost exactly 600 grams) in the country, and at 16 ounces in the cities. This level of consumption required the expenditure of 303 francs in the country and 296 francs in the city for a family of five persons annually. De Morogues estimates the annual income of a working class family, if "well off," at 600 francs in the country and 860 in the city. The proportion of bread in the budget, therefore, ranged between 35 per cent in the city and 50 per cent in the country. The author emphasizes, however, that these figures refer to workers who are above the level of need. To obtain this income of 620 francs, 300 days of work were required of the head of the family at a daily wage rate of 1¼ francs, 200 days of work of his wife at 75 centimes, and 250 days of work by the oldest of his children at 38 centimes a day.

After 1830, the importance of bread in the working class budget declined steadily. In Villermé's budget, bread still represents more than a quarter of total expenditures for the single worker in France and more than 35 per cent for families. In our time, the proportion of expenditures for bread in the working class budget has fallen to about three or four per cent. Furthermore, the price of bread today is a retail price set in

the urban bakeries, while formerly it was the price of wheat
delivered at the farm and the average housewife made her own
bread. There was practically no difference between the price
of a pound of bread and the price of a pound of wheat before
1800. With the development of commercial services, a difference has developed little by little. This is due to the fact that
the commercial services of distribution have not yet benefited
from technical progress in the same way as the services involved in the production of wheat. On the contrary, the number
of labor hours necessary to distribute bread in a city have
tended to increase because of the increasing size and complexity of urban conglomerations. In 1955, a kilogram of
bread was worth 55 francs and a kilogram of wheat only 33.
Thus, the difference between the two prices which was zero
in 1780, is now of the order of 40 per cent.

In the budget of a workman or a typist in New York, bread
amounts to less than one per cent. Nine-tenths of expenditures
for food are devoted to the purchase of "noble calories" such
as meat, milk and fruit. Accumulated expenses for all starches
do not amount to more than a fifth of all household expenditures. Schematically, the frigidaire, the automobile, and the
washing machine have taken the place, or are taking the place,
of his daily bread in the worker's budget.

Evolution of the Idea of Minimum Subsistence

As a result of these changes, the notion of minimum subsistence has been in flux for 150 years. When Vauban, Turgot,
or Arthur Young speak of a worker in easy circumstances, they
mean a worker who has enough bread to eat. The subsistence
minimum for them is that income which allows the purchase
of three pounds of wheat per day per capita, or the equivalent.
They have reference to a physiological minimum. Expenditures
for housing and for clothing appear negligible compared to
the costs of food, and it does not occur to them that the working classes might have essential needs over and above nutrition. They are aware that extra work allows the purchase of
the few earthenware pots and pans that constitute the equipment of the household. As for clothing, the miserable condition

of which will be discussed presently, it is furnished by means of an unusual outlay during a "good year." Housing is paid for by work. Its low monetary value corresponds to its extreme inadequacy.

After 1830, by contrast, sociologists modified the concept of minimum subsistence by calculating the physiological minimum more and more generously, with increasing importance allowed to the "noble" calories. Also, they bring in a steadily increasing quota of expenditures for lighting, heat, clothing and, after 1920, for entertainment and vacations.

Table VI illustrates three characteristic types of subsistence minimum: that of Vauban in 1698, that of Villermé in 1831, and finally a formula generally accepted by the labor unions in France in 1950. In studying these three types of subsistence minimum, the reader will be struck by the profound transformation of economic conditions which has occurred over the past 250 years.

To appraise these figures correctly, it must always be remembered that the subsistence minimum as stated by Vauban and Villermé did not represent a realizable possibility but *an ideal* whose attainment would solve every social problem. It was only after having observed that the average family income was 550 francs a year that Vauban states that an income of 750 francs would be required to place a family in easy circumstances. Similarly, Villermé notes that one out of two working class families do not achieve his budget minimum which he declares adequate on the grounds that those working class families who do achieve it declare themselves satisfied with their condition.[21] In sharp contrast to the foregoing, the modern concept of minimum subsistence implies a belief that no wage earner should receive a salary lower than that which will afford him the level of consumption described.

In other words, the subsistence minimum of Vauban is higher than the average actually observed for the nation; the subsistence minimum of Villermé is about equal to the average observed income; the subsistence minimum of 1950 is less than the actual average income observed for the nation.

From 1949 to 1955 the evolutionary tendencies have been somewhat upset in France. But the broad outlines of the phenomena studied above have evidently not been modified.

What conclusions may we draw from these facts? The most certain is that the purchasing power of a wage, if it is to have scientific validity, must be measured by specific enumeration of the purchases that are possible for the earners of that wage. This suggests that it is impossible to undertake a serious ap-

Table VI—Subsistence Minimum for an Adult Workman*

Food (per day)	France 1700	France 1831	France 1950
Wheaten bread	500 gr	1,000 gr	600 gr.
Rye bread	500 gr		
Cheese and butter	50 gr	100 gr	50 gr.
Portion of soup or stew		1 portion	
Milk, meat and lard			140 gr.
Potatoes			400 gr.
Dry vegetables			20 gr.
Fresh vegetables			350 gr.
Jug of dilute cider		1 "pot"	
Red wine			40 cl.
Fish			30 gr.
Fresh fruit			150 gr.
Sugar			25 gr.
Candy			10 gr.
Miscellaneous			60 gr.
Heat and Light (per year)			
Hours of lighting		1,000	4,000
Coal		100 kg.	500 kg.
Wood		50 kg.	250 kg.
Gas			175 m.
Clothing (per year)			
Wool suit		½	2/3
Overcoat			¼
Overalls			2
Cotton shirts		2	3
Socks and stockings		1 pair	6 pair
Handkerchiefs		1	6
Undershirts			3
Nightshirt			1
Swimming trunks			1
Tie		1	1
Sweater		1	1
Raincoat			1
Shoes		½ pair	1½ pair
Wooden shoes		2 pair	
Oversocks		2	½ pair
Cotton bonnet		1	

praisal of purchasing power before knowing the structure of the budgets of those wage earners whose purchasing power is to be measured.

Nevertheless, it would be ridiculous to carry a desire for

Table VI—Subsistence Minimum for an Adult Workman (Continued)

	France 1700	France 1831	France 1950
Maintenance (per year)			
Dishware:			
Plates			6
Cups			6
Laundry:			
Shirts		52	52
Sheets			12 pair
Stockings		12 pair	
Handkerchiefs		52	
Overalls			25
Scarf, collar, or bonnet		24 units	
Cleaning of three piece suit			1
Oilcloth			30 centimeters
Showers			50
Soap			12 kg
Haircuts			18
Comb		1	
Mending		10 hours	
Household linen:			
Towels			2
Tablecloths			1
Washcloths			2
Dish cloth			5
Sheets			1
Blankets			1/10
Mattress			1/5
Miscellaneous Expenses			
Newspapers (per day)			1
Magazines (per month)			4
Sports and spectacles (per month)			5 tickets
Cigarettes and tobacco (per month)			7 packs
Organization dues			equal to 1 hour of work
Commuting transportation (per day)			10 km
Vacation transportation (per year)			500 km
Other expenses			25% of total budget
Medical care, drugs			approximately 15% of the total budget

* See French edition for detailed sources of this and following tables.

precision to the point where nothing at all could be done. We must not be too exacting about the number of studies available, or about the methods they use, or about the reliability of averages. There is a real need for more studies and for more precise methods. On the other hand, however, we must be willing to use what results we have. Here, as elsewhere in the scientific domain, a measurement involving errors of the order of 20 per cent is worth decidedly more than no measurement at all.

This being the case, the development of purchasing power and, consequently, the rise in the level of living over the long run, can be measured by comparing the average consumption, at given dates, of the recipients of wages and other income. For example, Table VIII shows the difference in purchasing power of a salary of 450 francs in 1831 and of 161,500 francs in 1949. The former corresponded to a payment of one and one-half francs per working day—a figure close to the average paid to

Table VIa—Caloric Equivalents of Subsistence Minimum of 1950

Calories per gram	Items	Number of grams	Caloric Equivalents
2.4	Bread	600	1,400
2.8	Cheese	25	70
7.6	Butter	25	190
2.5	Meat	140	350
0.7	Potatoes	400	280
3.0	Canned vegetables	20	60
0.7	Fresh vegetables	330	245
Variable	Wine	40	Variable
0.8	Fish	30	24
Variable	Fresh fruit	150	Variable
4.0	Sugar	25	100
2.6	Candy	10	26
2.0	Miscellaneous	60	120
	Approximate Total		2,900

Caloric Equivalents of Villermé's Subsistence Minimum of 1831

Calories per gram	Items	Number of grams	Caloric Equivalents
2.4	Wheatbread	1,000	2,400
2.8	Cheese	75	210
7.6	Butter	25	190
	"Portion of stew or soup"		200
	Approximate Total		3,000

unskilled laborers in Paris. The annual salary of 161,500 francs in 1949 was almost the exact equivalent of the wages paid to an unskilled laborer in the metallurgical industry in a provincial center at an hourly rate of 70 francs for 50 weeks of work plus two weeks of paid vacation. Thus the annual salary of 1831 was given in return for 3,600 hours of work, that of 1949 for 2,250 hours of work.

Table VII—Cost of the Subsistence Minimum of 1831 in 1831, Compared with Hypothetical Cost of the Subsistence Minimum of 1950 in 1831

	1831 cost of the 1831 subsistence minimum	1831 cost of the 1950 subsistence minimum
A. For a single man		
Food	347	547
Housing	40	80
Heat and lighting	4	55
Clothing	41	90
Maintenance	18	73
Straw for bedding	1	
Miscellaneous expenses		68
Total per year	451	913
B. For a family of five, including three children		
Total per year	1,243	3,200*
Minimum average per capita consumption	249	640*
National income on the basis of the foregoing consumption	8	20*
Actual national income	8	

* Social security benefits would raise these figures by about 15% if taken into account.

Table VIII—Cost of the Subsistence Minimum in Current Francs for the Two Periods, for an Adult Workman

	Rouen (October-December, 1831)	Paris (April, 1949)
Food	347	58,000
Laundry and personal services	18	18,000
Clothing	41	27,000
Housing	40	4,500
Heat and light	4	10,000
Household linen	0	4,000
Miscellaneous expenses	0	40,000
Total	450	161,500
Amount represented by bread	110	5,100

Table IX—The Achievement of the Subsistence Minimum in Current Francs
for the Two Periods, for a Family of Five

	Subsistence Minimum	Average income of married laborers	Number of hours of work furnished for this income
Rouen, 1831	1,243	900	12,000
Paris, 1949	465,250	443,000	4,250

Table X recapitulates, by means of much less dependable data, the development of purchasing power for the repicient of a very high salary, 8,000 francs, in 1831. The table shows that to obtain the same commodities costing 8,000 francs in 1831, the amount necessary in 1949 would be 1,700,000 francs (and a little less than 3,000,000 francs in 1956). However, a family of five persons, having a net income of 3,000,000 francs after taxes at the present time, would not consume the same things as would have been selected in 1831 with 8,000 francs of income. Although the amount of food and housing is roughly the same, the relative importance of light, heating, and clothing in the budget has been considerably reduced. Miscellaneous expenses have been greatly increased and domestic expenses reduced as a result of a considerable disparity between the prices of items in these two categories. The domestic staff of this typical family has been reduced from three persons to one, while the proportion of the budget given over to miscellaneous expenses and maintenance has been doubled. These alterations in budget structure that are no less apparent in the working class budget than in the bourgeois budget will be further analyzed below. To appreciate the increase of the

Table X—The Budget of a Bureau Chief or Army Colonel with a Wife
and Three Children, 1831 and 1949[22]

	A The 1831 budget in 1831 prices	B The 1831 budget in 1949 prices	C The 1949 budget in 1949 prices
Food	3,000	450,000	400,000
Housing	1,200	25,000	25,000
Light and heat	1,000	100,000	70,000
Clothing	1,500	350,000	300,000
Maintenance	150	75,000	200,000
Domestic Service	500	400,000	120,000
Miscellaneous Items	650	300,000	585,000
Total	8,000	1,700,000	1,700,000

purchasing power of the high income wage earner, it must be remembered in studying the table, that a salary of 8,000 francs in 1831 was that of the permanent chief of a small government agency,* and that a functionary of this rank with three children was nowhere near a salary of 1,700,000 francs in 1949, or 3,000,000 francs in 1955. He earned only 900,000 francs in 1949 and 1,800,000 in 1955. However, if this official had benefited from the same relative increase of wages as the laborer, he would be earning more than 3,000,000 francs in 1949. The holders of high-salaried positions have suffered a loss of general purchasing power, measured either absolutely or relatively.

The study of the long-run changes in the level of living must therefore be based on at least an approximate enumeration of the goods and services actually consumed. Price distortions cause serious errors if one tries to relate income to the cost of particular products. Changes in budget structure lead to equally serious errors if income is related to the prices of a fixed consumption schedule.

On the other hand, in studying short-run changes in purchasing power and level of living, it is obvious that fixed patterns of consumption may be used as a basis. For example, it would be quite legitimate to take the items shown in Table VI to represent the consumption pattern of the Parisian laborer from 1947 to 1955. It would be possible to calculate a monthly index whose numerator would be the going monthly wages of such a laborer and whose denominator would be the total price of the goods listed in the quantities consumed during a given month. But if this index is carried beyond a short term of years, it leads to serious errors.

For similar reasons, it would be a mistake to suppose that an index calculated for laborers might be applied to high salaried workers. The cost of the commodities in the budgets of the prosperous do not vary in parallel with those in the working class budget. This problem will be taken up again later on. The following general principle may be introduced at this

---

* *Bureau,* but this is a smaller unit than the American *Bureau.* The latter is a major subdivision of a *Départment* and corresponds to the French *Direction.* A French *Bureau* is about equivalent to an American *Division.* T.C.

point: Since the working class budget in France is still dominated by expenditures for food, it is therefore controlled by the
retail price of food. By contrast, the budgets of the rich are
dominated by the products of luxury and by service items. *In
the short run* there is no necessary correspondence at all between the fluctuations in the price of food items and of tertiary
goods. Food products, being affected more strongly than most
others by technical progress, tend *in the long run* to show relatively lower prices. Thus, all other things being equal, any
index of the level of living of the comfortable classes and of
rich countries has a tendency—at a given rate of technical progress—to rise more slowly than the index of the level of living in
poorer classes and poorer countries. This fundamental economic law is a factor tending towards social equalization, at first
in any one country and eventually in the entire world, if technical progress proceeds normally in the agriculture of un-
developed countries.

The foregoing considerations, however simple they may
appear from a rational point of view, will nevertheless serve
to show the difficulties involved in the study of purchasing
power and level of living. The enumerations and the tentative
measures appearing in Tables I to X above are given only
as a basis for discussion and to illustrate the methods with which
this topic can be handled. The author will be grateful to
readers who call his attention to errors and omissions with the
aid of accurate and factual documents.

Before undertaking such a study, it is necessary to have a
clear idea of the development of the concept of minimum subsistence and its significance.

The investigation of the level of living requires extensive
research on family expenditures according to total income,
number of children, social class, educational level, occupation,
and so forth. Only a few such studies have ever been done. For
many long years, no French institution except the Academy of
Moral and Political Sciences had the material resources to
undertake such projects. Unfortunately, after having supported
the fine study of Villermé in 1831, the Institute completely
abandoned this task. The efforts of Le Play, so remarkable in
their conception, suffered from lack of funds and continuity

and produced only a few hundred fragmentary monographs. The General Statistical Office of France did not have the necessary resources. It has been necessary to wait until recent years to see really scientific work done on a large scale on the level of living. These studies have been done by the Haute Autorité de la Communauté Européenne du Charbon et de l'Acier, which was mentioned in connection with nominal salaries.[23] The study of the level of living should be the core of economic science. Instead, it has remained the sole concern of a few isolated students until very recent years. This is why the best available data for the study of the long term development are still such scattered observations as travelers' notes, censuses of production for certain countries, estimates of per capita consumption, statistical summaries, enumeration of certain manufactured products like automobiles, bicycles and radio sets.

These are the indexes that we shall now consider.

$\mathcal{N}otes$ to $Introduction$, $\mathcal{P}art$ I, and $\mathcal{C}hapter$ I

1. G. Friedmann, *Problèmes humains du machinisme industriel.* American edition: *Industrial Society* (Glencoe, Ill.: The Free Press, 1956).

2. An outstanding critique of these general ideas is *The Rise and Fall of Civilizations* by S. B. Clough (New York, 1953).

3. Preface to *Projet de Dîme Royale*, pp. 2, 3, and 4 from the duodecimo edition of 1707.

4. *Ibid.*, p. 83.

5. *Ibid.*, p. 135.

6. *La Méthode comptable dans la science économique: Prix de vente et prix de revient.* Cours autographié de l'École pratique des hautes études, 2° serie. (Paris: Domat-Montchrestien, 1949); *Documents pour l'histoire et la théorie des prix* (Paris: Armand Colin, 1958).

7. See French edition for detailed sources.

8. Le Roi, *Récit de la grande opération faite au Roi en 1686* (Versailles, 1851).

9. It is a question here only of the regular salary. It is certain that they received other large gratuities. The figures are taken from Vauban, *Projet de Capitation*, in *Projet de Dîme Royale*, p. 258. The Vauban text has one zero too

many in the salaries of the commissaries. This printing error becomes obvious from other calculations which follow.

10. Levasseur (*Histoire des classes ouvrières . . . II*).

11. Very good studies of nominal salaries are found in Simiand (*Le salaire, l'évolution sociale et la monnaie*) and in Labrousse (*Esquisse du mouvement général des prix et des revenus en France au xviiie siècle*). Among the original sources should be cited the work of Villermé, Hanauer, and Reybaud. Here is some data by Villermé on the salaries of spinning workers in 1835 and 1836.

In the spinning mills of Mulhouse, the average salary of an adult laborer is 1.57; at Sainte-Marie-aux-Mines, a worker earns an average of 8 to 11 francs a week and a child 1.50 to 4 francs.

At Lille a semi-skilled worker earns 1.5 to 2 francs a day. Among the skilled workers, the highest salary is that of the coppersmith at 4.50 to 5 francs a day. They represent a very small fraction of the working class.

Professional spinners earn:

at Lille, 2.5 to 3.5 francs a day,
at Sainte-Quentin, 1.5 to 3 francs,
at Calais, 1.5 to 3 francs,
at Rouen, 1.25 to 2 francs,
at Darnetal and at Elbeuf, 1.75 to 2 francs,
at Tarare, 1.40 to 1.60 francs,
at Lyon, 1 to 3 francs.

Flora Tristian confirms these amounts; she notes:

at Montpellier, 1.75 to 3 francs,
at Carcassonne, 1.5 to 2 francs.

Women nowhere earn more than 1.50 to 2 francs. The average is 1 franc a day; children earn 0.50 to 1 franc.

These studies give an idea of the difficulty of determining an average salary, above all on a national scale. The classical division between Paris and the rest of France, necessary though it is, is clearly insufficient for following the economic condition of the French working class.

For almost a century, the General Statistical Office of France, with the help of regional and local offices, has regularly published excellent studies on salaries. Therefore, there are many reliable and homogeneous series covering a long period of years.

Nevertheless, the economist who uses statistical series of salaries must always remember the many elements which enter into the problem of salary and real wage. In the period 1940-48, for example, cooperative enterprises, canteens, and the distribution of the products produced by the company and contingent companies to the employees have been an important part of the workers' remuneration. Such "advantages of nature" have always existed and probably always will. They often cause great inequalities between workers whose salaries are identical. Last and most important, there are the salary supplements such as the family allowance, the higher overtime wage rate, social contributions from the employer, and retirement benefits. All these cause a growing difference between the statistical hourly salary and the real wage. It is absolutely indispensable to take them into account, but they make numerical calculations very difficult. The statistical studies of salaries in eight nations by the CECA, done by the Division Statistique de la Haute Autorité, directed by M. Wagenfuhr, are models for the study of complex salaries. *Salaires et charges sociales dans les industries de la communauté* (Luxembourg, 1955). (Edited in the four languages of the European Coal Community: French, German, Italian, and Dutch.)

12. This study of Jaurès rests upon a large number of incontestable sources. For many consecutive decades in the eighteenth century, the worker's daily wage was a little lower than 1/20 of the average price of a *setier* of wheat. While the ten year average of the price of wheat was 25 *livres*, the average daily wage was from 18 to 20 *sous*. A *setier* of wheat weighed 240 pounds in Paris and in certain provinces a little less, sometimes as little as 210. A *setier* of rye weighed 195 to 200 pounds. The daily wage, in *sous*, is very close to the price of a *setier* of rye in *livres*. See *Essai sur les monnaies* (1746), p. 37; *Philosophie rurale* (1763), p. 185. These two works, the first by Dupré de St. Maur and the second by the Marquis de Mirabeau, are cited by Villermé, *Tableau de l'état physique et moral des ouvriers*, pp. 16 and 33. See also Meuvret, *L'histoire des prix des céréales en France dans le second moitié du XVIIe siècle* (Melanges d'histoire sociale, 1944). Villermé also cites the study of Turgot concluding that the worker from the province of Limousin can buy with his wages 3 *setiers* of rye per year—in time of scarcity. In normal times his wage was 10 *sous* and a *setier* of rye, by the Paris measure, cost 10 *livres*. The daily wage thus represented, in normal times, 1/20 of a *setier* of rye.

The order of magnitude of these figures has been confirmed by all of the recent studies: cf. notably C. E. Labrousse (*op. cit.*).

This stability over a long period of the relationship between the average price of cereals and the daily wage is a fundamental premise of traditional economics. This interrelationship, now broken, was related, as we shall see later, to the stagnation of technique and the stability of agricultural productivity.

13. The studies of Mme. Randouin of the Société scientifique d'hygiène alimentaire.

14. C. E. Labrousse, *Esquisse du mouvement des prix et des revenus en France au XVIIIe siècle*, p. 106. The price is given in *livres* and *centimes*. The original document (National Archives, F. 20105), gives the price in *livres* and *sous*.

15. Meuvret, "Les crises de substitance et la démographie de la France d'ancien régime," Revue *Population*, 1946.

16. In order to obtain one kilogram of pork, it is necessary to sacrifice 6 kilograms of grain or nutritionally equivalent fodder. The corresponding "cost" of beef is 12 kilograms; for milk it is 1.3.

17. The earliest date from French statistics on the number of acres under cultivation date from 1815. At that time, 11 million hectares of grain were under cultivation, of which 4 million were in wheat and 2.6 million in rye.

18. Cf. *Esquisse*, Table I, p. 173. The ratio over a long period of time of

$$\frac{\text{price of wheat}}{\text{price of rye}}$$

is affected by the stability of the ratio

$$\frac{\text{productivity of rye}}{\text{productivity of wheat}}.$$

The average of these two ratios is of the order of 3:2 and has not varied for a long time. Cf. *Documents pour l'histoire et la théorie des prix*, pp. 6-7.

19. Lavoisier, *De la richesse territoriale du royaume de France*. Original edition, printed by the order of the Constituent Assembly, about 1789, p. 14.

20. De Morogues, *De la misère des ouvriers et de la marche à suivre pour y remédier*, chap. III. Quoted in Villermé, Vol. 2. The original is difficult to find.

21. *Tableau de l'état physique et moral . . .* , Vol. I, p. 145.

22. The family of an office holder of this rank enjoyed an income in 1831

about six times as great as the subsistence minimum and six times as great as the average income of that time. In 1949, their income, including family allocations, was less than twice as great as the subsistence minimum and hardly superior to the national per capita resources for five people.

The figures in this table provide only a general idea of the change.

Although the level of living and the purchasing power of unskilled workers has greatly improved since 1830, this has not been the case for the higher salaried groups. It can be seen from Table X that in order to maintain the same volume of consumption as in 1831, the bureau chief or colonel with three children should have had 1,700,000 francs or about twice as much as his actual salary.

Thus, in France the improvement of the purchasing power of small salaries is due in some part to the reduction of the purchasing power of higher salaries. It is quite different in the United States where the purchasing power of low salaries has been increased even more than in France, but without any reduction of the level of living in any income group. The fan of salaries has also been closing in the United States, but without any actual reductions in purchasing power. There has been some progress for all groups, even if the lower brackets have progressed more rapidly. By contrast, in France, the fortunate, if one may use that term for bureau chiefs and their like, have had their budget diminished by nearly half.

As previously noted, the situation of white collar workers and officials in private enterprise has developed in a similar fashion as that of public officials.

23. *Première comparaison du revenu réel des travailleurs des Industries charbonnières et sidérurgiques de la Communauté en 1953* (Luxembourg: August-September, 1955).

Chapter II

GENERAL INDICATORS
OF THE LEVEL OF LIVING

ALTHOUGH systematic studies of the purchasing power of wage earners are practically nonexistent for earlier times, and although, under these conditions, it is even less possible to speak of *studies* of the average level of living of the total population, we do have a sufficient number of documents to form a rough idea of the changes in the economic environment of the average Frenchman during the past three hundred years.

These documents suggest a division of the history of the level of living into three major periods, each corresponding to one of the major types of consumption described in the previous chapter:

1) The era of the traditional level of living probably goes back to furthest antiquity and came to an end between 1750 and 1800. The level of living during that very long period was characterized by the irregular but frequent occurrence of famine bringing death to some fraction of the population. This stage was characterized by the predominance of coarse cereals in the budgets of wage earners.

2) The nineteenth century marks an important step forward in the French level of living. Bread replaces millet. The periods of high bread prices, still strongly felt by the population, affected the death rate only to the extent of small oscillations that become less and less distinct.

3) In the third period which began in France with the beginning of the twentieth century, the bread consumed occu-

pies only a small part of the total budget, and crises of agricultural underproduction go practically unnoticed except in
wartime. However the principal portion of the budget continues to be allocated to food.

The fourth type of budget, characterized by the predominance of non-food expenditures, has not yet appeared in France.

We shall thus describe here the first three stages of a development that is not yet finished. In retracing this development
in France, we must not lose sight of the fact that these major
types of evolution are not peculiar to France, but can be observed elsewhere and everywhere in the world. *At the present
time it is still possible to substitute comparisons between places
for comparisons between historical eras.* Millions of men in the
modern world—in China, in India, and in North Africa,[1] for
example—are still subject to the conditions prevailing in the
France of 1700. Modern Spain, the Balkans, and to a lesser
degree, Italy, show features analogous to the France of the
Second Empire. Finally, modern France itself can be fairly
compared to the United States in 1920.

In other words, it is hard to avoid the conclusion that the
present condition of various peoples, with respect to the level
of living, is the result of a historical development having a
common point of departure. Roughly, it may be said that before 1700 the nutritional situation of all the people of the
world was approximately the same. Everywhere the level of
living was controlled by the level of agricultural production. Everywhere the expansion of population was periodically
checked by famine that imposed upon the population the
Draconian and capricious rhythm of climatic disasters. Although the level of living has been raised practically everywhere since then, the rate of improvement has been extremely
variable from one nation to another. For some of them, the
situation is hardly different now than in the traditional period.
For others, it is so much altered that, scientifically speaking,
there is hardly any common measure between the original condition and the present state of affairs. Thus the nations are
spaced out along a single historical trail.

THE TRADITIONAL LEVEL OF LIVING

The small place given to famines by the historian is absolutely absurd. As soon as one has grasped the extent and the
frequency of the phenomenon, the resulting human suffering
and the limits imposed upon population, famines appear, in
a sense, as the fundamental events of traditional history. Their
description takes up only a few paragraphs in the thousands of
pages of classical history. What is even more serious is that the
historians have not observed the bond existing between famine
and other economic, social, and political facts. Famines are
treated like any other historical fact without any perception of
their determining character.

The writers of former times were not eager to describe an
evil whose horrors were familiar to everyone and that appeared
to be inevitable; the weather conditions that were the immediate causes were independent of human influence. However,
famines also have remote causes that might have been subject
to control had they been taken into account. These were the
numerical surplus of population and the lack of storage for
good harvests. Certainly the technique of storage might have
been perfected well before 1730 if the importance of the
problem had been understood and if there had been a real
effort to solve it. Here again, as with the water mill of Marc
Bloch, the essential problem was not the technology but the
mentality of the time.

Only rarely, then, did contemporary writers describe these
phenomena that to them were regular and appeared so natural. What attracts the attention of those chroniclers who describe a given famine is not so much the great loss of life which
is reported but the immediate circumstances: that, for example,
"it never rained from Easter Monday to Michaelmas"; or that,
on the contrary, "there was such a downpour on St. John's
Day that the grain rotted even as it was being harvested." Or
perhaps it was a hail storm at the beginning of spring. In general, the historians were so little interested that it now requires
a considerable amount of archival research to establish even
the dates of the worst famines. Horrible episodes that brought

the death of one out of five living beings are passed by in silence while every detail is given about the marriage of the Dauphin, the disgrace of a minister or a mistress. Our modern historians have often followed the well-beaten paths. It is easier to copy what others have written and what is incidentally pleasing to the reader than to examine half-destroyed parish records in the dust of the archives.[2]

There were no civil registers for those earlier periods other than the parish records which were badly done and often lost, and no general censuses which might have shown the full results of the famines. It is only by means of persistent research that the way can be opened for the discovery of the critical factors of history, in the abundant and sterile mass of narrative history.

Labrousse was one of the first to study and promulgate the importance of famines in the social history of the *ancien régime*. We have seen above that the essential feature in the history of the level of living before 1800 was the very great variability of the price of grain and the stability of nominal wages. The nominal wage varied only very slowly. In an average year it corresponded approximately to the price of 2,500 pounds of grain. But the current price of grain at various times deviated markedly from the average. The tables give an example of these variations for the period before 1740. Prices varied by a factor of one to three, but the variation had been still greater at an earlier time. Labrousse gives the following figures for the average *national* price of a *setier* of grain:

Table XI—National Average, Current Prices of Wheat, 1706-11

1706	13.7
1707	12.5
1708	12.4
1709	43.2
1710	31.0
1711	19.1

The amount of variation is understated by a national average and especially by one calculated for calendar years, since the crisis situation depends upon the state of harvests and is never exactly the same from one province to another.

Even in periods of low prices, the wage earner obtained a

bare physiological minimum of cereal calories. He had therefore no margin. It is easy to imagine his situation when, with
his wage remaining at a steady 100 francs a year, a *setier* of
wheat increased to 43 francs and the same amount of rye to
35. What then can be said of a situation shown by the gazettes
of Strasbourg as published by Father Hanauer?[3] These gazettes
record, between 1620 and 1646, variations in the price of
cereals whose range exceeds eight to one. The price in 1646
was the same as in 1620—5.3—but in 1635 it touched 45.2. A
sufficient number of historical documents have been preserved
to describe the social condition of the nation in the course of
these great eras of crisis.

The words poverty, misery, scarcity, and hunger, recur
constantly under the pen of those historians who turned their
attention to the social situation of the masses of the population
before 1800. We read what Vauban wrote at the end of the
seventeenth century: "There are not ten thousand small or
great whom one could call well off. . . . Close to a tenth part
of the population is reduced to beggery and actually begs, or
else are in no condition to give alms to these because they
themselves are very nearly reduced to this unfortunate condition." With the alternation of relative comfort and atrocious
misery, the situation described by Vauban appears to have been
continuous from the Middle Ages until about 1725. After that
date, an essentially different evolution occurred and foreshad-
owed modern times. It is therefore necessary to distinguish two
clearly different epochs in the history of the level of living
under the *ancien régime*.

A. From the Middle Ages to Louis XV

In 1643, St. Vincent de Paul wrote in a sermon addressed
to the Daughters of Charity of Paris:

> In many places bread is rarely eaten. In Limousin and in
> other places they live most of the time on bread made with
> chestnuts. In the region from which I come, they are nour-
> ished by a small grain called millet which is placed to boil in
> a pot. At the dinner hour, it is poured into a dish and they

of the house come around it to take their refection, and after-
wards they go out to work.

All of the accounts of those times report similar facts. Painting and sculpture give us an even more definite idea of the situation of the peasants in the rare cases where the artist was
willing to take models who did not belong to the aristocracy
or the middle classes. In this respect, the paintings of Le Nain
are invaluable. In the celebrated *Peasants' Meal* in the Louvre
(1642), Le Nain evidently did not wish to force the note of
poverty. One child holds a violin in his hands, two other per-
sonages are drinking a glass of wine. However, one of the peasants and one of the children are barefoot. The virtual absence
of household equipment and the shabbiness of ill-fitting clothing can be seen in the *Peasants' Meal* in the collection of the
Duke of Leeds. We see here an assemblage around a goblet and
a plate rather than a proper meal. The old man and the woman
have the air of dignified and courageous suffering that is found
in so many documents and descriptions of the time. The boy of
about fourteen, whose long hair hangs about his face, shows an
already adult degree of fatigue. The clothing of all of them is
worn and ragged.

In the *Cart* at the Louvre, not a single article of clothing
appears worn out. Obviously these are rich peasants. They
have a pack animal, three pigs, and a dog. Even the baby has
shoes. But the mother is seated on the ground and the coarse
garments are like those now worn by convicts. None of them
fit. The courtyard exhibits a squalid disorder.

The *Peasant Family* of the Louvre again shows barefoot
children. The oldest is dressed in a shirt that is twice large
enough for him, open to the navel. Their breeches are shape-
less. The mother, whose face is ancient although she can hardly
be more than forty, holds a glass of thin wine in her hand. This
premature aging of the female face was often remarked by the
chroniclers of the time. The father, whose clothes are frightfully
ragged, is cutting a lump of gray bread. The *Return From The
Baptism* of the same Le Nain, the *Peasants' Meal* of Adrien
Brouwer in the Museum of Basle, and of more recent date, the
Farmer's Family of Fragonard in the Leningrad Museum por-

tray similar settings. There is practically no difference as far as the level of living is concerned between these pictures of the seventeenth and eighteenth centuries, the miniatures in the Book of Hours of the Duke of Berri, and the sculptures of Gothic and Romanesque cathedrals.[4] As an objective summary of the description given by historians and chroniclers of the economic situation of the masses of the population in those times, I cannot do better than to reproduce the few paragraphs given over to this subject in the twenty volumes of Glotz's *General History*. In Volume II of the History of the Middle Ages, M. Augustin Flèche speaks of the misery "which was generally the fate of the rural classes in the tenth century."

The poverty of the peasant was shown in his house, a simple wooden hut with a straw roof and a floor of beaten earth, the stable joined to the living quarters; in his less than scant furniture, in his clothing, even in his food, which was limited to those products of the land which the lord was willing to leave to him and consisted mostly of black bread, of vegetables, of milk, more rarely of fish or of pork. There are many evidences of a rude existence, devoid of all comfort and all joy, which often amounted to a condition of total deprivation. One finds in the *Miracles of St. Benoit*, which provides a mass of valuable information about rural life, one of the abbey serfs fleeing to Burgundy because he is too poor, another committing robberies because he cannot find any work to support his aged mother, still others forced to beg because they have no means at all. If we remember that on the church lands, the situation of the serfs was regarded as favorable, it seems likely that often in the tenth century the land did not support its people. Besides, what use to cultivate when the crops served only to provoke seigneurial rapacity?

Always difficult, the situation of the rural classes became tragic at certain moments. In the annals of the tenth and eleventh centuries, the word famine appears repeatedly. According to Raoul Glaber, 48 years of scarcity were counted between 970 and 1040. Nor is this surprising. The decline of commerce having reached a maximum in the tenth century, it was enough for the weather to bring about a bad harvest or for a district to be ravaged by war, for the most elemental necessities to become scarce. Doubtless among the famines reported by the chroniclers, many were only on a local scale, but at times the affliction was general. Such was the great famine of the year 1000 which, writes Raoul Glaber, raged throughout the Romanesque world to such a point that there was no region which did not lack bread. The chronicler reports that in many places the people, prey to atrocious sufferings, went as far as to "eat not only the flesh of animals and of the filthiest reptiles, but also even that of women and children." In 1031, it was, in certain respects, even worse: "The weather was so unseasonable that no favorable time for planting or for the harvest could be found, in particular because of the water which invaded the fields. The ground was so inundated by the continual rain that for three years not a furrow suitable for planting could be made. At harvest time weeds and tares covered the entire country. A bushel of seed, in the soil where it did best, did not return more than a sixth of its own measure at the time of gathering and this sixth hardly amounted to a handful." Neither Italy nor Gaul nor England was spared. Everywhere were enacted those scenes of horror which the chronicler has admittedly dramatized, but without changing the reality of certain facts to which he was the desolate witness, like the sale of human flesh at the market of Tournus.

The famine had other consequences, too. The inadequate nutrition in time of scarcity was responsible for epidemics which were equally dreadful. In his account of the misfortunes of the year 1031, Raoul Glaber says that in Burgundy they made bread with a white earth in which was mixed a bit of flour or bran and that many people who tried to satisfy their hunger by means of this singular concoction swelled up and died. Such a diet must have had the most disastrous consequences for general health, and it is not surprising that this famine was followed by a plague which lasted three years and decimated the population of Europe. Almost at the same time, André de Fleury observed in Aquitaine a strange disease which he called *ignis sacer* and which attacked and ate into the bones. Leprosy, however, was rather rare. It did not spread until after the Crusades. (page 588)

Similarly, we find in Volume VII of the *History of the Middle Ages* by Calmette and Deprez the following observation:

Famine, scarcity, epidemics. The famine, scarcity and epidemics which raged in the course of the fourteenth and fifteenth centuries are only too well known, and to them must be added the less visible but equally certain phenomena of malnutrition and overcrowding of population into the fortified towns. All of these troubles crowded that unfortunate era with woeful scenes and paroxysms of commiseration.

Henri Pirenne describes in the same work the famine of 1315:

> *The famine of 1315 and the Black Plague.* It must be remarked that if the fourteenth century could not continue its advancement, the disasters which overwhelmed it were in large measure responsible. The terrible famine which overwhelmed all of Europe from 1315 to 1317 caused greater ravages, it appears, than any of those which had preceded it. The statistics which, by accident, have been preserved for Ypres, give some idea of its extent. We know that from the beginning of May to the middle of October of 1316 the city magistrates ordered the burial of 2,794 corpses, an enormous number when we reflect that the total population probably did not exceed 20,000. Thirty years later a new and more frightful disaster, the Black Plague, struck the world, which had hardly recovered from this earlier shock. Of all the epidemics known to history, this was undoubtedly the worst. It is estimated that from 1347 to 1350 it destroyed about a third of the European population. . . .[5]

These descriptions, however fragmentary they may be, leave no doubt about the reality of these evils. They also show that historians may easily confuse the manifestations of a problem with its causes. When Henri Pirenne writes, for example: "It must be remarked that if the fourteenth century could not continue its advancement, the disasters which overwhelmed it were in large measure responsible," it seems that he might as reasonably have written, "The catastrophes which overwhelmed the fourteenth century show the impossibility of advancement in the condition of the world of that time." In the same way Flèche seems to regard the rapacity of the landowners as the cause of the prevailing misery and does not speak of the general conditions of agricultural productivity except in connection with periodic crisis. He does not stop to think that even in the good years the harvest may have been so small as to limit the consumption of the masses. Not only is the solution of the problem of famines not perceived, but the problem itself is not scientifically posed and its economic importance is scarcely understood.

The economic system of the *ancien régime* was clearly characterized by the existence of a limited agricultural productivity. When productivity neared its limits, insecurity followed. The average level of living, hardly sufficient for the preservation of the race, was seriously threatened by climatic or political disturbances. These often led to major disasters.

We can retrace the large swings from relative prosperity to extreme misery in the course of the sixteenth and the seventeenth centuries. Studying the situation of the Parisian region under Louis XII and Francis I, Yvonne Bézard describes a time when the level of living of the people was really very high. But she notes that in less than fifty years the situation was seriously altered.[6] We shall return later to the causes of these cyclical variations.

The important fact emerging from this discussion is the existence throughout the course of many centuries of frequent periods in which the level of living fell so low that sizable fractions of the population died of hunger. Any one familiar with the resistance of the human organism to hunger and anyone who has studied the physical, intellectual, and moral conditions of the Nazi concentration camps can form some idea of the severe limitations set on human progress by the periodic impact of these famines. The mortality rates recorded at Ypres in 1315 or at Bourg-en-Bresse in 1709 are of the same order of grandeur as those of the worst periods at the Auschwitz Camp —15 per cent in six months, about one in three per year. The precarious situation of the peasant population lasted until the seventeenth century.

The last famine recorded in France was that of 1709. Labrousse was able to find the number of deaths recorded at Bourg-en-Bresse in the course of that period: There were 150 deaths in 1706, 200 in 1707, 230 in 1708, 550 in 1709, 300 in 1710, 120 in 1711.

After that date, the history of France does not exhibit another typical famine with general and severe overmortality due to hunger. After 1770, economic crises do not imply a reduction of the population. A new era begins to be discernible.

B. From Louis XV to Napoleon I

To say that large numbers of men no longer die of hunger does not mean that they have achieved the physiological minimum of 2700 to 3000 calories. It signifies only that the most unfavorably situated strata of the population are still able to obtain, during the worst months of scarcity, the 800 to 1000 daily calories by means of which death may be averted.

The average level of living under these circumstances remains so inadequate from our viewpoint that the reader may be tempted to minimize the difference between the era of famines and the era which followed immediately afterward. Nevertheless, it was really a new era for humanity. After 1709 in France whole cities and regions were no longer delivered entire to the furies of hunger. After 1709 we do not hear of children being eaten and human meat was no longer sold on the market of Tournus.

After 1709 the demographic expansion of the Western nations was progressively freed from the millenial rhythm of the famines. The brutal saw teeth of the old mortality curve gives way to curves with less rapid oscillations. The mortality excesses of famine years, formerly the predominant factor in demography and the sole determinant of the growth of population, disappear. Other factors, formerly present but negligible, take the place of this hyper-mortality—fecundity, the marriage rate, and infantile and general mortality.

We turn again to the works of Labrousse—this time in order to study the trend of the level of living in France in the course of the eighteenth century. Any reader who examines the extensive studies of this author and the mass of source materials on which they are founded is bound to be impressed by the solidity of his conclusions and the reality of the facts which he describes. In their essentials, they have not been challenged in any way and are now taken as authoritative.

As far as the level of living is concerned, the conclusions of Labrousse can, I think, be hastily summarized as follows:

1) From 1725 to 1789 the price of essential staples (wheat, cereals, other food products) rose faster than wages.

2) Rent and profit also rose faster than wages.

3) As a result the average level of living of the working masses was reduced, while that of the land owners rose. These trends were very slow. I would venture the estimate that the loss for the wage earner was from 10 to 15 per cent and the gain for the property owner was from 15 to 20 per cent between 1725 and 1780.

4) There were numerous periods of high grain prices but no famine during this time.

5) The average level of living of wage earners in the course of the period may be visualized by comparing the laborer's daily wage of one franc with the price of a *setier* of wheat at 25 francs.

6) The total population increased greatly, from perhaps 18 or 20 million to 27 million at the time of the Revolution.

We can say, then, that as far as the average level of living is concerned, the eighteenth century hardly differed from the previous centuries. If an estimate were attempted of the per capita purchasing power, measured in pounds of wheat, of the average wage earner from 1725 to 1789, compared to the period 1625 to 1725, the difference between these figures would be smaller than the errors involved in the calculations. Statistically, we must conclude that the average level of living remained at much the same level. But two essential and related facts can be observed in the eighteenth century:

1) The deviations above and below the average level of living were much reduced in comparison to former times.

2) Since there were no famines, the population grew rapidly and reached a density never known before.

The *average* level of living during the eighteenth century took on for the first time the character of an *habitual* level of living.

To get an idea of what this habitual level of living was like, the *Voyage in France* of Arthur Young is one of the few useful documents. Young had the true spirit of an observer and a sufficient awareness of concrete economic facts to give his attention to the important elements of agriculture and food production. Furthermore, as he was an Englishman, nothing in France appeared natural to him, and he often availed himself of that essential faculty of the scientific spirit—surprise. It is truly impossible to look for an explanation or even a clear account of facts unless one is surprised by their existence and does not take for granted the interpretations which are currently accepted.

On every page, Young compares France and England. He is astonished by the differences which he notes between the situation of the two peoples. France is much poorer than England. How? Why?

Without accepting Young's detailed answer to these questions, which is at least partly debatable, it is useful to look at his account of the facts.[7]

First of all, Young is struck by the poor quality of housing, the lack of paving and floors, the absence of windows. This is a point to which we will return in connection with housing. We cite only in passing this typical description of a worker's house in a favorably situated district in Savoy:

> The houses have a repulsive aspect . . . they are huts of mud, ugly, covered with straw, smoke escaping from a hole in the roof or even from the windows. Window glass seems to be unknown and these houses have an air of poverty which clashes with the general appearance of the country side.

Besides the inadequacy of housing, one fact obsessed our Englishman: the filthiness of human beings and particularly of the maids at wayside inns. For example, at Souillac:

> It is not in the power of an English imagination to figure the animals that waited upon us here, at the *Chapeau Rouge*. Some things that called themselves, by the courtesy of Souillac, women, were in reality walking dung-hills. But a neatly-dressed clean waiting-girl at an inn will be looked for in vain in France.*

---

* This and the succeeding quotations are in the language of the English original.

And the same at Pezenas:

> At supper, at the *table d'hôte,* we were waited on by a fe-
> male without shoes or stockings, exquisitely ugly, and diffusing
> odours not of roses; there were, however, a *croix de St. Louis,*
> and two or three mercantile-looking people that prated with
> her very familiarly. . . .

The words misery and poverty occur constantly in Young's
account:

> Poverty and poor crops to Amiens; women are now plough-
> ing with a pair of horses to sow barley . . . they plough and
> fill the dung-cart.
> Pass Payrac, and meet many beggars, which we had not
> done before. All the country girls and women are without
> shoes or stockings; and the ploughmen at their work have
> neither sabots nor stockings to their feet.
> To St. Martory is an almost uninterrupted range of well-
> enclosed and well cultivated country. For an hundred miles
> past, the women generally without shoes, even in the towns,
> and in the country many men also.
> There is a long street in the episcopal town of Dol, without
> a glass window. . . .
> To Combourg. The country has a savage aspect; husbandry
> not much further advanced, at least in skill, than among the
> Hurons, which appears incredible amidst enclosures; the people
> almost as wild as their country, and their town of Combourg
> one of the most brutal filthy places that can be seen; mud
> houses, no windows, and a pavement so broken, as to impede
> all passengers, but ease none; yet here is a chateau, and in-
> habited. Who is this Mons. de Chateaubriand, the owner, that
> has nerves strung for a residence amidst such filth and poverty?*
> To Montauban. The poor people seem poor indeed; the
> children terribly ragged, if possible worse clad than if with no
> clothes at all; as to shoes and stockings they are luxuries.

Young gives few descriptions of the people's food. Here
are two notes which are the most exact that I have been able
to find for that epoch:

---

* He was, among other things, the father of the great author and social
philosopher.

To Tonneins. . . . These people, like other Frenchmen, eat
little meat; in the town of Leyrac five oxen only are killed in
a year; whereas an English town with the same population
would consume two or three oxen a week.

. . . to Hasparren. Fair day, and the place crowded with
farmers. I saw the soup prepared for what we should call the
farmers' ordinary; there was a mountain of sliced bread, the
colour of which was not inviting; ample provision of cabbage,
grease, and water, and about as much meat for some scores of
people as half-a-dozen English farmers would have eaten, and
grumbled at their host for short commons.

In reading these words, the modern reader may believe
that Young was systematically vilifying France. On the other
hand, it is certain that a traveler in Calabria, in Sicily, in Sar-
dinia or Portugal, might have observed pretty nearly the same
situations around 1930, and even today might see worse things
yet in North Africa, in Egypt, in India, or in China. Present
reality provides evidence to verify the testimony of the past.
Moreover, although Young is manifestly imbued with characteristic British superiority and happy to show it, it is only fair
to say that the spirit of denigration is quite foreign to this
observer whose essential purpose was to improve the fate of
men by taking account of the natural forces which they faced.
As a matter of fact, when he did find less distressing conditions,
he pointed them out with enthusiasm, *as proof that it is possible
to obtain more satisfactory conditions of life* for a people. (An
example is Monein near Pau.) It was also with enthusiasm
that Young followed the efforts of the Duke of Larochefoucauld-
Liancourt. The quotation which follows seems to me to sum
up very nicely what Young thought of the situation of the peasant class in France and the spirit in which he made his observations:

Walking up a long hill, to ease my mare, I was joined by
a poor woman, who complained of the times, and that it was a
sad country. Demanding her reasons, she said her husband had
but a morsel of land, one cow, and a poor little horse, yet they
had a *franchar* (42 *lb.*) of wheat, and three chickens, to pay as
a quit-rent to one seigneur; and four *franchar* of oats, one

chicken and 1 *sou* to pay to another, besides very heavy tailles and other taxes. She had seven children, and the cow's milk helped to make the soup. But why, instead of a horse, do not you keep another cow? Oh, her husband could not carry his produce so well without a horse; and asses are little used in the country. It was said at present, that *something was to be done by some great folks for such poor ones, but she did not know who nor how,* but God send us better, *car les tailles et les droits nous écrasent.* This woman, at no great distance, might have been taken for sixty or seventy, her figure was so bent, and her face so furrowed and hardened by labour; but she said she was only twenty-eight. An Englishman who has not travelled cannot imagine the figure made by infinitely the greater part of the countrywomen in France; it speaks, at the first sight, hard and severe labour. I am inclined to think, that they work harder than the men, and this, united with the more miserable labour of bringing a new race of slaves into the world, destroys absolutely all symmetry of person and every feminine appearance. To what are we to attribute this difference in the manners of the lower people in the two kingdoms? To GOVERNMENT.

The situation thus evoked by Young, and confirmed by other writings of the economists of the time—notably Lavoisier —and confirmed also by what we have said about real wages and what will be said further on about the national product, leaves an impression of extreme precariousness. A brilliant but not numerous elite lived off an apathetic mass. The income of the great depended upon the extreme poverty of the small. Intellectual and artistic civilization could only exist for a minority; that minority could only assure its own security by the poverty of the masses, and its security was essential for its civilization. For if the population had not been very large and therefore very poor, the rent of the land would have been low.

With the eighteenth century, the era of millet came to an end for France. The time passed when the King of France could feed his workmen with two daily pounds of millet bread, a quart of wine and two bowls of gravy soup, *sometimes fat, sometimes lean.*[8]

FROM THE NINETEENTH CENTURY TO OUR OWN TIME

With the beginning of the nineteenth century,[9] and more particularly with the return of peace to Europe after 1820, the history of the level of living of the working classes enters a new phase.[10] This does not mean that misery disappeared, nor even that the subsistence minimum was achieved among the poorest wage earners. On the contrary, we will see that the 1830's offer the spectacle of numerous industrial centers where large parts of the population were clearly malnourished and where misery exercised its sway. But the general climate changed little by little. Problems which once had been crucial diminished; others appeared and took their places among the great social dilemmas.

In the first place, not only did famine not reappear, but even the periods of high wheat prices became less and less marked and their impact was less and less felt by the population. In the same way, the great epidemics ceased to occur.[11] On the other hand, unemployment not only persisted but appeared in conjunction with social crises of a new type which, although much less serious than the ancient famines, were perhaps less easily tolerated psychologically by the working class.

If we take in at a single glance the whole of the period 1820 to 1940, the improvement of the level of living of the working class appears substantial, but this improvement was so imperceptible in the short run and so often disturbed by regressive movement that it is difficult to give a definite idea of the trend except by comparing the situation of extreme years. This is what we shall do further on. In the meantime, it seems possible to distinguish three major stages in the social history of the last century:

1) From 1820 to 1871, the industrial revolution was getting underway. Heavy investments were made, but the consumption goods offered to the working class accumulated only slowly and sometimes diminished. Population increased so rapidly that despite a small increase in agricultural productivity, the entire product of the whole of French soil was necessary to support the inhabitants. The migration of the peasants toward the

cities did not involve the depopulation of the countryside, but
was supported by a surplus of births among the rural population.

2) After 1871, there was a new explosion of technical progress—what G. Friedmann has called the second industrial revolution—as a result of the introduction of electrical power in
industry. At the same time, the mechanization of agriculture
began to be felt. The output of the land and the productivity
of labor increased markedly, and since at the same time population ceased to expand,[12] the area necessary to support it decreased and the countryside began to empty. The level of living
rose faster than in the previous period as a result of the cumula-
tion of gains in both the agricultural and the industrial sectors.
However, the rhythm of expansion remained slow. Interrupted
by World War I, it recommenced rather feebly after the war.

3) After 1929, a third phase opened under the unfavorable
auspices of a world economic crisis. Nevertheless, this was a
period of lively technical improvement and consequently of
rapid improvement in the living conditions of the worker.
World War II interrupted this phase, but did not terminate
it. The war and the resultant ruin effected a profound regression lasting until 1950 or thereabouts. Since then the pre-war
level has been regained and one can see the re-establishment of
an ascendent and relatively accelerated trend that began about
1930.

A. The Level of Living of the Working Class
   in about 1830

Besides such historians as Ernest Levasseur and Paul Louis
who studied the condition of the working class after the French
Revolution, a number of contemporary studies of undoubted
scientific value tell us something about the average level of
living in the France of 1830. Among the conscientious observers
were Villeneuve-Bargemont, Guerry, Angeville, and above all
Villermé who, in his great *Inventory of the Physical and Moral
Condition of Workers Employed in the Manufacture of Cotton,
Wool and Silk*, gives us the best data for analysis. Although it
is not possible here to enter into the details of a subject so huge,

we shall try to sum up the observations made available by grouping them around three topics: The nutrition of the working classes, the problems of the most disfavored fraction of the population and—in spite of the clearly unfavorable impression which the first two studies will give—the slow but incontestable improvement of the general level of living in the course of the first half of the nineteenth century.

1) *Nutrition.* As noted above, the fundamental fact which emerges from a study of the nutrition of workers in 1830 is that such terms as "millet" and "buckwheat biscuit" are no longer employed. We have seen above, in discussing the subsistence minimum of Villermé, what pattern the author ascribes to the food budget of a working family which is "not in need." The standard ration of Villermé actually gives a number of calories equal to or greater than the subsistence minimum of 2700 to 3000 calories per capita per day. Villermé gives many examples of the actual consumption of working families, based on meticulously detailed inquiries. There is, for example, the ration of a family of six persons as shown by the studies of the Industrial Association of Mulhouse.

This is how Villermé summarizes his observation for that same region of Mulhouse:

> With respect to nutrition, and in other respects as well, the workers in cotton can be divided into several classes.
>
> For the very poorest, those of the spinning and weaving mills, and some day-laborers, the diet is commonly composed of potatoes as a base, some thin soup, a bit of poor milk, bad "pasta" and bread. Fortunately this last is of fairly good quality. They do not eat meat or drink wine except on pay day or the day after, which is to say, twice a month.
>
> Those who have a better position, or, who having no dependents, earn 30 to 35 *sous* a day, add to this diet some vegetables and sometimes a small quantity of meat.
>
> Those whose daily wage is two francs or more eat meat with vegetables almost every day. . . .[13]

The working class diet was similar practically everywhere in France, somewhat better at Sedan, worse at Lille, and Sainte Marie-aux-Mines. The average food allowance varies around

the following quantities: two pounds of bread, 100 grams of
cheese or butter, vegetable soup, meat and meat soup on pay-
days. The drink was diluted cider at best, wine was an exceptional treat. In the poorer districts, the menu recalls that of
the eighteenth century even more. Villermé describes the diet
of workers on the shores of the Swiss lake of Zurich in this way:

> . . . Their habitual food is made up . . . of the following
> items: potatoes which are the base, and which are eaten with
> everything in the form of bread, when they are not eaten
> alone. A bit of bread which is usually of good quality. Meat-
> less soups and broths made with flour, oatmeal and so forth
> . . . dairy products. Some fruit. Eggs from time to time. Some-
> times fish in certain localities. Finally, chicory coffee with milk
> for the women's breakfast. Meat is a rare food for them. They
> do not eat it at all, or at most have it once a week.

Such a situation is easily understood if we recall that the nominal wage of a large part of the working class was only one
franc a day, while the price of bread varied between 30 and 40
centimes a kilo.

According to a remarkable study mentioned by Villermé:

> In a Rouen factory, two-thirds of the workers did *not*
> earn the 450 francs a year necessary to have the following menu
> every day—two pounds of bread, seven cents worth of cheese
> or butter, a portion of meat and soup, or gravy soup at the
> cook shop. Diluted cider as a beverage.[14]

However inadequate this diet might be, it had one essential
advantage for the working class—its relative stability. After 1820
the price of bread maintained a relatively constant level unknown before. The average national price began to assume a
definite direction as a result of the extent and the regularity of
exchanges between provinces. While the variations recorded
before 1789 often reached the proportions of one to four
within very few years, and variations of one to two in short
periods were common before 1800,[15] the absolute minimum
price of bread for the period 1820 to 1845 was 20.16 per quintal, while the absolute maximum was only 30.05. In the course

of this period of 25 years, there was only a single rapid increase in the price of wheat, that which carried the price from 20.90 in 1825 to 29.38 in 1828. The price remained high from 1828 to 1832, but it never exceeded 150 per cent of its lowest level.[16]

2) *The crises* of overproduction began to be more feared than the crises of underproduction. In the course of the crises of the new type, the manufacturers abandoned the workers whom they had snatched from the countryside during the period of prosperity. Unemployment swept the industrial centers. The men most recently hired were let out without warning, the others had their working time reduced. On the whole, the sufferings caused by the fluctuations of earnings became more important than those due to variations in the price of bread, and the problems imposed upon the working class by industrial crises began to substitute in men's minds for the traditional threat of agricultural crises. Thus, there was still great poverty and in several respects the fate of the average worker appeared more unfavorable during this initial period of industrial progress than during the final stages of the traditional period. Doubtless white bread replaced black bread almost everywhere, and doubtless if the peasant came to the

Table XII—Major Fluctuations in the Price of Wheat in France from 1820 to 1914*

YEARS OF		VALUES	
Minimum Values	Maximum Values	Minimum	Maximum
1822	1823	20.66	23.36
1825	1830	20.90	30.05
1835	1839	20.16	28.90
1841	1843	24.95	27.40
1844	1847	25.96	38.22
1851	1856	19.04	40.47 Max.
1859	1861	22.13	35.40
1863	1864	25.35	33.00
1865	1867	21.70	36.00
1869	1872	23.65	30.50
1875	1878	25.00	30.00
1885	1886	19.15	21.61
1887	1888	19.60	20.10
1889	1891	19.70	23.05
1895	1898	13.50 Min.	23.00
1903	1905	16.65	18.50
1906	1910	17.36	22.75

* Francs per Quintal.

city it was because the level of living there appeared to him
to be higher than in the country—at least psychologically. The
city of 1830 was an America where one might try his luck. But
what hardships were reserved there for those who did not suc-
ceed! The peasant house, poor, but in the open air, was exchanged for an insanitary warren. The hardships of peasant
labor, supportable in the fields, were transported to the odorous
and unhealthy factory. The moral and social framework of the
village disappeared for the new anonymous masses, thrown into
inorganic suburbs. It was the hideous era of proletarization.

Villermé, Flora Tristan, Jules Simon, and Noiret encountered misery everywhere. Villermé gives a description of the
workers of Mulhouse which deserves to be famous:

> The workshops of Mulhouse alone reckoned in 1835 more
> than 5000 out of about 11,600 workers who lived in the sur-
> rounding villages. These workers are the least well paid. They
> consist principally of poor families encumbered with young
> children, who come from everywhere during times of indus-
> trial activity. They come to Alsace and hire themselves out to
> manufacturing. One must see them arriving each morning in
> town and leaving at night. Among them there are a multitude
> of women, pale, thin, walking barefoot through the mud, and,
> when it rains, having no umbrellas, covering their heads with
> an apron or a skirt to protect their faces and necks. There are
> an even greater number of young children no less dirty, no less
> emaciated, their rags covered with oil from the machines. The
> children do not even have on their arms, like the women, . . .
> a basket with their provisions for the day. They carry in their
> hands or hide under their vests or where they may, the lump
> of bread which must nourish them until their return home.

> Thus, to the fatigue of a working day which is already
> excessively long, being at least 15 hours, there is added for
> these unfortunates, the discomfort of a regular and painful
> trip back and forth. The distances are from three to six miles
> and sometimes even more. The result is that they arrive home
> in the evenings overwhelmed by the need to sleep and leave
> the next morning without having completely rested.

The situation is no better for the weavers at Reims, Lille,
or Rouen. At Sainte-Marie-Aux-Mines, Villermé makes this
frightful comment:

If my information is correct, the workers of the factory of Sainte-Marie-Aux-Mines are generally discontented with their lot; however, the weavers who are the great majority, are too weak and have too little energy for this discontent ever to be feared.

At Sedan, the situation was better. It was, in fact, the best in France because of the solid tradition of worker-employer relations, and even more because of the proximity of Belgium where, since wages were then lower than in France, the price of food was correspondingly less. For the only time in the course of his travels in France, Villermé was able to see at Sedan child workers at play:

> . . . The day of my arrival at Sedan, *I was surprised*, in passing the door of a woolen factory at the moment when the bell signaled the return to work after the dinner hour, to see there a great number of children . . . playing, running, jumping with a gaiety and a petulance which, even without their thriving appearance, would have already shown me the most evident proof of their excellent state of health. At the sound of the bell, all of them hurried into the courtyard. The poor children, even younger, by the way, who worked in the cotton spinning mills, do not resemble these at all. . . .

The total impression which one gets from an attentive reading of the documents of the time may be summarized thus: More than a third of the working class of the cities, living in horrible dens, heaped on pallets without covering, without light, without fire, without water, suffered from "frightful indigence, brutalization, vices, and a profound degradation." The popular tongue gave the name of "white Negroes" to these exhausted, thin, and dirty creatures. Villermé, a thorough bourgeois, concluded that their condition could not be blamed on their vices, but rather their vices on their condition, and that, in general, "they deserve all of the sympathy of men of good will, for their good qualities and the respectable cause of their misery."[17]

3) *The symptoms of improvement.* Sad as this situation may have been as described by impartial observers, it does not appear worse than the fate of preceding generations. In fact,

none of these authors presents the condition of his time as more unfavorable than that of the previous years. Moreover, we must take into account in this matter a psychological factor that is extremely powerful and that each of us can verify easily and daily—the passage of time colors old memories in rose. This influences many people today in their recollections of "the glorious epoch" before 1914. Many of us have a tendency to describe favorably the remembered conditions of childhood or youth, whether it was a worker's apprenticeship or a boarding school. Some former prisoners even come to the point of remembering with a certain melancholy not devoid of wistfulness, their years of captivity in Germany!

The testimony of old workers who have described the improvement of the material conditions of life has therefore a special value. Such testimonials are not rare in the social literature of 1830 to 1840. They are certainly more frequent than in the social literature of today. Villermé interviewed at Reims and in other cities a number of old people who recognized a substantial improvement: In clothing, woolen cloth had replaced cotton in winter, cleanliness had been diffused among the workers' daughters, white bread had taken the place of coarse bread:

> Fifty years ago, the woolen workers of Reims were in a deplorable state of poverty, like those in other occupations. Those of them who were best off, piled into tiny rooms, badly fed, badly clothed, would seem very poor today. It is said that those who ate meat and meat soup once a week were envied, while today every worker who is reasonably well off has them twice a week. Finally, the health of the Reims worker in former days was not as good, in general, as we see it now.[18]

Evidence that improvement had been felt can be found in a great number of the memoirs of the time.[19] Even housing, however inadequate, did not seem to represent a regression. The hut of the peasant to the north of Loire, windowless or with a narrow window sealed by wooden shutters all through the winter, with its floor of beaten earth, was not necessarily more wholesome nor agreeable than the workers' housing. Characteristically, the dark, narrow, and tortuous streets, in which the working class was heaped, were in many places made up of houses originally constructed for another class of inhabitants. The development of a quarter of Paris like the Temple is typical in this regard. There, the working class took the place of the aristocracy. Of course, the density of the population increased greatly during the transition, but without exceeding the normal density in other kinds of workers' housing. One must not forget the mediocrity of hygiene and comfort in middle class houses under the *ancien régime*. With regard to housing, as we shall point out later on, France is a lazy beneficiary, or victim, of her past. Our ancestors have left us the houses which they constructed. We would rather dwell in them than to make the effort of building new ones. Many a worker family still lives in the house of a merchant or citizen of the *ancien régime* and in many of our southern cities, even *of the Middle Ages*.

Such are the general indicators of the level of living of the working classes around 1830. It would obviously be worthwhile to extend this description and to apply it to each of the succeeding decades from the Restoration to our times. This would be quite possible, since there are many sources. It has been done in part by Duvau in his notable thesis on *The Life of Workers under the Second Empire*. This book, to which the reader is referred, excuses me from describing the two fascinating decades between 1850 and 1870.

It must be noted, however, that the number of objective and quantitative studies, instead of increasing from 1830 to our day, decreased until about 1930, with some sign of recovery in recent years. Here, as elsewhere in economic science, the intellectual school has done its worst. The doctrinaires have triumphed over the observers and theory is preferred to experiment.

In this preliminary sketch of a quantitative measure of the level of living we must limit ourselves to certain landmarks. At least the principal tendencies of the complex beginnings of the industrial revolution must be taken into account. We shall review in very general terms the facts observed from 1830 to 1930, and then we shall discuss a few statistical indexes that allow us to measure the changes observed between these dates.

B. From 1830 to 1930

In 1830, *machinisme* had just been born. The social structure was practically the same as in the previous century. There
were yet no railroads. Steam engines were strange novelties.
Only the textile industry had entered a new period of activity.
However, the essential scientific discoveries had already been
made. It remained only to implement them. In other words,
the necessary conditions having been satisfied, the technical
progress that was formerly unthinkable became possible. Furthermore, the viewpoint of the ruling classes favored the effort.
The Renaissance, then the eighteenth century, and finally the
Revolution had profoundly transformed traditional mentality.
In the words of Jean Marchal, the individual had become
Faustian before the state. He knew he was able to transform
nature and he desired such a transformation.

We may describe the century from 1830 to 1930 as the first
century of technical progress. Certainly there had been some
measure of technical progress in the course of previous centuries, but the evolution had been much slower, the elements
affected by progress were much fewer, and for the daily life
of the average man, much less essential before 1830 than after.

Nevertheless it would be a mistake to think that the decisive progress accomplished first by coal and steam, later by
electric power and the internal combustion motor, had any
drastic influence on the level of living. It was rather the style
of life which was changed during this century. The improvement of the level of living was so slight that it could scarcely
be felt from one decade to the next, and there would even be
uncertainty about the direction of the trend if a comparison
of the periods at both ends of the century did not settle the
matter.

The first century of technical progress can be divided in
France into two almost equal intervals. During the first stage,
population grew very rapidly and the level of living was checked
by this very growth. During the second stage, technical progress reached the countryside and a permanent agricultural
crisis appeared to lower the level of living of the peasant class.
In effect, a pendular movement was produced. The great capi-

tal investments that were indispensable for technical progress were supported at first by the labor of the urban working population. Later they weighed more heavily on the peasants. World War I not only prolonged but aggravated the problem of completing the technical transformation of the French nation.

It is not possible to review here the economic history of France during the past century—at least, not in the light of these leading ideas. It is likely that it would be possible to establish a series of causal relationships as yet unnoticed.[20]

Such a study would describe the peasant prosperity under the Second Empire related to the high price of wheat, the building of rural roads, the clearing of new lands, the large scale construction of rural housing, and the creation of new farms and new villages. The sharp decline of the 1880's would be brought into focus. Wheat, which under the Empire had maximum prices of more than 30 francs per quintal and minimum prices of more than 20, fell suddenly to the range between 13.5 and 23. The peasant exodus began, the villages were abandoned, the houses fell into ruins, and the newly cleared lands went out of cultivation.

The collapse of the price of wheat, the cause of the emigration of the rural population, was itself attributable to the increase in productivity of cultivated land and the halt in demographic expansion. The last year when the average hectare in France gave less than ten quintals of wheat was 1879. The three years, 1894, 1895, and 1896, each exceeded 13 quintals. Fourteen quintals per hectare were reported in 1898 and 1899, 15 in 1903, 16 in 1921, 17 in 1929, and 19 in 1938. The productivity of the average hectare in 1938 was triple that of 1815 and more than double the average of the period 1815 to 1880.

The population, which grew from 27 to 39 million between 1800 and 1880, increased only from 39 to 42 million between 1880 and 1939. The area planted with wheat, which had increased steadily from 4.5 million hectares around 1815 to about seven million in 1880, necessarily reached a plateau and then declined after 1880. It had fallen to five million hectares by 1938. The determinism of technical progress shows

itself here in full strength. It would be fascinating to study it
in detail and to show its relation to that other variable engine
of human economy—demographic movement. We must limit
ourselves here, however, for lack of time and for lack of the
material means of research, to the investigation of the level of
living in its essential aspects. For this, we must first investigate
the trend in the purchasing power of the working masses, then
the development of real national income per capita; finally we
shall examine the numerous indicators of the level of living,
which after 1830 provide us with more and more accurate statistics.

1) *The purchasing power of the working masses.* The general outline for the study of the real earnings of workers in the
last 150 years may be found in Chapter Two of my *Civilization
de 1975* and in Chapter Nine of the *Grand Espoir du XX
Siècle.* The reader is referred to these texts, whose conclusions
can be summarized thus:

a) The evolution of real earnings is very different if we
consider hourly wages instead of daily, weekly or annual wages.
Between 1830 and 1938 the length of the working day was
lowered from 12 to 8 or 9 hours. The length of the working
week was reduced from 72 to 40 hours. These figures represent
orders of magnitude rather than exact averages.

b) The evolution of real earnings is very different measured in relation to wholesale or retail prices and differs generally in relation to the prices of products with great or small
possibilities of technical improvement. The fact is that *no improvement of purchasing power can be observed with reference
to any product or service whose methods of production have
not changed since 1830.*

A given wage may take on very different measurements of
purchasing power, according to the articles of consumption to
which it is related. This relationship dominates the study of
the level of living, because it permits us to identify the reasons
for the improvements that have taken place. We shall return
to this matter in a later chapter. Here it is sufficient to notice
the reality and the extent of the observed disparities in price
movement. We may take as an example the evolution of purchasing power since 1700, measured on the one hand with

reference to a commodity such as mirrors, subject to great technical improvement, and on the other hand, with reference to a service that still requires the same work as formerly—a private lesson, a medical visit, a seat at the opera, the execution of a portrait by an artist, the defense of a case before the courts, the signing of a notarial act, the creation of a dress or of a hat by a dress maker or a modiste, a square yard of tapestry, the binding of a book by hand, an architect's plan, or a haircut.

In 1702 it required 42,500 laborers' hourly wages to buy a mirror four meters square. In 1850 it still took 7,200, while in 1950 it required only 200. By contrast, it still takes more than half of an hourly wage to pay the barber.

Purchasing power has been multiplied by 210 as far as mirrors are concerned. During the same period it has decreased by 35 per cent at the barber's. The key to the mechanism determining any average level of living is to be found in these few figures.

These figures suggest that the measures selected for the level of living must be specified with care on pain of arriving at complete confusion.

Expressed in kilograms of wheat at the wholesale price, the average hourly wage of carpenters and cabinet makers at Paris went from less than one kilogram in about 1800 to about 1.2 kilograms in 1830 and nearly eight kilograms in the period 1930 to 1935.

On the other hand, the daily wage in kilograms of wheat increased much less—from 10 kilos around 1800 and 13 kilos around 1830 to 65 in 1930-35. The annual wage follows the same trend as the weekly wage, because vacations, when they exist, are now paid.

But the gains in real earnings are less when they are expressed in average retail prices of food and other staple commodities. Setting values of 100 for 1750 to 1760 and 140 for 1800, the real average weekly earnings of skilled laborers of Paris did not exceed 250 at their maximum point in the period 1930 to 1935 and fell to lower levels thereafter. Happily, the provincial worker and the miner have gained appreciably more. Measured by retail prices, the annual earnings of a workman in the mines tripled between 1820-40 and 1931-38. The annual wage of a country laborer doubled between 1801-10 and 1931-38.

The salaries of high ranking personnel, far from improving, fell off considerably over the same interval. The salary of a Councilor of State is a good index of the earnings of senior executives also in private industry, because if serious gaps develop between the salaries offered by private enterprise and by government, too many high officials would leave the public service. The purchasing power of the salary of Councilors of State was reduced by half between 1801-10 and 1938-39.[21]

Table XIII—Disparities in the Trends of Purchasing Power

	1700	1850	1950
Hourly wage rate for unskilled labor in the provinces	1 sou, 4 deniers	0.17 francs	74 francs
Price of a mirror, 4 meters square	2.750 livres	1,245 francs	15,000 francs
Price of a haircut in Paris	7-9 deniers	2 sous	60 francs
Purchasing power index of the hourly wage in mirrors	100	580	21,000
Purchasing power index of the hourly wage in haircuts	100	85	65

The ordinary studies of the level of living, which have begun to appear in recent years in France and abroad, generally refer to a working class consumption that is constant in time and consists principally of food items at the retail prices of the urban markets. We have the costs of a uniform style of life for France, calculated by Simiand, by the General Statistical Office, and by Kuczynski.

The following table shows the estimates of the General Statistical Office and the clearly less optimistic estimates of Kuczynski. The indexes are not corrected in any way for unemployment, illness, or taxes. However, Professor Kuczynski has tried to take note of the fluctuations due to changes in the duration of work at the time of cyclical crises.[22]

The discrepancies between this table and certain comparable measures are not surprising if we recall the divergence from 65 to 21,000 recorded in Table XIII. It is only necessary to include different kinds of consumption to arrive at different indexes. But even according to Kuczynski's table the long term improvement of purchasing power is clear beyond argument if 1850 and 1935 are compared. The development, unmistakable in the long term, is very irregular in the short term. There are numerous regressions which have the effect of removing from people's minds the feeling of progress. It should also be noted to what extent the years 1878 to 1880 mark a change in the pace of development.

2) *Average per capita real income.* The foregoing consid-

Table XIV—Indexes of Real Daily Wages in France, 1830-1957

Dates	Index*	Index†	Index‡
1830		54	62
1850	68	60	87
1856	52		
1859	75		
1860		63	75
1865	77		
1868	71		
1869	78		
1870		69	
1871	65		
1872	74		
1874	71		
1875	84		
1878	79		
1880		74	75
1888	99		
1890		89	
1891	93		
1893	102		
1894	99		
1900	100	100	100
1902	115		
1903	108		
1906	122		
1907	120		
1909	120		
1910		106	100
1912	107		
1914	112		
1929	105		
1930		130	115
1935	112		130
1939		160	145
1949		125	125
1957		180	185

* Adapted from Kuczynski.
† Estimates of the General Statistical Office of France up to 1910, of the author for 1930, and later.
‡ Provincial wage rates for unskilled labor.

erations leave no doubt whatsoever of the fact of substantial improvement in the purchasing power of the skilled worker in France. This improvement can be estimated, between the beginning of the eighteenth century and our own time, as the tripling of the hourly real wage, and the doubling of weekly earnings, measured in relation to the classic staples. As for the average laborer, his hourly wage has been multiplied by 3.5 and his daily wage by 3 (see Tables VI and VII).

However, the preceding study raises certain questions. Has the improvement of the urban worker's level of living been achieved at the expense of the peasant? Is it related to the closing of the fan of salaries, the reduction of the purchasing power of high officials, and of high salaries generally, or in other words, to a more egalitarian distribution of income?

Only a study of real per capita income will allow us to answer this question. Unfortunately, estimates of national income are subject to serious errors. Until recent years, the only figures available for France were obviously too low. Happily, the problem of estimating national income was partly solved after 1946 by the statisticians of the General Planning Commission under the inspiration of Jacques Dumontier. Since 1950, official estimates of French national income have been calculated with increasing accuracy by the national accounting service of the Ministry of Finance. The figures given in the second line of Table XV are those of M. Froment, except for 1830. They are by far the best available, and appear to me to be valid within a margin of perhaps twenty per cent.

By dividing these estimates of national income by the national population at each date, and then dividing the result by the cost-of-living index, we obtain the real per capita income, expressed in 1913 francs.

As the table shows, real per capita income was only 290 (standard) francs in 1830. It has exceeded 1,100 francs since 1900. After 1900, progress was much slower, no more than 1 per cent from 1900 to 1913, compared to an average of about 2 per cent in the previous century. World War I brought a setback. The level of 1930 was hardly above that of 1913. Even more serious was the new stagnation of 1930 to 1938, an interruption in progress which, as we shall see in the next chapter, was unique to France. These results are based, as we have just noted, on new estimates of the national income. On the whole these confirm the estimates of foreign economists, notably Colin Clark who dates the "loss of momentum" in France from the turn of the century.

These figures also serve to show that the improvement in the condition of wage earners was not achieved at the expense of the other classes of the population. On the contrary, from 1830 to 1938, per capita real income quadrupled, while the laborer's daily wage scarcely tripled. In a closer view, it appears that although the average urban worker earned less than the average Frenchman from 1830 to 1913, he earned much more between 1913 and 1938. However, it should be noted that the work week had generally been reduced from six days in 1913 to five days in 1938, so that the worker's real annual earnings were only 10 per cent higher at the later date. The improvement in the condition of the French working classes during this period had been almost exclusively applied to a reduction of working hours. The level of living had been voluntarily— that is, by legislation—sacrificed to the style of life.

Of course, these figures are only meaningful with reference to the group of goods and services included in the cost-of-living indexes used. With reference to manufactured products, the improvement of the wage earner's purchasing power, as well as that of the average Frenchman, appears much greater. For example, the average hourly wage was worth only half a kilowatt of electricity in 1900, against three kilowatts in 1938. In 1900, it required 40 hours of a laborer's wages to buy a bicycle pump, but only two hours in 1938. The bicycle itself cost 100 days of work in 1900, and only ten in 1938.

The findings thus obtained, which appear on line four of Table XV are not very different in general trend from those presented by Colin Clark in 1940 when he published *The Conditions of Economic Progress*.

Aside from short-term fluctuations, Clark's estimates confirm the long-term trend towards the improvement of the level of living in France. In spite of World War I, the average

Table XV—Some Indexes of Change in the Level of Living During the First Century of Technical Progress in France

	1830	1850	1860	1880	1900	1913	1920	1938	1953-54
Population (millions)	32.4	35.6	36.5	37.5	38.9	39.8	41.6	42.0	42.7
Total income distributed (in billions of current francs)	8	14	23	32	37	51	340	370	11,000
Retail price index (1913 = 100)	85	70	85	100	85	100	600	700	17,500
Real national income per capita (in 1913 francs)	290	560	740	850	1,140	1,280	1,360	1,250	1,500
Hourly wage rate of unskilled labor (current francs)	0.17	0.19	0.20	0.23	0.29	0.34	3.18	5.90	136
Daily wage rate of unskilled labor (current francs)	1.8	2.15	2.25	2.60	2.90	3.40	25	48	1,100
Daily real earnings of unskilled labor (1913 francs)	2.1	3.0	2.6	2.6	3.4	3.4	4	6.9	6.3
Price of 100 kilograms of wheat (current francs)	30	19	33	30	17	21	116	197	3,300
Retail price of 1 kilogram of bread (current francs)	0.40	0.30	0.33	0.40	0.30	0.40	2.15	2.81	55
Price of a cubic meter of illuminating gas or its equivalent in coal (current francs)					0.25	0.20	0.95	1.35	30
Price of a kilowatt-hour of electricity or its equivalent in other light sources (current francs)					0.70	0.57	1.62	1.75	26
Percentage of illiteracy among conscripts	53	39	33	17	6	4	8	—	1.5
Number of students in secondary schools (in thousands)	45	50	60	90	100	140	185	280	544
Number of college and university students (in thousands)	—	—	—	—	30	41	74	75	148
Number of teaching certificates issued	—	1,200	950	1,500	2,200	2,500	3,800	4,900	9,525

Table XV—Some Indexes of Change in the Level of Living During the First Century of Technical Progress in France (Continued)

	1830	1850	1860	1880	1900	1913	1930	1938	1955
Number of doctors	—	—	—	14,800	17,200	20,800	25,400	26,000 (1936)	38,000
Number of pharmacists	—	—	—	6,400	10,200	11,600	11,000	12,000 (1936)	17,000
Number of dentists	—	—	—	—	1,700	2,900	7,000	8,600 (1936)	13,000
Credit balance of savings banks (francs per capita)	1.15	3.8	10.5	34.7	111	147	950	1,600	23,000
Same, in hourly wage units	9	20	50	150	380	435	295	320	168
Same, in kilograms of bread	4	13	30	85	365	370	440	560	418
Value of sea fish caught (millions of francs)	—	—	—	87	106	157	1,832	1,312	29,500
Weight of fish caught (in standard tons)	—	—	—	230	260	250	530	550	—
Salt consumed (thousands of tons)	—	560	620	700	1,100	1,300	2,000	2,100	2,639
General index of freight movement	—	8.4	215	375	680	940	—	—	—
Domestic railways (kilometers of line in service)	50	3,000	9,400	23,700	38,000	40,800	43,600	44,000	41,000
Railway passenger-kilometers (billions)	0.0	0.8	2.5	5.9	14.1	18.2	29.3	27.1	26.0
Airline passenger-kilometers (billions)	0.0	0	0	0	0	0	15	66	2,500
Bicycles in service (millions)	0	0	0	10	1,000	3,500	7,800	8,900	—
Automobiles in service (thousands)	0	0	0	0	3	100	1,100	2,000	2,800
Letters posted (millions)	63	160	265	530	980	1,750	1,760	1,740	2,200
Postcards posted (millions)	40	95	180	700	1,450	1,970	4,500	3,900	2,300
Telegrams sent (millions)	0	—	0.7	17	40	51	45	35	31
Telephone conversations (millions)	0	0	0	0	195	430	835	960	1,913

Table XV—Some Indexes of Change in the Level of Living During the First Century of Technical Progress in France (Continued)

	1830	1850	1860	1880	1900	1913	1930	1938	1955
Value of gifts and inheritances (billions of francs)	2	2.7	3.5	6.4	7.8	7.0	—	—	—
Trials of voluntary homicide cases	600	600	400	450	500	600	500	—	—
Trials of other criminal cases	7,800	4,800	5,000	4,200	3,300	3,100	450	—	—
Minor criminal charges (thousands)	180	200	175	185	200	235	220	—	—
Number of convicts in the central prisons (thousands)	—	20	21	17	8	7	6	5 (1935)	22.7
New business corporations	—	—	—	5,000	5,600	7,150	11,700	—	6,600
Estimates of annual per capita consumption:									
Simiand's composite index for five major commodities	—	52	64	83	116	145	—	—	—
Charcoal (quintals)	0.7	2	4	7.8	12	16	21	16	13.5
Oil and electricity (in charcoal quintal equivalents)	0	0	0	0	0	1	2	4	8.7
Matches	—	—	—	750	700	1,200	1,350	950	—
Tobacco (kilograms)	0.3	0.5	0.8	0.9	0.9	1.1	1.3	1.2	1.3
Beer (liters)	9	11	18	23	28	32	35	28	19
Tea (grams)	3	4	7	11	28	30	35	31	32
Coffee (hectograms)	2.5	4.3	9.4	15	21	29	43	44	38
Cocoa (grams)	20	56	120	290	450	695	890	1,150	1,120
Sugar (kilograms)	2.3	3.2	5.5	8.6	12	18	22	23	26
Grain (decennial averages in quintals)	1.4	1.8	1.9	2.3	2.4	2.4	2.2	2.2	1.9
Potatoes (quintals)	1.0	1.6	1.8	2.8	3.1	3.4	3.4	4.1	3.5
Wine (million liters)	26	59	47	71	92	100	121	116	137
Cotton (kilograms)	0.9	3.1	2.4	4.1	4.0	6.8	8.7	6.9	—
Wool (kilograms)	1.5	—	2.6	4.0	5.2	6.7	7.4	5.5	—

level of living in the course of the decade 1925 to 1934 was almost exactly twice as high as in the decade 1850-59, even though the average duration of work in the cities had been reduced from 70 hours a week to 48.

All the figures of Table XV confirm the reality of this improvement. The reader may do well to study them. They give some idea of the complexity and the variety of economic life. Without any detailed commentary, and without returning to the major trends, we may here note certain of the most remarkable conclusions. The credit balance of savings accounts, per capita, represented the equivalent of four kilograms of bread in 1830 and 560 kilograms in 1938. France had three times as many automobiles in 1955 as it had bicycles in 1900. The consumption of sugar per capita increased from 2.3 kilograms in 1830 to 26 kilograms in 1955. That of grain from 1.4 to 1.9 quintals, potatoes from 1 to 3.5 quintals, coffee from 2.5 to 3.8 hectograms. The average consumption of tobacco quadrupled, that of beer tripled, that of wine more than quadrupled, that of chocolate was multiplied by 50. In 1938 every Frenchman used seven times as much cotton and three times as much wool as in 1830. The number of doctors at the service of the

Table XVI—Real Product per Capita* in France, 1850 to 1958
(in thousands of francs, at 1938 prices)

Years		Years	
1850-59	2.9	1944	4.9
1860-69	3.5	1945	5.2
1870-79	4.5	1946	7.8
1880-89	4.8	1947	8.4
1900-09	5.5	1948	8.8
1910	6.3	1949	9.9
1911-13	7.6	1950	10.6
1920	6.9	1951	10.9
1921-25	8.2	1952	11.0
1926-30	10.1	1953	11.1
1931-35	9.3	1954	11.7
1938	9.0	1955	12.5
1939	9.7	1956	13.2
1940	8.2	1957	13.9
		1958	14.2

Sources: A. Sauvy, Report to the Economic Council, March 1953. Series extended before 1900 and after 1952 by the author.

* See note to table XXa.

French people more than doubled, while the dentists increased ten-fold.

The number of students in secondary education quintupled, the number in higher education tripled. The future intellectual character of our civilization was assured by a change without precedent in the history of humanity.

$\mathcal{N}$otes to $\mathcal{C}$hapter II

1. "The average national production of India does not suffice to nourish two inhabitants out of three . . . even supposing that they had no need for clothing, lodging or transportation, and eating the coarsest of foods." Shah and Khambata, *La richesse de l'Inde et sa capacité fiscale.*

2. M. Meuvret, *op. cit.*, who is the great specialist of social history of the reign of Louis XIV, states that many deaths were not registered during famines because so many of the dead were transients. Men and women, made homeless by disaster, died on the roads. . . . Many were not taken to the church or buried by the priest who in that case would usually not register them in the Death Register.

2a. It was only in 1955 that the Institut National d'Études Démographiques published a guide for historical research in the old civil registers. See Michel Fleury and Louis Henry, *Des registres paroissiaux à l'histoire de la Population.*

3. Hanauer, *op. cit.*, p. 96.

4. Among the most instructive sculptures are "La mouture du blé" (on the capital of Vézelay), "Les Mois," of the cathedral of Amiens and those of Notre Dame (the reaper carries his hay on his back, as the peasants of Lake Como still do).

5. Henri Pirenne, Gustave Cohen and Henri Focillon, *Histoire du Moyen Âge*, t. VIII, p. 167. There are many descriptions of famines. For example, it is estimated that in the winter of 1438, one-third of the population of Paris died of famine or disease (cf. *Histoire des famines à Paris*, by François Vincent, chap. III). Short, in his valuable book, *New Observations on Bills of Mortality*, numbers famines from the Christian era to the year 1800 at 239. Short's work, which is now quite old, would be a good point of departure for modern research on this important problem.

6. Yvonne Bezard (*La vie rurale dans le sud de la région parisienne de 1450 à 1560*) writes that in order to buy a hectolitre of wheat, a workman must work "5 days under Louis XII, 10 days under Francois I, and 4½ days in 1914." One hectolitre of beans took 3 working days under Charles VIII, 10 days under Henri II, and 15 in 1914. According to Bezard, a cow took 12 working days under

Charles VIII, 43 days under Francois I, and 133 in 1914. Thus, it would appear that the situation of a man of average income under Charles VIII and Louis XII was quite favorable.

Unfortunately, these averages are not real averages. She adopts, for example, as the price of one hectolitre of wheat, 11 *sous*, 6 *deniers* under Louis XII; 1 *livre*, 17 *sous*, under Francois I; 2 *livres*, 2 *sous* under Henry II. But she reports that the price of wheat-maslin was 30 *sous*, 4 *deniers* in 1482 and 8 to 9 *sous* in neighboring years. She makes the mistake of not understanding that if the price of wheat quadruples in two years, it is because something serious has happened and averages are meaningless.

Furthermore, the era of Louis XII was a time of very high level of living. It did not last very long and did not avoid famine during its short duration.

7. From our point of view, Young is much closer to the realities than the classical economists of our day. In reading his pages, the notion of the productivity of work leaps to mind. It would seem that given a little systematic reflection, he might have formulated a valuable theory on the level of living. The same can be said for Lavoisier.

8. Cf., *Comptes des bâtiments du Roi*, published by Guiffrey (I, p. XX), the food order for March 22, 1684, "to feed the workers on the buildings of His Majesty at Versailles."

9. The time passed when the troops of Louis XIV, sent to Larhaix to put down a peasant revolt, could roast children on a spit. All is not beautiful in the machine age, and horrible things still happen. But this occurred among Frenchmen and in the age of Corneille. (Lavisse, *Histoire de France*, t. VII, pp. 214-17.)

10. We have several documents of economic and social research under the First Empire in various Departments. According to an annual report on the Department of l'Orne for 1809, an official document which had no interest in blackening the facts, this was the state of the peasant: "Housing is in general unhealthy, low and humid, with no opening but the door. Breakfast is bread and butter: and dinner, soup made of a vegetable, often chestnuts. Most people drink water. The more prosperous use fat in cooking. Beef appears on the table only for an important holiday. They make their own cloth, which is coarse. They wear cotton leggings and wooden shoes. The furniture is scant and they all sleep in the same room. They are superstitious and immoral. One sees many child-mothers."

The portrait is not flattering, but the author adds, "the situation is much better in the east and the south of the Department than in the north and the west," (Levasseur, *Histoire des classes ouvrières et de l'industrie de 1789 à 1870*, pp. 510 and 511). See also the important research of Gautier, *Pourquoi les Bretons s'en vont?* (1950).

11. Leprosy was conquered in France in the fourteenth and fifteenth centuries, smallpox and typhus in the eighteenth century, and cholera in the nineteenth.

12. The population of France was 27.5 million in 1801, 38.5 million in 1870 and 42 million in 1939.

13. Those who received two or more francs a day did not number more than 10 per cent, and those who had no dependents were extremely rare.

14. This is the minimum diet as studied by Villermé (cf. Villermé V. I, p. 180). The investigation (which followed) with the May 25, 1848 decree, describes a situation which differs very little: "For the class of the poorest workers, the diet consists almost entirely of potatoes. In general, meat is too expensive to be eaten.

For some, the same as far as bread is concerned. Housing and clothing as poor as the diet." (Manuscript of the National Archives, cited in Rigaudias-Weiss, *Les enquêtes ouvrières* . . . , p. 223.)

15. Cf. Table V. For example: Amiens 1786: 16.60; 1789: 33.75.

16. The last rapid rise in the cost of wheat was between 1851 and 1856, when it doubled. It is the only time it reached this high in that century. It is, of course, a question of a rise in the price of wheat without a concomitant variation in wages.

17. In the preceding discussion I have taken Villermé as a base rather than Buret (*De la misère des classes laborieuses en Angleterre et en France*, 1840). However, Hilde Rigaudias-Weiss in *Les enquêtes ouvrières en France entre 1830 et 1838,* much prefers Buret to Villermé.

If I had taken Buret's book as my base or those of other worker or socialist authors, I would have arrived at a much more pessimistic description. For example: Leroux (*De la plutocratie*), estimates at 8 million the number of indigents in France about 1830 (or one inhabitant in four). Buret estimates that there were three and a half million (or one in 9.7). Buret estimates that one inhabitant in 4.2 should have been helped (Buret, I, p. 265). Villermé, however, limits himself to the official figures, one in thirty for the entire country and one in 12.3 for Paris. In using Villermé as a reference, the situation in France in 1830 is the most optimistic that the studies permit.

Villermé seems like a more scientific observer than Buret. He has no doctrinnaire ideas to defend, but is sceptical and conscientious in his work. Villermé gives more concrete evidence than does Buret. Buret himself said "it is not enough to know what happens; it is necessary to know what should happen," (II, p. 125). My job here is to describe what is, and to leave to others the necessary but difficult job of describing what should be.

18. Levasseur, II, p. 295.

19. Cf. Rainneville, *Du travail* (Amiens, 1837).

20. Current economic histories are purely descriptive. One of the best economic histories of Europe is Shepard Bancroft Clough and Charles Woolsey Cole, *Economic History of Europe* (3rd ed., revised; Boston, 1951). The best world economic history of the period 1880 to 1900 is that of Colin Clark, *The Conditions of Economic Progress* (2nd ed.; London, 1951).

21. Same sources. The retail price is measured for this evaluation by the General Index of Retail Prices which, since 1913, has been computed by the General Statistical Office of France; from 1801 to 1913 it was computed by Simiand, and before 1801 it is an index calculated by the author. An estimation of the index for 1750 to 1760 is given in *La civilisation de 1975*, p. 54.

The militant syndicalist Paul Louis concludes his study of the working class level of living since 1800, in his valuable *Histoire de la classe ouvrière en France,* with the following comments:

"We shall try to present the trend of real income for the past century and a half in summary form, taking the case of a skilled worker of Paris, a mason or watchmaker, for example, and determining what that worker was able to buy with his daily earnings at various dates. Here are the results of this inquiry:

"With his daily earnings, the Parisian worker was able to obtain:

"In 1801, 10 kilos of bread, or 5 kilos of meat, or 3.5 kilos of butter, or 120 eggs, or 100 kilos of potatoes.

"In the period 1850 to 1855, 16 kilos of bread, or 4.25 kilos of meat, or 3.70 kilos of butter, or 60 eggs, or 87 kilos of potatoes.

"In the period 1882 to 1884, 18 kilos of bread, or 4.88 kilos of meat, or 2.20 kilos of butter, or 94 eggs, or 77 kilos of potatoes.

"In the period 1910 to 1913, 26 kilos of bread, or 5.60 kilos of meat, or 2.70 kilos of butter, or 71 eggs, or 64 kilos of potatoes.

"In 1925, 18.50 kilos of bread, or 2.60 kilos of meat, or 1.90 kilos of butter, or 58 eggs, or 29 kilos of potatoes."

Obviously, this summary leaves an impression of great confusion. Gains are recorded for bread, and sometimes for meat, but appreciable losses appear for eggs and potatoes. These disparities are incomprehensible at first sight, and call for explanation. The method used also raises certain questions.

a) A summary of this kind ought to give not only the result of the calculations, but also the figures on which they are based, like the price of the various items at each period, the quality chosen, the amount of daily earnings. Even the month of the year from which prices are selected has a considerable influence, and ought to be shown. Without these data, any evaluation of the figures is nearly impossible.

b) In taking the skilled Parisian worker for purposes of reference, M. Louis happened to take the category least favored by the trends of the time. Our index of wages for this group ranged only from 48 to 670 between 1810 and 1930, while the index for the unskilled provincial worker ranged from 54 to 965 during the same interval.

c) 1925 was an inflation year, in the course of which wage earners were at a particular disadvantage, as prices rose more rapidly than earnings. Moreover, the regression caused by World War I was still felt in 1925, although a rapid recovery took place in subsequent years. See Tables XIV, XV, XVI.

d) The daily earnings of 1801 refer to a working day of twelve hours, those of 1925 to an eight-hour day.

e) As we shall see later, the disparities in trends which appear (e.g., cheaper bread, dearer eggs) are related to disparities in the technical progress achieved in sectors of agriculture and transportation. In selecting products which have benefited from much or little technical improvement, it is possible to obtain results much more divergent than these. Among food products, the extremes seem to be sugar on the one hand, potatoes and tobacco on the other. To estimate trends in purchasing power, it is necessary to take account of the worker's total budget, and not just a few food products.

f) Whatever reservations there may be about the statistics for 1801, it is clear that the reduction of the price of bread, even supposing that there had been only regressions with respect to other food items, is crucial; *it is precisely this reduction which permits the worker to buy other food items,* formerly unavailable to him by virtue of the sole fact that he could not buy enough calories to nourish his family even in the most convenient form—bread.

22. J. Kuczynski; *Labour Conditions in Western Europe, 1820 to 1935* (1937).

Chapter III

THE LEVEL OF LIVING
IN THE WORLD

THE PRECEDING CHAPTERS have demonstrated the appreciable rise in the level of living made possible by technical progress in France during the past two centuries. We turn now to the situation of the other countries of the world. Does France occupy a privileged situation? Has there been a like improvement in the purchasing power of wages in other countries, and if so, to what extent?

The answers to these simple questions would have been difficult to supply only 15 or 20 years ago.

The credit for pointing out the scientific and human interest of comparative studies of the level of living belongs to the economic staff of the League of Nations. However, it was Colin Clark who had the honor to first prepare a general table of the levels of living achieved in the modern world and to state the essential questions about the causes and conditions of the observed discrepancies (in *The Conditions of Economic Progress,* 1940). Even if he did not distinguish all of the conditions and even though he may have been mistaken about some of the causes, his book will always have an important place in the history of economic science. In proposing other formulations than those of Mr. Clark, and even in criticizing many of his principles, we are only exploring a territory that he pioneered.

Since 1940, by the way, the available statistics about levels of living, national income, and purchasing power have become much more abundant. These measures permit a ready answer to the question raised at the beginning of this chapter about the relative situation of France among the nations. Many nations today have a level of living far above that of France; many have a level of living far below.

Some of these, like India and China, have a level of living not much different from France in 1800. Others have a level of living two or three times higher than France in 1950. All of this comes about as if the nations were spaced out *along the route of time.* The development that France has undergone since 1750 is one pursued by all of the nations of the world, but some of them mount the ascending slope with great speed, and others very slowly. Several nations are in advance of France, the majority remain behind. Thus, the time differences in the speed of the process explain the spatial distribution at any given moment.

These facts will appear clearly in the following four sections which describe successively the four fundamental aspects of the problem of comparative levels of living: nutrition, average total income per capita, real earnings, and indexes of consumption.

COMPARATIVE NUTRITION
IN THE MODERN WORLD

Half of today's world is still living in the age of millet. Two-thirds of the human beings now alive are undernourished. These incontestable facts emerge from all of the contemporary studies and especially from the simultaneous investigations of several agencies of the United Nations.[1]

The normal average ration of a normal population consisting of children, adults and old people is—as noted above—from 2,700 to 2,800 calories per head. The total agricultural production plus the possible importations furnish something less than 2,250 calories per head in enormous regions that include more than half of the earth's surface. These are almost all of Asia, a large part of Africa, some parts of Central America and South America. Only three-tenths of all humanity have more than 2,750 calories daily. These are the great nations of the West, the Soviet Union, and the British dominions. The general situation may then be summarized in the following table:

Less than 2,250 calories	Age of millet or of rice	Half of the human race	Asia, Central America, large part of Africa
From 2,250 to 2,750 calories	Age of wheat	Two-tenths of the human race	Fringes of above areas, mediterranean Europe, Balkans
More than 2,750 calories	Age of varied diet	Three-tenths of the human race	Soviet Union, western Europe, United States, the British dominions

The U. N. experts have estimated the average nutrition of those nations which were willing to furnish basic statistics as shown in the following table. (The original numbers have been rounded.)

Table XVII—The Scale of Average Daily Food Consumption

	1934-38	1946-48
Denmark	3,400	3,200
New Zealand	3,300	3,000
Argentina	3,250	3,600
United States	3,250	3,400
Sweden	3,200	3,000
Norway	3,200	3,000
Australia	3,150	3,000
Switzerland	3,100	3,100
England	3,100	2,800
France	3,000	—
Netherlands	3,000	2,700
Belgium	3,000	2,700
Finland	3,000	2,600
Germany	2,900	2,000
Rumania	2,800	2,400
Czechoslovakia	2,700	2,400
Poland	2,700	2,300
Italy	2,600	2,100
Brazil	2,500	—
Chile	2,500	2,600
Greece	2,300	—
Japan	2,200	1,600
China	2,200	1,800
Peru	2,100	2,100
Indonesia	2,100	1,750
Colombia	2,000	2,100
India	2,000	1,800

If we remember that 2,000 calories corresponds to about 850 grams of wheat per capita and per day, it is evident that the two most numerous populations of the earth, the Chinese and the Indians, occupy a situation with respect to nutrition which is very similar to that of the French under Louis XIV.

The differences in level of living in the modern world are plainly considerable. The average differences are greater in some cases than the differences among individuals in the same nation. *There are not 200,000 Frenchmen as badly nourished today as the average of 700 million Asians.* The daily food of an average Chinese or Indian would cost 50 francs in France, which is the wage paid for 20 minutes of a day laborer's work. Put another way, every French laborer would be able to provide himself with the average ration of an Indian by working only 120 hours a year. Inversely, if a Frenchman were to offer 120 hours of gratuitous work to a Chinese, he would be able to double the latter's ration; if this same Frenchman were willing to limit himself to the same diet, he would be able to accept the responsibility, in working a normal year, for no less than 19 Chinese, so that, making all due allowance for costs of transportation, the 21 million French workers would be able to double the food allowance of the 400 million Chinese by working 19 out of 20 hours for the Chinese.

This example is intended only to illustrate the extraordinary differences that have developed between the levels of living of different peoples. The study of real per capita income confirms the existence of these disparities.

NATIONAL INCOME PER CAPITA

The best estimate of the average level of living of a population is obviously that which is based on an estimate of the real national income per capita.[2]

Although the measurement of nominal national income, expressed in current money, has made great progress since 1940, this measurement still includes, as may be imagined, a large component of error. Moreover, the conversions necessary to

translate nominal national income into real national income
are themselves productive of sizable errors. The facts adduced
in the previous chapters show that the structure of consumption
varies with the volume of that same consumption, and that the
prices of different goods are very far from any parallel evolution in time or any stable proportionality in space. It is quite
impossible to develop any unit of consumption that is valid
both in time and in space. Furthermore, it is impossible *in
principle* to establish from year to year and for each nation the
price of a standard consumption unit that will remain comparable between countries and from one era to another.

I have discussed in another book[3] the important problem
of real income. Here it is sufficient to recall that the concept of
real income has a tendency to dissolve as we attempt to make
it more exact. This does not mean, however, that real incomes
cannot be compared when the differences are of sufficient magnitude. It is possible to chart large scale changes in real income
by relating nominal income to the cost of a fixed cluster of
currently consumed goods, selected to be as representative as
possible of the average habits of a given people at a given time.

We shall examine first the orders of magnitude of the estimates given by Colin Clark for the past fifty years. We shall
then present additional evidence about the recent development
of the level of living in different nations, based in part upon
the studies of the United Nations, and in part upon the investigations of such contemporary economists as Kuznets.

1) *Differences in real national income per capita in the
modern world.* Colin Clark has expressed the nominal national
income per capita of a very large number of countries in international units of "constant purchasing power," by estimating
the price of a defined cluster of goods and services in each
country and at each epoch. He arrives thus at a table of equiv-
alence of currencies like the following: One U. S. dollar, 1934,
equals 15 French francs, 1934; or 17 French francs, 1935; or
30 French francs, 1936.

Working in the opposite direction from such a table, he
is able to provide an estimate of the real national income for
all of the countries of the world and for all the years considered,
expressed in 1934 dollars. As a matter of fact, the unit of ref-

erence that he uses is the average purchasing power of an American dollar in the period 1925 to 1934. Despite the serious reservations that must be made about this method of converting currencies, using as a base a cluster of commodities that may correspond to the real habits of one population and not at all to the habits of another population or another area, it is nevertheless certain that the calculations made in this way are useful as first approximations, the more so because Clark's method is relatively unfavorable to the rich countries in comparison to the poor countries. In poor countries the gap between the cost of luxuries like meat, and the cost of staple products like cereals, is much less than in rich countries. For example, in France in 1850, an average pound of meat did not cost more than three times the price of a pound of bread, while in modern France meat is worth at least six to eight times its weight in bread. There is nothing complicated, of course, about this phenomenon. It does not make sense to say that one people has a level of living which is twice that of some other, since in reality no people consume twice as much grain, twice as much milk, twice as many vegetables, twice as much meat at the same time. Nevertheless, the figures in Table XVIII provide a rough but suggestive idea of the distribution.

The figures in this table confirm the scale of the international differences previously noted with regard to the level of living. Between China and the United States, the difference is of the order of 1 to 12. It would be 1 to 30 if it were measured with reference to rice or wheat. Still more impressive, if purchasing power is measured with reference to a manufactured product such as a bicycle, a radio set, an automobile, or an electric motor, the disparity between China and the United States will increase to 1 to 50, 1 to 80, or even 1 to 100. On the other hand, with regard to such commodities as haircuts, legal fees, medical expenses, or handmade objects, the differences will be much slighter and sometimes even to the advantage of the Chinese, although these are precisely the goods and services that the Chinese is hardly able to obtain because all of his income is devoted to food. It little matters that some services are cheap if, in fact, they are out of reach of the mass of the people.

These remarks show at the same time how much in these figures is arbitrary and how much is representative. In scientific terms, they can only be summarized by some such statement as the following: The statistical studies of real national income confirm the studies of nutrition alone. The differences existing at the present day between the nations are such that in some countries, most people do not have enough to eat because all of their income is devoted to the consumption of cereal, while in other countries, the average man not only consumes more expensive foods, but also a host of other products and services, so that the cereals which take more than 80 per cent of the

Table XVIII—Real National Income Per Capita in Colin Clark's International Units, with an Assumed Working Year of 2500 Hours

NATIONS	PER CAPITA INCOME OF LABOR FORCE		PER CAPITA INCOME OF TOTAL POPULATION			
	1935-38	1909-13	1921-24	1925-29	1930-34	1935-38
United States	1,389	484	506	590	438	545
Canada	1,350	402	459	550	435	529
Argentina and Uruguay	1,150	297	382	446	403	488
South and Central America	—	—	—	130	—	—
Great Britain and Northern Ireland	1,206	434	403	502	488	584
Eire	770	262	238	281	284	311
Norway	682	154	208	215	220	279
Sweden	800	165	240	275	301	367
Denmark and Iceland	800	229	242	264	297	347
Finland	500	94	64	125	168	200
France	804	279	302	310	316	358
Spain	600	200	240	245	250	260
Portugal	370	115	100	110	120	125
Holland	850	288	345	357	306	335
Belgium and Luxemburg	700	197	209	261	270	315
Germany and Austria	780	263	279	292	261	343
Switzerland	1,000	285	396	463	410	455
Italy	410	132	134	152	149	158
U. S. S. R.	323	102	57	95	90	108
Baltic States	350	100	68	100	100	117
Poland	350	117	84	117	117	117
Czechoslovakia	450	141	147	169	161	161
Hungary	420	92	120	145	135	161
Balkan States	300	81	85	102	102	102
Australia	1,200	330	416	476	425	521
New Zealand	1,612	440	512	550	530	710
Japan	380	46	72	102	113	139
India, Burma and Ceylon	198	—	—	64	—	—
China, Korea and Formosa	—	—	—	44	—	—

budget of the average Chinese do not absorb more than four per cent of the budget of the average Frenchman and two per cent of the budget of an American.

2) *Short term changes in real national income.* The preceding facts, it seems to me, do not leave the slightest doubt about the fundamental direction of contemporary economic evolution: a long term rise in everybody's level of living. Some nations have barely begun this development, due primarily to their huge population growth, but in all the countries of Christian civilization, it was well under way before 1900. The speed of improvement may vary considerably. The general direction is the same everywhere.

However, it is obvious that the movement has little or no

Table XVIIIa—Annual Production Per Employed Worker, in Clark's International Units, Various Countries, 1940-47

By Country	1940	1943	1944	1945	1946	1947
United States				2,308		2,566
Canada				2,080		2,247
Eire			660			
Great Britain				1,540		1,383
Belgium						791
Turkey						419
Switzerland		696				
Italy				243		354
Germany			1,227			
Norway						930
Denmark						823
Sweden						1,500
Hungary		395				
Japan			579			
Australia					1,503	1,511
New Zealand				2,014	2,281	
South Africa				566		
Spain				825		
Brazil					297	
Argentina				1,002		
Venezuela	508					
Dominican Republic			148			
Ecuador	293					
Cuba				500		
Colombia	222					445

This table is not comparable with the previous table because of differences in the method of calculation, and because this table is based on labor force and the previous table on total population. The full procedures of calculation are not given in the original source, but the results are useful nevertheless.

Source: Based on the 1951 edition of Colin Clark, *The Conditions of Economic Progress.*

regularity. It is often the case that the short term shows regression in relation to the long-term secular trend. Some of these regressions are due to economic crises such as unemployment. Others, much more serious, are due to war or revolution.

The following table shows the regression due to the crash of 1929, and the regression in Germany and most of the other countries of Europe, caused by World War II.

The figures show that the regressions attributable to the crisis of 1929 reached an order of magnitude of 25 per cent. Those due to the war were very much greater. Hungary experienced, in 1945, a fall of 50 per cent from the 1939 level.

The findings about real national income per capita are further confirmed by studies of real earnings in various countries.

REAL EARNINGS AND
THE PURCHASING POWER OF WAGE EARNERS

The study of real earnings is, as we have seen, complex. To the difficulties arising from the duration of work, the skill of the workman, and the nature of the goods consumed, there must be added for international comparisons the difficulties that arise from occupational organization, methods of work, and customary wage arrangements, involving such matters as perquisites, the "thirteenth month," family allocations, social wel-

Table XIX—Recent Trends in National Income and the Cost of Living in Several

	1929
South Africa:	
National Income (millions of pounds sterling)	260
Cost of living (Index, 1948 = 100)	72
United States:	
National Income (billions of dollars)	87
Cost of living (Index, 1948 = 100)	71
Canada:	
National Income (billions of dollars)	4.7
Cost of living (Index, 1948 = 100)	79
Germany:	
National Income (billions of Reichsmarks)	76
Cost of living (Index, 1948 = 100)	77

fare payments, taxes and so forth, as well as differences in the traditional style of life.

We shall not return here to the principles which we developed in the *Civilization of 1975*[4] concerning the fundamental distinctions between hourly wage rate, daily wage rate, and annual wages. We shall not return, either, to the comparisons based on the prices of a quintal of wheat, which show great disparities from country to country. Instead, we shall give other evidence on real earnings which is less familiar and less accessible, and which confirms our previous conclusions.

Since 1926, the *Revue Internationale du Travail*[5] has been publishing a very remarkable series of statistics on the wages observed in twelve of the world's great cities, and on the prices in each of these cities of the "basket of food" of working families. As baskets of food are not composed of the same assortment in different countries, the study has used five types of baskets. Francois Simiand prepared a paper on this investigation which, as far as we know, was never published. The accompanying graph is taken from that paper and is based upon figures furnished by the *Revue*.[6]

Between Milan and Philadelphia, the discrepancy was of the order of 1 to 3.5. The basket in Great Britain (the basket of a relatively rich worker) costs relatively more than those of other and poorer countries and less than those of richer countries. The difference in the price of different baskets is not very great except in Australia where it reaches 30 per cent.

Countries

1930	1938	1939	1946	1949	1953	1956
235	395	435	700	923	1,252	1,546
70	68	68	91	104	130	140
75	67	72	179	216	308	344
69	59	58	81	99	111	113
4.2	4.0	4.3	9.8	13.2	19.0	23.0
79	66	65	80	104	120	123
70	82	90	48	63	109	147
74	64	64	82	107	108	114

At a more recent date, Lehoulier has published in the *Bulletin of the General Statistical Office of France* an excellent study on real weekly wages in various countries.[7] Lehoulier has found the average of weekly earnings in the various nations for six well-defined occupations in six industries—coal mining, metallurgy, construction, lumber, textiles, and printing. He related these nominal salaries to the price of a certain number of food staples taken in definite quantities.

The results obtained by Lehoulier are summarized in Table XXII, which compares the purchasing power of each group to that of the French workman of 1914 taken as 100.

The difference between the United States and the other countries is immediately evident. England and Sweden form

Table XIXa—Real Per Capita National Income

	United States 1923 prices (dollars)	Great Britain 1900 prices (pounds)	Germany 1929 prices (marks)	France 1929 prices (francs)	Australia 1929-30 prices (dollars)
1819	(180)	—			
1869	246	—			
1870	—	24.6			
1899	501	—			
1900	—	42.7			
1901	—	—	1,074		408
1909	580	—			
1910	—	43.5			
1911	—	—	1,136	5,030 (1913)	
1929	717	—	1,118	5,940	569
1930	625	50.0	1,134	5,550	
1931	535	—	1,005	5,370	
1932	419	—	889	5,160	
1933	418	—	931	5,060	525
1934	493	—	1,023	4,720	
1935	567	55.8	1,095	4,980	
1936	623	57.7	1,210	5,270	
1937	682	57.7	1,338	5,880	
1938	631	(58.8)	1,481	6,730	539
1939	683	(61.8)	—	—	
1945	1,439	(75.7)			
1946	1,124	(76.4)	543	(7,440)	
1947	1,062	(82.5)	708	5,910	690
1948	1,092	(84.0)	590	6,670	700
1949	1,068	(81.0)	762	7,000	729
1950	1,140	(87.1)	(880)	(7,000)	—

Source: W. S. and E. S. Woytinsky, *World Population and Production, Trends and Outlook*, The Twentieth Century Fund, 1953.

another group still very favored in relation to the third, consisting of France, Germany, and Italy. We see further that, while the three first ranking nations gain from 20 to 30 per cent between 1914 and 1938, the three others have either gained very little, like the 15 per cent for France, or even lost —more than 10 per cent for Italy. Finally, it should be noted that the great progress of the United States was accompanied by a marked sensitivity to crises. From 1929 to 1932, the purchasing power of the American worker fell from an index of 271 to an index of 182, or 30 per cent. This regression is greater than that shown by the real national income. It occurs because Lehoulier's index uses industries that are especially vulnerable to crises. An index of earnings of white collar workers in commercial establishments would have shown somewhat less decline. Whatever the exact amount of this regression may have been, it seems certain that severe short-term regressions were associated with strong long-term progress. The most progressive economies appear to be the most fragile. However, it is worth remembering that even at the worst of the depression of 1932, the index of purchasing power of the American

Table XX—Recent Trends in Real Per Capita Product in Several Countries (Indexes, 1953 = 100)*

	1938	1947	1950	1955
Canada	56	86	92	100
France	90 (?)	—	93	111
Germany	86	—	82	117
Italy	89	74	86	111
Japan	104	52	78	110
Netherlands	85	81	94	113
Switzerland	83	90	95	—
United Kingdom	—	86	93	107
United States	59	84	91	102

Source: Statistical Annual of the United Nations, 1956.

* These figures were obtained by applying to the national income, expressed in current monetary units, a correction intended to eliminate the influence of monetary fluctuations. The corrected national income is divided by the population, so that, in principle, the index measures the *physical volume* of the goods and services available to the average citizen.

Obviously, this procedure gives us only a crude approximation to the phenomenon we are trying to measure. The very nature of the research precludes precision since it is scientifically impossible to obtain a single, numerical measure of the physical volume of a complex product. Specialists interested in this point are referred to the relevant monograph, Jean Fourastié, Productivity, Prices and Wages (O.E.C.E., Paris, 1957). Others take the figures of Table XXa, and similar figures elsewhere in this work, as only roughly descriptive.

worker stood at 182 compared to the maximum of 120 which the French worker achieved in 1935.

Dessirier has published a series of studies on the real earnings of various nations. He estimates at 10 to 20 per cent the possible error of his figures. These calculations confirm the findings of Lehoulier, and furthermore they apply to a number of other nations. Using France, 1913, as the base of 100, the indexes reached the following orders of magnitude in 1939 and 1944:

	1939	1944
France	110	75
United States	300	450
Canada	275	350
England	175	225
Sweden	175	175
U.S.S.R.	75	
China	25	20

It must be noted that all the earnings entered in the above calculations were full-time earnings, without any allowance for partial or total unemployment. The national income per capita, on the other hand, automatically takes account of unemployment in the nation.

Table XXI—Per Capita Income, Various Countries, in U. S. Dollars around 1948

United States	1,525	Spain	182
Switzerland	950	U.S.S.R.	181
New Zealand	933	Chile	180
Canada	895	Hungary	163
Australia	812	Turkey	143
Sweden	805	Japan	143
Denmark	781	Colombia	132
United Kingdom	777	Bulgaria	113
Belgium, Luxemburg	646	Brazil	112
France	418	Mexico	106
Czechoslovakia	345	Guatemala	103
Germany	336	Greece	95
Uruguay	331	Peru	82
Venezuela	322	India	(75)
Argentina	315	Bolivia	55
Italy	225	China	(50)
Poland	190	Philippines	41

Source: W. S. and E. S. Woytinsky, World Population and Production (The Twentieth Century Fund; New York, 1953), pp. 395, 399.

All of the foregoing calculations, those of Simiand, Clark, Lehoulier and Dessirier, are based alike on expenditures for food. We have sufficiently stressed the point so that the reader will certainly recall that one arrives at entirely different figures in measuring purchasing power against manufactured objects, clothing, rentals, services, and so forth.

On the other hand, it is certain that the consumption of food, in "baskets of provisions," gives a vivid and socially relevant image of the facts.[8]

The correlation of the average real income per capita and of average real earnings must be explored. This has been done

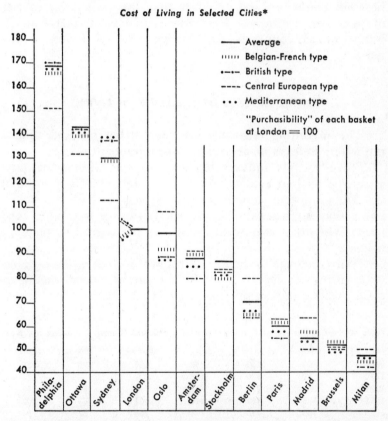

Cost of Living in Selected Cities*

* Graph by Francois Simiand, based on data published by the International Labor Office in 1926.

by Brousse.[9] The findings are fairly consistent and permit the
following comparisons for the period 1925 to 1934:

Average Level of Living

	Index of Real Wages	Index of Real Per Capita National Income
France	100	100
United States	230	215
England	175	170
Germany	100	104
Italy	75	50

This table serves to confirm both the disparities that exist
between countries, and the fact that the purchasing power
of wages determines—at least approximately, and at least in
industrialized countries—the average level of living of the
nation.

OTHER INDEXES OF THE LEVEL OF LIVING

The preceding estimates may be further checked against
numerous indexes of apparent consumption.

These various indexes confirm, on the whole, the facts
already placed in evidence in this chapter. Hardly a third of
the human species now alive can be said to have a level of
living that surpasses the simple satisfaction of minimum food
needs. The other two-thirds are still in the vegetative phase of
history.

France belongs to the first third, but in spite of the progress
made in the last 200 years, she is far from the head of the movement. Among the nations comprising this first third, and which

Table XXII—Comparison of Purchasing Power in Several Countries between the Wars

Years	France	United States	England	Germany	Italy	Sweden
1914	100	202	152	109	90	155
1920	88	220	173	—	—	175
1929	109	271	177	112	80	211
1932	105	182	195	101	80	202
1935	120	238	191	100	77	194
1938	113	265	188	102	79	189

are considerably dispersed from the United States at one extreme to the Soviet Union at the other, it can hardly be said that France occupies an average position, for, in fact, she seems to be closer to the Soviet Union than to the United States.

The most striking result of this inquiry is that in 1956, nations still existed whose level of living had remained practically the same as during the long centuries of the traditional era, while at the same time others had transformed their living conditions. The world of today simultaneously contains communities that have hardly evolved at all in 2,000 years and others that are in full transition to a new human condition.

What are the causes of this progress? Why have certain peoples been able to reach and maintain a pioneer position? Why are the others barely capable or even incapable of imitating them? What is the dynamic element in contemporary economic evolution?

It is customary to give arbitrary indexes for the level of living of populations. However arbitrary, they convey a clear picture. We know by various means—through tax records or direct enumeration—a whole series of material facts that are unquestionably related to the level of living and the purchasing power of nations.

Table XXIII gives certain statistical fragments of this kind. The figures invite commentary and criticism. Some of them are representative and exact. Others are questionable. Such as they are, they nevertheless bring out orders of magnitude that cannot be challenged.

The four first columns of the table present estimates of the consumption of food items typical of rich nations: sugar, tobacco, tea, coffee, cocoa, oranges, tangerines, bananas. The longitude of the country involved must, of course, be taken into account. The consumption of sugar is one of the most informative items. We saw above that in 1880 the French consumed 8.6 kilos per capita per year, the same as the present-day consumption in Italy. The United States, Great Britain, and the British Dominions were close to 50 kilos per capita per year in 1938, about double the figure for France. During the occupation and postwar rationing, the per capita sugar allotment in France was 6 kilos per year.

Table XXIII—Various Indexes of the Level of Living, around 1938

	Consumption of sugar (kilos per capita)	Consumption of tobacco (kilos per capita)	Consumption of tea, coffee, cocoa (kilos per capita)	Consumption of oranges and bananas (kilos per capita)	Telephone instruments (per thousand of the population)	Telegrams dispatched (per thousand of the population)	Radio sets (per thousand of the population)	Automobiles (per thousand of the population)	Locomotives (per thousand of the population)
United States	49	2.7	8	27	160	161	189	190	52
Great Britain	46	1.7	11	16	58	123	171	37	48
Canada	46	–	–	–	70	–	122	100	–
Australia	–	–	–	–	100	–	131	100	–
Sweden	36	–	–	–	100	–	151	30	–
Norway	27	0.9	7	8	68	123	–	18	21
Holland	41	3.3	13	10	42	65	–	17	17
France	23	1.8	5.6	7	35	99	77	45	50
Germany	25	1.8	3.3	6	50	44	–	14	37
Italy	9	1.2	1.3	11	9	74	15	8	14
Spain	11	1.2	1.4	17	9	62	–	8	16

Table XXIIIa—Various Indexes of the Level of Living, around 1953

	Consumption of sugar (kilos per capita)	Consumption of tobacco (kilos per capita)	Consumption of tea, coffee, cocoa (kilos per capita)	Consumption of oranges and bananas (kilos per capita)	Telephone instruments (per thousand of the population)	Telegrams dispatched (per thousand of the population)	Radio sets (per thousand of the population)	Automobiles (per thousand of the population)	Locomotives (per thousand of the population)
United States	44.5	5.5	10.3	41.3	369.4	134	990	382	28.7
Great Britain	36.5	2.8	7.2	10.7	112.7	119	360	81	41.9
Canada	43.5	4	6	24.6	214.6	150	565	242	34.3
Australia	66.6	2.1	5	25.6	161.2	493	–	251	–
Sweden	43.1	1.4	8.1	18	240.4	116	330	94	21.4
Norway	26.9	1.3	6.8	17.9	144.8	222	270	57	12.9
Holland	37.9	2.8	10.6	12.3	85.5	76	235	57	29.2
France	25.2	1.9	4.9	18.7	59	60	220	88	27.9
Germany	25.5	1.7	3.1	10.8	54.3	53	255	42	27.9
Italy	13	1.5	1.8	19	27.9	77	115	23	13.1
Spain	–	1.6	0.5	19.3	26.1	70	55	7	13.2

$\mathcal{N}otes$ to $\mathcal{C}hapter$ III

1. See also, C. Clark, *The Conditions of Economic Progress;* Office of the United Nations, *Enquête mondiale sur l'alimentation* (1946); *Programmes européens de remise en état et d'amélioration de l'agriculture* (1948); International Emergency Food Council, *Reports of the Secretary General to the Meetings of the Council.*

2. For a discussion of the errors inherent in estimates of real national income, see J. Fourastié, "Sur la mesure des quantités économiques," *Revue d'Économie Politique,* January, 1956.

3. J. Fourastié, *Productivity, Prices and Wages* (1957).

4. *La Civilisation de 1975,* p. 44 ff.

5. July, 1926.

6. We wish to thank Georges Luftalla, to whom Simiand gave his files, who permitted us to use the unedited writings of this great economist, and who authorized the publication of this graph on the level of living.

7. *Bulletin of the General Statistical Office of France,* June-September, 1944.

8. The *Bulletin of the U.S. Bureau of Labor Statistics* published early in 1950 an evaluation of the purchasing power of one hour's wages for food, with the United States equal to 100. The range is from 109 for Australia to 18 for the U.S.S.R. France has an index of 35. China and India are not in the table. The study also indicates "how much time a workman must work to receive a certain product." It can be seen that the spread between the rich and the poor countries is weaker for food than for manufactured products, and weaker for housing and services than for food.

There have been numerous publications on this subject in the past several years. See especially Margaret J. Hagood, "Exploration of Technics for Measuring Economic Density of Population," *Actes du Vᵉ congrès mondial de la population,* Vol. III, pp. 315-31.

9. H. Brousse, *Le niveau de vie en France* (Series, *Que sais-je?*), p. 25.

Chapter IV

LEVEL OF LIVING AND THE PRODUCTIVITY OF WORK

THE CONCLUSIONS of the three previous chapters may be summed up in two essential facts:

1) The average level of living of the population of several great nations has been appreciably improved in the course of recent centuries, in spite of reductions in the duration of work, and increases in the density of population.

2) This improvement in time has created a disparity in space, due to the fact that the levels of living of the different nations of the world have been raised at very different rates. Since the disparities in space can be reduced to disparities in time, the essential problem of the level of living is to find out how the improvement in time occurred.

The observed facts allow us to clarify the problem further. During a long sequence of centuries, the level of living seemed to be controlled by the density of the population. Alfred Sauvy has brought to light the fundamental principle of the population optimum.[1] Below a certain density, economic life was non-existent or at least precarious, but as soon as the population became too dense on a given territory, its level of living decreased because of the decreasing productivity of work. A given square kilometer of land which supports 30 workers and their families with ease, supports 50 less well.

As soon as the population reaches a higher figure, let us say 40, life becomes more difficult, even if the 40 men now work harder than the first 30. The least disturbance in the weather may now provoke famine. Famine leads to the struggle for existence. This struggle may first be under the social form of the defense of the rich against the poor, later under the national form of attack by the peoples who have not yet suffered famine upon those who have just suffered it, are going through it, or are about to go through it. The history of the Middle Ages, and of the *ancien régime* should be reviewed with this insight into the function of the level of living. Without denying the influence of purely human and political facts, such as inheritances and the quarrels of royal families, the wisdom or the foolishness of kings and ministers, it cannot be doubted that famine has played a crucial part in history, although often unperceived by contemporaries and by historians.

The problem that we face is to discover how this famine mechanism was broken; what were the causes, in the scientific sense of the word, that intervened and stimulated, at least for some nations, a parallel increase of the population and of the level of living, although the two phenomena had hitherto been inconsistent as soon as the population reached a certain density? The same causes must explain how it was possible to raise the average level of living of some populations incomparably higher than the highest of those that have come down to us in records of the past.

It is obvious that the search for this factor is of capital interest, not only for economic science but also for political action and, in consequence, for the very life of humanity. If we are able to identify the cause of improvement in the level of living, and if this turns out to be a factor at least partly dependent upon human initiative, we will be able in affecting it, to affect the level of living itself. *We shall know how to improve the level of living of any people.*

The observed fact that must serve as our point of departure, and that the previous discussion most certainly brought to light, is that the level of living of a population is simply the average per capita production. It is, therefore, by studying production and related factors that we will be able to solve the problem. Taking into consideration the essential element of life, *time,* leads us from the notion of production to the notion of productivity. We define *productivity* as production by units of time, or in other words, as the velocity of production.

The study of productivity will turn out to be a satisfactory way of explaining the evolution of the average level of living, the disparities in space, and the differences observed in relation to various forms of consumption. We shall still have to examine the distribution of actual levels of living on both sides of the average. This will lead us to study the function of rents and profits and to show that these rents and profits are themselves results of the phenomena of productivity, in the sense that *the countries of low productivity are the countries of high rents*. Hence, they are also those with a widely opened fan of incomes.

PRODUCTION AND CONSUMPTION

The first theorem of the level of living is that *consumption in a closed economic system cannot permanently exceed production*. (A closed system is that of any area whose exterior commerce plays a minor part.) This fact is logically obvious and also, more important, it is experimentally demonstrable by the comparisons that can be made for any era and for any country, between total consumption estimated directly or indirectly and total production also estimated directly or indirectly. For example, the average consumption of the masses of the French population around 1725 to 1750 can be estimated from the purchasing power of wages at one and one-half pounds of bread per head and per day. This represents for the kingdom an annual consumption of wheat equal to 50 or 55 million quintals. But the area of all the cultivated land, taking account of that lying fallow, multiplied by the average output of the time, also gives 50 million quintals. In the same way, agricultural production can be related to effective consumption at any time whatever.

More generally, when we studied the level of living of the French working masses toward 1830, we noted that the French national income at that time was eight billion francs, which gave the sum of 250 francs as the per capita national income, corresponding quite closely, as we have seen, to the subsistence minimum of that period. In order to give each Frenchman, from 1831 onwards, the subsistence minimum of 1939, it would have been necessary to suddenly raise the national product of France from 8 billion to 20 billion francs.

It is quite impossible to raise the average level of living of a people without raising their output. If the effort is limited to a redistribution of income, the most that can be done—and this with certain difficulties which we shall examine later—is to reduce the dispersion of the observed purchasing powers around the average level; it is not possible to raise the average. For example, it might have been theoretically possible, by a strictly egalitarian distribution, to give to each Frenchman in 1830 the subsistence minimum of Villermé. Even the strictest equalization of income could not have done any more than this. To do better, it would have been necessary to influence production. Leaving for a later section then, the question of the distribution of levels of living on both sides of the average, we shall first study the factors which determine this average.

The second theorem of the level of living is this: *Not only does total production determine total consumption, but in the short term the structure of production also determines the structure of consumption.* Within a closed economy in the course of a period when stored supplies cannot play an important part, it is impossible to convert one commodity into another rapidly. For example, if 1,000 quintals of wheat have been produced, the consumption of wheat will not be able to exceed 1,000 quintals before the next harvest. Moreover, if more than 1,000 quintals are wanted for consumption the following year, it will be necessary to take advance measures to see that the ground is sown to grain. And as always, the crop will be attendant upon the frivolities of the weather.

In this way, the structure of production and the structure of consumption are closely tied to each other, and can only develop jointly and through their effect on production, a form of action *which takes time.*

More exactly, the problem of the development of the structure of production is a *problem of manpower.* If we want to increase the production of wheat, we must have more laborers.

If we want to increase industrial production, the number of workmen must be increased. To get more refrigerators, more refrigerator-makers will be needed.

In sum, *the structure of consumption depends upon the structure of the labor force,* and since the structure of consumption changes when the level of living rises, *any rise in the level of living of a people presupposes mobility in its labor force,* or in other words, is accompanied by changes in occupational distribution.[2]

THE NOTION OF PRODUCTIVITY

It appears that the average level of living of a nation cannot be raised unless per capita production itself is increased. Since the structure of consumption changes as the level of living rises, the structure of production must also change as per capita production increases.

These postulates, expressed as functions of time, take the following form: In order for the average level of living of a people to rise, the total annual production per interval of time must increase, and the labor force must change in such a way that the structure of production adapts itself gradually to the changing structure of consumption.

If we use the term productivity for production per unit of time, we see that the level of living cannot rise except by an increase of productivity, unless the duration of work is increased. On the other hand, if the productivity of labor increases in any sector of the economy, while productivity and duration of work in the other sectors remain constant, the level of living must rise because the total annual production has increased. Either the increase of productivity enlarges production in a direction matching the development of the structure of consumption, and then the rise in the level of living takes place without any shift in the labor force, or the supplementary production is not easily consumed. In the latter case, a crisis of overproduction in this sector will cause a shift of labor to some other unsaturated sector. The level of living will eventually rise because of the increasing consumption of the goods produced by this other sector.

The rise of the level of living, the increase of productivity, and the shifting composition of the labor force are three closely knit phenomena. For each degree of productivity in the different sectors, there is a corresponding value of the average level of living, which correlates to a particular structure of consumption and a particular distribution of the labor force. If, on the other hand, one starts with a profile of average consumption, there will be a corresponding degree of productivity in each of the great sectors of production and a corresponding distribution of the labor force.

Of course, these statements are only applicable to closed economic areas, and indicate only general tendencies. We have noted that differences of custom, climate, and so forth introduce disparities between one country and another. Moreover, the secular trend is greatly influenced in the most backward countries by certain characteristics of the most advanced, so that, for example, although the distribution of the labor force must be about the same in India today as in Europe of 1750, there are already in India a certain number of refrigerators and automobiles, and consequently, though paradoxically, some electricians and some auto mechanics.

The connection between the three phenomena, level of living, labor force, and productivity, being thus recognized, it is not difficult to determine which of them plays the determinant part. Obviously, the level of living can only be a resultant of the two others, and as far as the labor force is concerned, it cannot begin to shift freely from one occupation to another until the time arrives when it is not entirely occupied in the production of food. The mechanism for the improvement of the level of living is then the following: The sciences—first, mathematics, then the physical sciences, finally, the biological sciences and behavioral studies of man at work —provide the necessary means. Man uses these means to increase his influence over things. Scientific progress thus engenders technical progress.

Technical progress so defined, that is, in the broadest possible sense of the term, permits an increase in the productivity of work, which is to say, the output obtained per unit of time. As soon as productivity is sufficiently high so that the people are protected from famine, the realignment of the labor force begins. The distribution of labor changes so that the structure of total production responds to the demands of increasing consumption. Historically, this shift of the labor force was accomplished, it should be noted, at the cost of great suffering for the people involved, for in a laissez-faire system, the movement was seemingly imposed by a social situation whose principles were not understood. It was only by financial ruin and by unemployment that men were informed that their production had been refused by the community.

This is not the place to expand upon all of the elements of this scheme which encompasses so much of economic life. It is only necessary to note the relation between the level of living and the level of productivity, by showing that *no increase in the average level of living is possible without an increase of productivity*. Moreover, empirical observation shows that *there is no increase of the purchasing power of the wage earner with reference to commodities that do not benefit from technical progress*.

PRODUCTIVITY AND PURCHASING POWER

Purchasing power is, as we have seen, the ratio of an income to the price of a consumption item. Up to this point, we have insisted on taking the price of a total schedule of consumption as the denominator of this ratio, for example, the cost of the subsistence minimum, or the typical budget of a working class family in a given country and at a given time. We have already observed that the value of the level of living is closely dependent on the observed structure of consumption, because of important discrepancies in the evolution of the prices of different commodities.

It is now necessary to examine more closely the variations in purchasing power which arise from the nature of the commodities consumed. More exactly, instead of measuring the level of living by reference to a total unit of consumption, we must now examine the results obtained by relating income to the price of specific goods and services.

A. Divergent Secular Trends of the Prices of Various Commodities

Classical economic science has always been attached to the study of the general movement of prices. The work of Simiand, of Hauser, of d'Avenel, of Hanauer, as well as the work of Kugner and of other modern economists, is dominated by the idea that a general price level exists. They have searched in vain for the causes underlying this general price level—in the movement of precious metals, credit, the issue of paper money, and many another phenomenon. If there were such general price trends, it would be possible to derive an *absolute* measurement of purchasing power, by relating average earnings to the general price level. The observed facts stand in absolute contradiction to the idea of a general price trend. More exactly, they show that there are as many "general" movements of prices as there are indexes to measure prices. In other words, the usefulness of an index of prices depends entirely on the elements that constitute the index. To really understand the general trend of prices, it would be necessary to set up an index based upon the totality of observed and observable prices in the entire economy. This is either practically impossible and therefore scientifically meaningless, or it results in a calculation of the national income in current prices. By dividing current wages by current national income we do not arrive at an index of level of living. The product of average salary times total employment always gives an approximation of national income.[3]

As a matter of fact, even the studies of the classical economists showed fundamental divergences in the movement of some prices in relation to others. In his work at the École Pratique des Hautes Études, "New and old studies of the general movements of prices from the sixteenth to the nineteenth century," Simiand encountered these divergencies at every turn, and it was only by virtue of an extremely powerful preconceived idea that he was able to speak at all of a general price movement. A glance at the diagrams published in this book will show that there is no parallelism at all between the different categories of commodities. His diagram number 5, whose data are reproduced in Table XXIV, shows beyond all possible argument the complete divergence between, for example, the price of spices, with an index of 85, and of lumber, with an index of 910. From the year 1500 to 1875, the price of wood was multiplied by nine, the price of crops by six, while the price of metals was multiplied by only 2.7, that of textile products by 2, and that of spices by 0.85.[4]

How is it possible to avoid the explanation of technical progress for this fanning out in the general trend of prices? The fall in textile prices began with the creation of the first factories by Colbert. The fall in spices is related to the development of navigation and the establishment of overseas colonies. The fall in the price of metals is related to progress in mining and processing of minerals. Technical progress in agriculture, not absent but very feeble until 1789 (the iron-axled cart was practically unknown in France before the Revolution), made great strides after 1810. The lumber industry did not benefit from technical progress until about 1900, except for the improvement of transportation.

It is immediately evident that if we measure purchasing power in relation to spices, in relation to manufactured textile products, or in relation to stove wood, we will get results that differ in a ratio of one to ten. The series of Father Hanauer and of Simiand do not include any category of wages, which is a grave omission. It is difficult to see how these authors went

Table XXIV—Index of Current Prices of Various Commodities in Alsace from 1450 to

	1500-25	Average 1500-1600	Circa 1600
Crops, excluding hay	95	200	310
Meat	110	160	200
Wood	90	185	220
Metals	100	165	210
Building materials	85	110	140
Spices	175	160	175
Textile raw materials	—	—	—
Textile manufactured products	75	100	125

* Based on the work of François Simiand.

about constructing a general index of prices, without taking account of this essential price. If they had included an index of the average earnings of laborers, its value, taking 1450-1500 as 100, would have been around 1000 for the period 1850-75. Thus the development of the level of living between these two periods exhibits the following values: in relation to meat and other agricultural products, 1.5; in relation to construction materials and textile raw material, 2; in relation to metals, 4; in relation to finished textile products, 5; in relation to spices, 12. These facts confirm the conclusion reached in Chapter Two. The improvement of purchasing power seems to have been extremely variable, depending upon the commodity taken for reference. The improvement is directly related to the effects of technical progress. For convenience of explanation, we shall call those commodities that have benefited from only slight technical improvement in the course of modern history *tertiary*. We shall term primary or secondary those products which have benefited from great technical progress, reserving the term *primary* for agricultural products and the term *secondary* for non-agricultural products.[5] With this terminology, we can formulate the following propositions: The average purchasing power and the average level of living of a people are not improved except in relation to consumption which corresponds to products that have benefited from an improvement in the productivity of labor. *Purchasing power grows slowly with regard to the consumption of tertiary goods. It increases to a much greater extent with regard to primary and secondary goods.*

1875* (1450-1500 = 100)

Average 1600-1700	Circa 1700	Average 1700-1800	Circa 1800	1800-50	1850-75
370	280	270	410	500	640
250	250	270	380	500	620
240	190	325	590	750	910
225	210	215	250	300	270
240	210	250	430	475	490
250	165	100	120	120	85
—	—	275	430	460	520
175	160	150	165	180	200

These general conclusions are confirmed and elaborated if we attempt to measure the level of living, not only with reference to a group of items of the same type, but also in relation to a good or a service taken alone, as, for example, a quintal of wheat, a square inch of window glass, a haircut, and so forth.

B. The Development of Purchasing Power with Regard to Specific Commodities

In ancient times among the Greeks, an iron cooking utensil was worth more than a woman and more than four cows. In Carolingian times, "a good horse was worth less than his bridle." Thus has technical progress made itself felt since before 1800! A kilogram of pig iron, so unimpressive today, was worth several hundred hours of work in the Middle Ages. The fall of the price of iron in relation to hourly earnings began to be conspicuous after about 1560. However, the long term correlation of the price of wheat and hourly wage rates—indicative of a striking causal relationship—continued, as we have seen, until about 1800. A great number of products began to decrease sharply in comparison to hourly wages after 1830. This category includes practically all manufactured products. A ton of steel was worth 80 dollars on the world market in 1873. It fell to 20 dollars in 1886 after the introduction of the Bessemer process. A kilo of aluminum was worth 80 gold francs in 1886 and 2.5 in 1910. A meter of merino wool sold at Reims for 16 francs in 1816 and 1.45 francs in 1883. Chilean nitrate brought 187 francs a ton in France when artificial nitrate was offered at 125 francs. A kilogram of sugar was sold at five francs in 1811, the date at which Delessert established the first refineries for beet sugar. It was worth 0.6 francs in 1910. These examples can be multiplied almost indefinitely. They cannot be fully appreciated unless we take into account the slow but continuous increase in hourly wages between 1810 (0.15) and 1910 (0.35), so that there was an improvement of purchasing power in the course of this period not only in relationship to all of the commodities whose price in francs had fallen, but even in relationship to all the commodities whose price had not increased more than two fold.

Instead of piling up examples, we shall examine a little more closely the history of certain items of consumption, some of which have benefited from great technical progress while others have not progressed at all.

Productivity and Selling Price. If it takes 1,000 hours of human labor to produce a commodity, it cannot be sold for long for less than 1,000 times the hourly wage of the workman.

Since it still takes a quarter of an hour to cut a man's hair and ten minutes to shave him, the prices of barbers have remained exactly parallel to wage rates for the past 300 years. The price of a haircut varies, according to the luxury of the establishment, between two-thirds and three-thirds of the hourly wage of the journeyman barber.

On the other hand, increases in productivity often cause astronomic falls in price.

The price of glass and mirrors. A bead from a necklace of Queen Hatshepsut fixes 1400 B.C. as the oldest date in the history of glass. The glass makers who are represented on the walls of the Hypogeum of Beni Hassoun, blow through pipes of the same model as the glass makers of 1900. Until about 1650, glass panes were made by blowing. It was necessary first to start an enormous bottle. The two ends were then removed and the remaining cylinder was cut along a line and stretched out flat. Towards 1850, important technical progress had been made in handling pieces in process, abolishing the work of those unhappy children whom the workmen called "the fire meat." After the end of the seventeenth century, glass could be made to flow, but it was only in 1902 that the Frenchman Fourcault introduced a workable industrial process for manufacturing window glass by extrusion.

Since severe conditions of temperature, of homogeneity, and of transparence were to be met, we can understand how the production of a large piece encountered numerous obstacles before the development of modern techniques. It is quite clear why, until 1900, window glass and mirrors remained very much more expensive, by weight, than goblets and bottles.

In 1702, a single mirror of four square meters required, on the average, 35,000 to 40,000 hours of work. These were the largest which could then be produced. The mirror surface re-

quired even more work than the glass pane. It was polished
with sand and emery, before being coated.

It was not until the twelfth century that the glassmakers
discovered how to obtain the necessary temperature conditions
to make *transparent* glass panes or stained glass of a few square
centimeters. Before that, no house and no church, however
rich it might be, had glass windows. This can be seen by an
examination of the paintings of the old masters.

As far as the house was concerned, the fourteenth century
was the century of transition. Formerly, there was no glass.
The windows were closed only by full shutters, by wooden
trellises, or by waxed cloth. The Romans, they say, used horn
in their palaces, or mica, a translucent mineral which comes in
thin layers. Panels of horn have also been discovered in some
French castles. Leaves of oiled parchment were sometimes used.
Giotto, Fra Angelico, and all the painters before 1400 show
the windows without any covering. The celebrated madonnas
Benois and Litta of Leonardo da Vinci in the Museum of Leningrad, and the "Annunciation" of Cima da Conegliano in the
same museum, still show windows without any glass, although
in very richly furnished rooms.

The oldest painting I know that shows a window entirely
covered with glass is the "Annunciation" of an unknown old
master, at the Museum of Basle, dated by experts at 1470. But
this is not a matter of window panes. These are clumsy lumps
of glass, translucent but not transparent, such as one still sees
in old Alsatian houses.

Glass remained so dear until about 1600 that even the
richest houses could only provide panes for the upper part of
the windows. The lower part was closed with a full shutter of
wood, sometimes lightened by a small opening in the center.
This arrangement can be seen in hundreds of paintings of the
great Italian, French, and Flemish primitives. One of the most
interesting in this respect is the "Annunciation" of the Master
of Flémalle, of about 1428, in the Mérode collection at Antwerp. One sees very clearly in this picture the glass panes at the
top of the window. The lower part is provided with wooden
trellis work, while the middle part cannot be closed except
by full wooden shutters.[6]

Thanks to the accounts kept by Colbert for the Château of Versailles, it is possible to know the going price of mirrors at the time the palace was constructed. By a privy seal contract executed January 2, 1684, between the royal administration of buildings and Messrs. Pequot and Guymont, agents for the factory recently established at Paris which became the Saint-Gobain Company, the following prices were charged:

	Regular price	Special price to King
14 inch mirrors	3 livres, 4 sous	2 livres, 15 sous
44-45 inch mirrors	470 livres	352 livres

We see the enormous differences of price occasioned by small differences of surface. The hourly wage of the average workman was then about 18 *deniers,* equal to 1.5 *sous* or to .075 *livres.* Louis XIV himself could not have mirrors longer than 45 inches for Versailles. Each of these mirrors was worth 352 *livres,* or 5,000 hourly wage units of a laborer, or more than 7,000 dollars. In the construction of the fine mansions of the time, the mirrors cost commonly as much as the furniture and the upholstery. For the Hôtel d'Avary, in the rue de Grenelle, constructed in 1718, the expenditure for mirrors reached 28,400 *livres,* as against 16,700 for upholstery and 60,000 for all the woodwork and furniture.

The continued increase of productivity led to a steady decline in the price. The four-square-meter mirror which cost 2,750 *livres* in 1702 (close to 40,000 hourly wage units), was worth only 1,245 francs in 1845 (6,900 hourly wage units), and 262 francs in 1862 (1,000 hourly wage units). After 1900, the introduction of the turntable method put the bureau with a mirror within reach of the average worker. The four-square-meter mirror was sold in 1905 for 60 francs, or about 200 hourly wage units. It cost some 20,000 francs in 1955, or 135 hourly wage units. In 1567, the stewards of the Duke of Northumberland still dismounted the glass windows of the castle during the master's absence, but in 1945, window glass had ceased to be a serious item in the budget of a workman.

Thus, measured in four-square-meter mirrors, the purchasing power of a laborer has improved by better than 200 to 1. *The Accounts of the Château of Versailles* allow us, on the other hand, to measure the evolution of purchasing power with regard to a service that has not benefited from any technical progress until the most recent years—the waxing of wooden floors. To wax ten square meters of floor in 1685 took three *sous* or about two hourly wage units. To do the same in 1955 by non-mechanical methods cost 300 francs, or still two hourly wage units. The stagnation of purchasing power is empirically observed to be perfect, as theoretically expected.

So we see that economic evolution shows us the progressive reduction of the price of commodities subject to great technical progress in comparison to the price of commodities subject to little or no technical progress. A commodity or a service that has not benefited from any technical progress since 1700 must cost as much today—in hourly wage units—as under Louis XIV.

We are led to ask if the difference that we observe today in the level of living between the different countries of the world does not have its source, and therefore its cause, in differences in the intensity of technical progress achieved in those countries. As soon as it is proved that the evolution of the level of living is caused essentially by technical progress, it is evident that the different countries of the world, not having arrived at the same point along the route of technical progress, must show appreciable disparities of price among themselves.

Factually, it is known that in a country like the United States, technical progress has gone much further than in France, while countries like China are near the point where France was in 1850.

If this hypothesis is correct, we ought to find that goods or services not subject to technical progress or at least to very little progress (what we have called tertiary goods and services) cost about the same amount in all countries. Put another way, the price of this given good or this given service, divided by the hourly wage of the place where it is produced, should give the same or similar figures in all countries. By contrast, the price of commodities subject to great technical progress, those which are secondary or primary, should present differences relatively great insofar as the countries compared have arrived at different stages of industrialization.

These expectations can be completely confirmed in the

world of today. Towards the end of 1947, the hourly wage was
about one dollar in the United States and about 60 francs in
France. A frigidaire of 150 cubic decimeters, a secondary product, was worth 150 dollars in the United States, or 150 hourly
wage units, and 60 thousand francs in France, or 1,000 hourly
wage units. On the other hand, a haircut, a tertiary service,
was worth one dollar in the United States, or one hour's salary,
and sixty francs in France, or again, one hour's salary.

The international money market introduces into these real
prices a disturbance which makes them appear anarchic. In
effect, the exchange rate is an average rate, intended to permit
an approximate equilibrium in the balancing of accounts. This
rate of exchange does not serve to equalize the hourly wage
rates except between countries that have attained a similar
technical level.

Between countries of very different technical levels, like
France and the United States, the exchange rates make hourly
wages appear to be very high in the rich countries and very low
in the poor countries. This permits the exchange of products
costing three or four hours of work in the poor countries against
products that require only one hour of work in the rich countries. At the official rate of exchange, one dollar equals 350
francs. The hourly average wage of a laborer in industry was
450 francs in the United States and 150 francs in France in
1955. With such an exchange rate, France was able to compete
on the world market with American producers, with all products for which her productivity was more than one-third of
American productivity. An incidental consequence is that tertiary products and services appear very expensive in the United
States in relation to their cost in France.

Table XXV below, which compares prices on the basis of
the official rate of exchange in the cities of Paris, Cairo, and New
York, shows that in countries of little technical progress, tertiary
commodities are less expensive than in countries with great
technical progress, while on the other hand, secondary products
are much more expensive in Cairo than in New York. *This
is the explanation of the important phenomenon of price disparity in the modern world.*

In the same way it follows from the preceding considerations that the purchasing power of the hourly wage of the laborer, expressed in tertiary goods, is the same in all the countries of the world, and is fixed in time. The improvements in the differences of purchasing power are only shown in relationship to primary and secondary goods or services.[7]

The bonds of cause and effect linking technical progress, the productivity of labor, and the average level of living of a people, show themselves clearly. If an object is sold at one time at a price equivalent to 200 hourly wage units and at another time at 50 hourly wage units, it is probably because its cost of production was close to 200 hourly wage units during the first period and later was close to 50 units. Furthermore, if an object is sold in one country for 200 hourly wage units and in another at 50, it is because its manufacture and distribution take about 200 hours of average labor in the first country and about 50 in the second. Here we encounter the problem of cost of production. Selling price differs from cost of production by variable quantities that may be considerable when positive and may occasionally also appear as negative. These are rents and profits. It is entirely obvious that rents and profits cannot explain differences as large as that of the 200 to 1 which we have noted for the price of mirrors. Nor can they explain the differences of the order of one to five, ten, or twenty shown in

Table XXV—Disparity of Prices in the World*

	Cairo	Paris	New York
Secondary Products:			
Radio set, popular model	$102.30	$58.10	$30.20
Wool blanket for single bed	17.20	9.30	7.90
Automobile tire, 600 x 16	27.90	15.80	14.90
Electric current, 1 kw-h at household rate	.09	.07	.04
City gas, per cubic meter	.07	.05	.02
Tertiary Products and Services:			
Monthly wages of unskilled laborer	16.30	44.20	139.50
Haircut	.14	.28	1.00
Hourly rate of domestic cleaning woman	.11	.23	.93
Mixed Products and Services:			
Electric permanent wave	8.10	3.20	9.80
100 kilometers of railway travel,			
second class or coach	1.60	1.50	2.00

* See French edition for detailed sources. The figures refer to the period about 1948. Francs have been translated into dollars at the official rate for May, 1948.

Table XXV between the U. S., France, and Egypt. A radio costs about ten to fifteen hourly wage units in the United States, 80 to 120 in France, and 600 hourly wage units in Egypt.

THE DISTRIBUTION OF LEVELS OF LIVING
ABOVE AND BELOW THE AVERAGE

It was said above that the available documents show an objective trend toward the closing of the fan of salaries in France. This tendency is verified by the observation of backward countries like China and India.[8]

It is interesting to see how technical progress does away with traditional rents and profits. The example of land will show this clearly.

Let us take the case of a territory in which internal commerce is not important and outline the history of the formation of rents and of their later disappearance:

1) As long as the country is technically backward, during the traditional period the first occupants of the country will occupy the best lands. Let us suppose that 100,000 inhabitants cultivate 100,000 hectares of very fertile land. They live comfortably, their food is abundant, they proliferate. There is no rent.

2) The youngest sons begin to occupy the less good land adjacent to that of the oldest. Since they cannot cultivate more ground than their brothers in the course of the year, and in fact must cultivate less because it is poorer land, their per capita productivity falls, together with the output per hectare. The elder brothers enjoy a rent relative to the younger.

3) As the population grows, this is accentuated. The good lands are much sought after. Their proprietors can hire them out and demand rent in cash or kind. Political power grows out of this economic power founded in property and rent, together with social "exploitation" in the Marxist sense.

4) The more densely the country is settled and the more backward its technique, the greater the necessity of cultivating marginal lands. The stony and broken ground of the Causse

is then cultivated at the same time as the marvelous river bottom of the Lot. The former yields one unit, while the latter gives five. The proprietor of the river bottom can easily rent it out for 3 or 3.5. He becomes a baron and builds the chateau that keeps the frightened serf respectful of the arrangement. Besides, the serf knows that he cannot find a better income elsewhere. The regime is politically stable.

5) A famine or an epidemic reduces the population. The men of a certain hilly district where the soil yields two or three units, die off. The serfs of the valley desert and occupy the vacant land. The rents of the proprietors of poor land disappear. Those of the proprietors of good land are reduced.

As the population grows again, a new cycle begins.[9]

6) Let us suppose now that by means of technical progress the average output of the land is doubled. If the population does not double, a grave agricultural crisis develops. Schematically, let us suppose that the population is constant. More than half of the fields become useless. The peasant proprietor of poor land, ruined, looks for work in town. Meanwhile the rent of the proprietors of good land falls accordingly.

The limits can be readily seen. If 100,000 hectares produced sufficient food to feed 40 million Frenchmen, only the 100,000 best hectares of France would have any value at all. Moreover, this value would be low, since the output of marginal land (the 100,001st hectare), would be very close to the output of the best hectare.

This model explains land devaluation in technically progressive countries, and can be observed in all the regions of France since 1880. In the course of the nineteenth century, the general movement of the price of land reached a maximum around 1880, which corresponds to the date when the phenomenon *technical progress* became more important than the phenomenon *growth of the population*. Today, the real price of good cultivable land in France, that is to say, the price of a hectare expressed in hourly wage units, is four to six times lower than in 1880.[10]

This mechanism also explains the facts observed by Simiand and Colson who were not able to explain them. The income from unbuilt-upon real estate was equal to ten billion hours of work in 1850, compared to 15 billion in 1880, and only five billion in 1925.

The same mechanism accounts for industrial profits. As long as the progress of productivity is restricted to a fraction of the economy, it creates rents for the benefit of those producers whose productivity has advanced. The selling price tends always to be fixed at a point above the cost of the least efficient producer whose production is necessary to satisfy the demand. In the long run, however, technical progress tends to cancel profits by increasing the productivity even of marginal producers, and above all, by increasing the volume of production of the best equipped producers. Every improvement in productivity creates a profit for its initiator, but at the same time destroys the profit of outmoded forms of production.

In the long run, this outcome is inevitable. But in the short run it can be delayed at the insistence of the producers, in the very common situation of imperfect competition. Either the producers combine to maintain the selling price as if no technical improvements had been introduced, or the price maintains itself because of the tacit restrictions of the producers, or even sometimes of the merchants who sell the commodity to the public. In general, it is an economic crisis that forces the sellers to give up their open or covert combination. The crisis is not, as the classic economists believed, the cause of falling prices, but only the occasion. If there had not been an improvement in productivity, there could not be any permanent decrease in selling price, depression or no.

We note that around 1929 the real value of French land (expressed as usual in hourly wage units) was less than a quarter of the value for 1879-81. The houses and castles had fallen by 1924-25 to 70 per cent of their value in 1851, and 40 per cent of their value in 1889. Only the factories and personal property had increased their real value from 1851 to 1925, but even in these categories there had been an appreciable decline after a maximum reached around 1912.

These facts, hardly noticed by the economists, were attributed to "currency devaluation." But they were appreciable before 1912, and could be observed also in the United States.

Table XXVI—Evolution of Capital, Interest, Hourly Wages, and National Income
in France from 1850 to 1925

	VALUE OF PRIVATE CAPITAL		RETURNS FROM PRIVATE CAPITAL		
	in billions of current francs	in billions of hourly wage units	in billions of current francs	in billions of hourly wage units	HOURLY WAGE RATE
About 1850	90	460	3.0	15	0.195
1879-80	186	810	6.6	29	0.23
1890	200	800	7.3	29	0.25
1900	206	710	7.5	26	0.29
1910	240	730	10.0	30	0.33
1924-25	735	365	46	23	2.0

In our opinion, they are really the direct result of the action
of technical progress on rents and profits.

*The consumer's budget, the labor force, and the national
income.* Even if there were as many rich as poor, the level of
living of the poor could not be raised to that of the middle
income group by distributing total income equally among all
citizens. The total food consumption of rich and poor together
adds to 1,000 plus 360, or 1,360. The average is 680 instead
of the 900, which is the food consumption of the average worker
(see Table XXVII). In contrast, the consumption—and therefore also the production—of miscellaneous items would amount
to 6,000 plus 60, or 6,060, for an average of 3,030, although
a middle income budget would require only 900 for miscellaneous expenditures. There would therefore be too many
"other" commodities and not enough food.

Table XXVII—Model of Private Expenditures in Relation to National Output

	Food	Housing, Furniture and Clothing	Miscellaneous	Total
The Rich:				
% of budget	10	30	60	100
Amount expended	1,000	3,000	6,000	10,000
The Middle group:				
% of budget	30	40	30	100
Amount expended	900	1,200	900	3,000
The Poor:				
% of budget	60	30	10	100
Amount expended	360	180	60	600

Thus, to equalize the income of a population composed of two classes equal in number, one rich and the other poor, it would be necessary not only to equalize their money incomes but *to modify the structure of production,* and especially to obtain a greater volume of food. However, this is not always possible. For example, it was impossible in France before 1800. In the cases where it is possible, it always implies a transfer of manpower which takes time, and then of investments which require accumulation. It also involves the training or re-training of workers.

Economic problems are labor force problems. The average production of rice in a country is 500 grams per capita. If the Maharaja is exiled and his income is divided among the hundred thousand poor Hindus, the nominal monetary income of each one is doubled, but the production of rice does not increase, and so the consumption of rice remains at 500 grams per capita. The price of rice doubles.

Table XXVIII—The Paradox of the Maharaja and the Poor Hindus

	1 Maharaja	100,000 Poor Hindus
Annual per capita income	40,000,000 money units	400
Daily per capita caloric intake	5,000	1,000
Daily per capita consumption of rice	100 grams	500
Total annual consumption of rice	36 kilograms	18,250,000
Non-alimentary consumer expenditures	39,800,000 money units	0
Total income of the "class"	40,000,000 money units	40,000,000

In order to raise the level of living of the 100,000 poor Hindus, it is necessary to change the occupation of the individuals to whom the Maharaja gave an opportunity to perform non-agricultural labor by buying their secondary or tertiary production—always supposing that there is enough land to increase the output of rice.

In any case, the total national production will be considerably diminished. In order to obtain a very small increase in agricultural production, it will be necessary to virtually ruin secondary and tertiary production, which will ultimately have grave repercussions for primary production as well. Hence the stability of high-rent regimes in very poor countries.

The only practical solution to the problem is an increase of productivity which is a long-term solution. One must have the courage to say that *in the short run, there is no solution.* By itself, the removal of the Maharaja cannot raise the level of living of the poor Hindu.

Table XXIX illustrates the fundamental relationship between the budget structure of the low-income population and the structure of national production and therefore of the labor force.

It is impossible to increase the people's consumption of manufactured products, housing, and so forth, without altering the structure of production. Conversely, the average level of living of a people without exterior commerce can be deduced from the distribution of the labor force alone.

The disparities that may be observed between the structure of the worker's budget and the structure of national production are due in part to the consumption of the prosperous classes and even more to savings for productive investment.[10a] However, since the working classes form the mass of the nation,

Table XXIX—The Structure of National Consumption and National Production
(Percentage Distributions)

	At Farm Prices (primary)	FOOD Processing Services (tertiary)	HOUSING & Other Services	Other— Goods (secondary)	TOTAL
France, 1800:					
Structure of the worker's budget	78	5 ⌣ 10		7	100
Structure of the national product	70	18		12	100
Structure of the labor force	80	12		8	100
United States 1950:					
Structure of the worker's budget	20	20 ⌣ 25		35	100
Structure of the national product	18	55		28	101
Structure of the labor force	20	50		30	100

these disparities are necessarily slight. They might even be nil in a socialist society.

The disparities noted between the structure of national income and the structure of the labor force have to do with differences of wage rates and average incomes in different occupations. Agriculture is in general the least favored, while tertiary occupations are the most favored. Here, too, the more a country approaches socialism, the more these disparities diminish.

The fundamental relationship, expressed by Table XXIX, among the level of living, national production, and occupational structure, is mediated by the common element in all of these phenomena—technical progress. *Technical progress is the independent variable of economic life.* It has as much influence under a liberal as under a dictatorial government, in a capitalist as in a collectivist system. This determinism obviously extends also to the secondary manifestations of economic life: prices, salaries, taxation, and so forth.

The figures of the table show that the problem of purchasing power cannot be resolved by changing the income distribution alone. Suppose a social revolution had taken place in 1830. Even if it had succeeded in equalizing the revenues of the whole population without disorganizing production, it would have had no permanent effect unless it led to a new distribution of the labor force in order to adapt production to a new structure of consumption. It is certain, in any case,

Table XXX—Minimum Subsistence, Compared to Per Capita Consumption
(kilograms per year)

	Sugar	Wheat	Coal	Wine
Subsistence standard of 1831	0	220	150	0
Average consumption of 1831	2.3	154	70	26 liters
Subsistence standard of 1949	7.3	100	500	73 "
Average consumption of 1938	23.8	222	1,600	116 "
Production which would have been required to guarantee the subsistence standard of 1949 to each Frenchman of 1831 (thousands of metric tons)	237	3,250	16,250	2,400
Production achieved in 1831 (thousands of metric tons)	75	4,300	2,300	817

that it could not then have provided the level of living that is considered a bare minimum at the present time.

For example, to give 7.3 kilograms of sugar to each inhabitant—the amount now considered as a minimum subsistence ration—it would have been necessary to produce 237,000 tons of sugar. The actual production was then 75,000. The same may be said of all other products except for the classic commodities of the poor—wheat, potatoes, barley, and rye—of which there would have been a small surplus.

Men of the traditional era gradually came to a fairly clear perception of the cause and effect relationship between consumption and production, between the structure of consumption and the structure of production, and finally, the labor force. As a matter of fact, at least eight-tenths of the population did not consume anything but the product of their own work or, rather a part of that product. Technical progress has concealed this determinism by separating work from consumption. The workmen who make automobiles do not eat automobiles, but bread, meat, and so forth. I produce books, courses, lectures, and I consume bread, meat, and many other commodities. The worker is thus led to regard his consumption as independent of his own work, and consumption in general as independent of production in general. His salary alone seems to determine his purchasing power, even though a general revision of salaries only amounts to a change in the monetary unit.

In *The Man with the Forty Crowns,* Voltaire showed that in his time the essential determinism of the level of living had been perceived. "The Geometer" in the scene is Deparcieux:

THE MAN WITH 40 CROWNS: Do me, I beg you, the favor of telling me how many animals with two hands and two feet there are in France.

THE GEOMETER: There are supposed to be about twenty million, and I should like to adopt this likely figure, at least until it is verified, which would be very easy and which no one has yet done because it is never possible to keep track of everything.

THE MAN WITH 40 CROWNS: How many acres do you suppose are contained in the territory of France?

THE GEOMETER: 130 million, of which half are in roads, in

cities, villages, moors, heaths, swamps, dunes, barren land, useless woods, pleasure gardens more agreeable than useful, uncultivated land, bad land badly cultivated. We can reduce the productive land to 75 million square acres, but suppose we reckon 80 million. It is little enough to do for the fatherland.

THE MAN WITH 40 CROWNS: How much do you suppose that each acre produces in a fair year, taking one with another, in wheat, in grains of all kinds, wine, fisheries, wood, metals, cattle, fruit, linen, silk, oil, including all expenses, and without counting taxes?

THE GEOMETER: If they produce 25 *livres* each, it is a great deal. However, let us say 30 *livres* so as not to discourage our fellow citizens. There are acres which produce 300 *livres* consistently. There are others which produce three. The proportional mean between 3 and 300 is 30. As you can see, 3 is to 30 as 30 is to 300. It is true that if there are many three-*livre* acres and very few at 300 *livres,* our account will not balance, but once more, I do not wish to haggle.

THE MAN WITH 40 CROWNS: Very well, sir, how much will the 80 million acres produce in money income?

THE GEOMETER: The calculation is already made. They will produce annually two billion, four hundred million *livres* at current values . . .

THE MAN WITH 40 CROWNS: I understand. But you have told me that there are 20 millions of us, men and women, old and young. How much for each one, if you please?

THE GEOMETER: 120 *livres,* or 40 crowns.

THE MAN WITH 40 CROWNS: You have guessed my income exactly. I have four acres which, counting the idle years together with the productive years, are worth 120 *livres*. It is very little. Imagine if everyone had an equal portion as in the Golden Age, everyone would have only five golden *louis* per year?

THE GEOMETER: Not more, according to our estimate, which I have made a little generously. Such is the state of human nature. Life and fortune are strictly limited. Taking one with another, we do not live more than 22 or 23 years in Paris. Taking one with another, we do not have more than 120 *livres* per year to spend, that is to say, that your food, your clothing, your housing, your furniture, may be represented by the sum of 120 *livres* . . .

THE MAN WITH 40 CROWNS: . . . If we decided to have twice as many children as we do have, so that our population was doubled, and we had 40 million inhabitants in the place of 20, what would happen then?

THE GEOMETER: Either we would each have only 20 crowns on the average to spend, or the soil would have to produce twice as much as it now produces, or there would be twice as many of the poor, or we would have to have twice as much industry and gain twice as much by foreign trade, or send half of the nation to America, or half of the nation might eat the other.

THE MAN WITH 40 CROWNS: Let us then be satisfied with our 20 million people, and our 120 *livres* per head, distributed as God pleases, but still this situation is sad and your century of iron is a hard one.

THE GEOMETER: No nation is better off; there are many in worse condition. Do you think that they have enough in the North to give the equivalent of 120 *livres* to each inhabitant? If they had had that much, the Huns and Goths, the Vandals and the Franks, would not have deserted their home lands to go and settle elsewhere, with fire and steel in their hands.

THE MAN WITH 40 CROWNS: If I let you go on, you will soon persuade me that I am happy with my 120 francs.

THE GEOMETER: If you thought yourself happy, then in that case you would be so. . . .

THE INFLUENCE OF THE ECONOMIC CRISIS
ON THE LEVEL OF LIVING

If we examine the statistics of the level of living since 1830 or 1850, in a period of crisis, that is; if we compare, for example, hourly wages with the price of basic commodities, we find only weak effects. The purchasing power of wages varies little during periods of crisis. On the other hand, if, instead of speaking of real wages, we consider the average real income of the whole of the population, we observe an appreciable decline in the average level of living of the nation.

On the one hand, wages do not decline more than prices and often less. On the other, the average total income certainly declines during depressions.

Why does income fall more than the average wage rate? For two important reasons. The first is that crises in the modern period are manifested principally by the fact that a large number of wage earners lose their jobs or are no longer employed full time. It is the fundamental characteristic of crises in the present era to cause very serious unemployment.

The second reason is that the profit of entrepreneurs, and the returns from investment suffer a veritable collapse. This is due to the distress selling of inventories and to the fall of prices generally.

Consequently, the wage earners who do not lose their position maintain a purchasing power that is not very different from what it was previously even if their earnings are reduced, since prices have also been reduced. But the unemployed lose their wages and, in the liberal economies of the nineteenth century, they had no other resources. In the more developed economies of today, the unemployed receive insurance or relief, but their level of living falls considerably nevertheless.

Profits decline more during a crisis than wages. As a matter of fact, it is because of the fall in profits that unemployment occurs. When managers see their businesses threatened and limited, and their sales made with difficulty, they lighten their payrolls and operate on a reduced scale. It may be that the enterprise comes to a complete halt and disappears. *Crises can only be remedied by shifts within the labor force.*

In conclusion, the facts that appear to be capital for the scientific study of the causes of improvement in the level of living are the following:

1) There has been an appreciable improvement during the past 150 or 200 years in all of the countries of the world, but according to very different time schedules. As Karl Marx wrote, "The country which is most developed industrially shows to those which follow on the industrial ladder the image of their own futures."

This circumstance gives the economist a research situation that is close to the experimental condition: Wherever the rise in the level of living is most rapid, there the causes of the movement will operate with greater force.

2) The improvement, within a given country, is very irregular when we consider a range of commodities. With respect to certain commodities, no improvement at all can be seen, while for others, the improvement in 150 years has been of the order of 1 to 200.

These two facts enable us to identify the causes of the improvement in the level of living. By comparing very different sequences of development (for example, bicycles and tapestries since 1890), we can discover the determinant factor which affects one case and not the other.[11]

An experimental analysis of this kind makes technical progress appear to be the *principal* cause of the improvement of the people's level of living and of the purchasing power of the working masses, at least such technical progress as increases the productivity of human labor. It is very easy to observe and to verify empirically that all the products for which there has been improvement in purchasing power have also benefited from an increase in productivity (mirrors, lighting, transportation, bicycles, manufactured and agricultural products in general), while the commodities associated with little or no improvement in purchasing power (the cost of hospital care, tuition fees, haircuts, tapestry, book bindings, objects of art, handicraft objects, services in general) have not been subject to any major improvement in productivity.

These experimental facts are easy to understand rationally. Since productivity is the ratio of a volume of production to the direct or indirect labor time necessary to obtain that volume of production, it is simply the reciprocal of the cost of production expressed in hours of labor.[12] If productivity is constant, the cost of production is proportional to wages.

Consequently, with a constant productivity, the improvement of purchasing power cannot be obtained except by a reduction of the difference between the cost of production and the selling price. For all of the important products and services in today's market, this gap turns out to be negligible compared with the gains made possible by the improvement of productivity. On no important product or service, in fact, was the rate of profits ever higher in France than about 20 per cent of the selling price. More often it is of the order of two to five per cent. Yet the gains made possible in the past century by the improvement of productivity for these same products are of the order of 100, 200, 300, and even 10,000 per cent. *The effects of productivity are more important than the effects of profit, in the middle run as well as in the long run,* so far as the improvement of the level of living of the masses is concerned.[13] Among the factors that determine the value of a commodity (labor, scarcity, need, profits, surplus value, etc.), the factor of labor turns out to be predominant for a great number of essential goods.

It would be obviously absurd to conclude from this that there is no problem of profits. In the first place, even when they are small in relative value, they may be large in absolute amount. Again, profits may be slight in comparison to the gains of productivity, but considerable in relation to the cost of production. Finally, for a great number of products, contrary to what occurs for others, *the phenomenon of profit is more important than the phenomenon of productivity.* It would be extremely useful to make a list of products in rank order of the rate of profit. This does not appear impossible to do. By analyzing the annual accounts of enterprises over a sufficiently long period—thus permitting hidden reserves to appear —we would have at least an approximate list. One could then identify some cases where an effort to improve the level of living would have to be directed principally to the reduction or suppression of profits, along with those cases where the improvement of productivity is called for. It is already certain that many of the important commodities in the worker's budget fall into this latter category. It is also certain that in those cases where profits are important, such profits are more often commercial than industrial or agricultural. The struggle for the reduction of profits, like the effort to improve productivity, is linked to the rational distribution and utilization of the labor force.

Since the level of living is in large measure determined by the productivity of labor, and since this productivity also controls economic development in general—the movement of prices, crises, foreign commerce, government fiscal policy, and the duration of work—it is easy to understand the close relation, in a closed economic system, between the level of living and each of the essential factors of economic life. For example, in a closed economy, with a high level of living, it will always be found that the labor force has shifted towards tertiary occupations and that, nevertheless, tertiary services appear scarce and are very expensive in relation to primary and secondary goods.

Notes to Chapter IV

1. Alfred Sauvy, *Théorie générale de la population*, Vol. I.

2. This important fact reveals the obstacles that make it difficult to raise the level of living of the masses by the suppression of high incomes alone. We have seen that spending habits vary a great deal with income. The poor spend from 60 to 90 per cent for food. The upper income groups, on the contrary, spend 60 to 80 per cent for services and luxuries. If the highest incomes were divided among the poor, the latter would not buy services or luxuries, but food. Therefore, food would not be more abundant because high incomes were suppressed. It would be necessary that the men who provide services change their work.

For example, if, at the present time, we wanted to raise the level of living of the population of India by suppressing the high incomes of the local princes, the nominal income of each worker could probably be doubled. They would then try to buy double the amount of rice they now consume. Since the production of rice would not have been *ipso facto* changed, the price of rice would double, and there would be no improvement in real buying power. There could only be an improvement by returning to work on the land the labor force responsible for the services and luxuries of the Maharaja. But since the land capable of growing rice is already under cultivation, and since the law of diminishing returns would come into play, such action would be rather ineffective. It must be realized, too, that this transfer of population would not be easy, and that the new arrivals would be ill-adapted to agricultural labor. The controls and the police necessary for this change would absorb an important fraction of the labor force. Furthermore, the average level of living being insufficient to provide for education, it would be necessary to reconstitute a privileged class entitled to education. This example, while completely theoretical, suggests the necessary conditions for efficacious political reform. In brief, *it is not taking away Mr. Rockefeller's box at the opera which provides more steak for the poor, but rather the production of more steak.*

These facts give some insight into the difficulty of solving the problems of a technically backward country. They evoke the essential problems of present day China and India.

3. J. Fourastié, "Indirect Measurement of Productivity," *Productivity, Prices, and Salaries* (OEEC, 1957).

4. It is instructive under these conditions to see how Simiand, dominated by his thesis, neglected these differences. A different frame of reference would have made him see them in a different light and helped to explain them. A scientific attitude, sincerely believed to be "objective," is in reality influenced by general ideas and even more strongly so because they are latent. Objective attitude? But what objects should be observed? The mind must choose. It is this opposition between the limited mental process and the multiplicity of the external world that sets the limits of science. The criterion of success is not to take in all observable facts (which is still impossible), but first to identify and then to relate those that are important for the proposed action.

One must always be aware of the subjective quality of objectivity. It is indispensable to scientific research. If Simiand had been aware of this, he would have been guided by facts other than those which captured his attention. He would have seen that in the matter of the evolution of prices, disparity was more important than parallelism. The observation of disparities would have revealed the causes of parallelisms to him and led to a solution of his problem.

It is interesting to follow the development of his thoughts in his book. At times he was so close to the solution that another step would have solved the problem. Thus when he wrote:

> We have, on the other hand, price changes of industrial materials, or even of industrial products, which would indicate a relatively very low level:
> Is this not due to a grouping of economic conditions, evidently of great importance for industrial exploitation, and which might have a connection with the changes leading to the dimunition of cost of production—change in the organization of work, change in the utilization of other means of production, or in other words, the group of factors which we call "the industrial revolution"?

Unfortunately Simiand stops here; he does not develop this idea. He returns immediately to the general consideration of modifications in income and relative levels, of the economic conditions of consumption and distribution, etc. (*Op. cit.*, p. 198).

5. It might seem more logical to use only two adjectives here, one for technically progressive products and one for technically unprogressive products. But it will be seen further on that among the technically progressive products it is useful to distinguish between agricultural and non-agricultural items. The distinction between degrees of progress is itself somewhat arbitrary, since we are dealing with a continuum.

The reader will recognize the terms "primary," "secondary," and "tertiary" as those of Allen B. Fisher. Although I give these words quite a different meaning from his, I hope that Mr. Fisher will think it legitimate.

6. The fundamental question of window glass will be taken up later. We can speak here of the "civilization of glass."

Among the paintings showing the history of glass, the following are particularly representative:

a) Paintings representing windows with no system of closing:

> Giotto (1276-1336), *Announcement Made to St. Anne* (Chapel of Sacro Vegni).
>
> Leonardo da Vinci (1452-15519). *The Benois Madonna, The Litta Madonna* (Leningrad Museum); *The Last Supper* (Milan).
>
> Botticelli (1441-1510), *Portrait of St. Vespucci* (Berlin, Private collection).
>
> Metzys (1466-1530), *Virgin with Cherries* (Cincinnati, Private collection).
>
> Schaufelein (1480-1540), *Portrait of a Man* (Basle Museum).

Maître de Moulins (1498), *Peter II with a Patron Saint.*
b) Pictures representing richly furnished interiors, with the windows partly covered with small translucent squares of glass:

Maître de Flémalle (1428), *The Annunciation.* (Merode Collection at Antwerp.) [The painted window in this picture is typical; the top part is of stationary stained glass panes, the middle of wooden shutters, and the bottom of wood lattice.]

Carpaccio (1456-1525), *The Celestial Apparition to St. Ursula* (Academy of Venice).

Van der Weyden (1399-1464), *Annunciation* (Louvre).

Cima da Conegliano (1459-1517), *Annunciation* (Leningrad Museum).

Froment (1484), *The Resurrection of Lazarus* (Uffizi, Florence).

École d'Avignon (XIV), *The Altarpiece of Thouzou* (Petit Palais, Paris).

Bouts (1420-75), *Annunciation* (Leningrad Museum).

Maître de Moulins (1490), *Portrait of Margaret of Austria, fiancée of Charles VII* (Lehmann collection, New York).

These pictures prove that in this era even the richest men could not completely cover their windows with glass.

c) Paintings representing casement windows made entirely of translucent glass.

Van der Weyden (1400-64), *St. Luke drawing the portrait of the Virgin* (Leningrad Museum).

Also, his *Virgin and Child* (Royal Museum, Brussels).

Bouts (1420-75), *Altarpiece* (St. Peter's Church, Louvain).

Memling (1435-94), *Annunciation* (Lehmann collection, New York). *The Virgin of Martin van Nieuwenhoven* (St. John's Hospital, Bruges).

Metzys (1466-1530), *The Banker and His Wife* (Louvre).

French School (XVI), *Gabrielle d'Estrée* (Condé Museum, Chantilly).

Van Eyck (1380-1440), *Virgin of Autun* (Louvre).

Tintoretto (1518-94), *The Birth of St. John the Baptist* (Leningrad Museum).

From the seventeenth century on, paintings of rich interiors almost always showed windows with glass that could be opened.

d) Pictures representing peasants' houses without glass windows. There are many such pictures up to about 1800. Often there is just a wooden lattice:

Brueghel (1525-69), *Children at Play* (Vienna).

7. This fundamental fact was demonstrated in *Le Grand Espoir du XX° siècle.*

8. On the situation in ancient Rome, cf. J. Carcopino, *La via quotidienne à Rome à l'apogée de l'Empire,* p. 36 ff.

9. This explains the phenomenon observed by Labrousse: from 1730 to 1789, rents went up while real wages went down. The income of the agricultural worker is related to the productivity of marginal land. It decreases as the cultivated area increases. On the other hand, rent goes up when the countryside is prosperous and the peasants are poor.

10. See *Le grand espoir du XX° siècle,* Chapter V, and *Recherches sur l'évolution des prix en période de progrès technique* (1st Series), pp. 30-33.

10a. Space precludes the treatment of this important matter of investments in this book. See J. Fourastié, "La Prévision Economique au Service de l'Entreprise et de la Nation."

11. If economic factors acted equally on all forms of consumption and production, the improvement in the level of living could be seen in haircuts and

bread as well as in window glass. The number of haircuts would be greater in one country than another, according to the political and social regime.

12. Since the selling price is the price of a unit of production.

13. For example, the profit of the first manufactured glass was about 20 per cent. In suppressing this profit (and supposing that this had no effect on productivity), a piece of glass four meters square might have been sold for 32,000 hourly wage units instead of 200 as at present. The same principles apply to many other commodities, none of which would modify the level of living of the people to any extent. This explains why a political revolution, even a radical one, as in China, does not improve buying power. It also shows why, as Lenin said, the true revolution would be the electrification of the country, and why the nationalization in France of various industries did not lower their prices.

The purchasing power of the worker's hourly wage in the United States has increased as follows in the past 150 years despite the system of private profit.

Wheat	1000 *per cent*
Bread	700
Transportation	10,000
Lighting	10,000

PART TWO

Style of Life

THE PRECEDING CHAPTERS have only been able to present rather incomplete comments of complex phenomena. We have tried to give some indexes of an evolution so little known that in the Latin countries of Europe the very idea of economic progress is often contested, or considered more as a political slogan than as a scientific fact. Nevertheless, the problem of the level of living is simple in comparison with that of the style of life.

Styles of life are extremely diverse. The climate alone establishes profound differences. There is practically no resemblance between the living arrangement of the Negroes of the Cameroon and the Eskimos of the frozen North. The temperature, the length of days and nights, and the available foods are so different that the people hardly seem to belong to the same species. Differences in traditions, customs, and beliefs all add to the great disparities of geographic conditions.

How then shall we be able to treat scientifically a group of facts whose heterogeneity seems to restrict us to merely anecdotal description? Science consists of bringing causal relations to light, but what causal relations can possibly appear in such a welter of unrelated facts?

First of all, we must limit our subject matter. We are not

abstractly concerned with the customs of all the inhabitants of this planet, but only with the influence of technical progress on the style of life. This obviously excludes the study of the style of life of those peoples who have not yet profited from industrialization. More exactly, we are led to compare the situation of countries and even of individuals before and after technical progress.

One of the most striking facts, when one tries to compare a highly mechanized style of life—such as begins to be realized in a few places in our world—with the style of life existing before 1800, is that this development does not seem to follow any simple principles. Doubtless, evolution has had some leveling effect. As the French love to point out: the clothing, the coiffures, the fashions, the diet, the use of leisure, are much more homogeneous since 1900 in the countries affected by technical progress. New means of transportation and of communication destroy the originality of regional folkways. There is an unquestionable tendency to homogenization along geographic lines. However, something must be added to this, which is less well understood and which therefore we must stress, namely that *this inter-regional uniformity is accompanied by increased local differentiation.* Before 1800, 80 per cent of the French population lived a peasant existence. In different costumes the styles of life from Dunkirk to Port Vendres were fundamentally the same—rising at dawn, sleeping at sundown, the somnolent winter, the busy and joyous summer. Everywhere the same preoccupations, the same fear or love of hail, rain and sun; the same church bells, the same prayers, the same general stability of conditions. The 20 per cent of the French who escaped this determinism of the land were in part the beneficiaries of profit, in part the merchants, the artisans, and the tiny industrial labor force. Furthermore, the style of life of this minority was not so different from that of the peasants as one might think. The absence of transportation, the scarcity of artificial lighting, the weakness of the media of intellectual communication, gave to the life of the cities a general atmosphere which was very little different from that of the country. Madame de Sévigné reports that at her friends, the X's, they used two candles per day, which means that it was necessary to dine at 4:30 in the winter and to go to bed before 6:00.

Occupational factors introduce powerful elements of differentiation into the style of life and consequently into the minds of men.

These occupational factors eventually determine the whole evolution of the style of life. If the great majority of men had been forced to continue to work the earth, as they did before 1800, none of the transformations of the modern world could have occurred. The cities would not have grown, and there would be nobody to render the essential services of modern life: transportation, medical care, education, personal services. Nor would it have been possible to build the domestic machines which little by little are transforming the life of the housewife.

Subsistence is an inescapable problem for everyone as long as the essential needs of food and clothing are not satisfied. But as soon as these elementary problems of the level of living are resolved, men begin to attach more importance to the style of life. And very soon, they are ready to sacrifice some part, even an important part, of their *level of living* to improve their *style of life*.

It is thus that, since 1900, by voluntarily reducing the duration of work, we have unwittingly reduced our possible level of living by about half.

If we have sacrificed our level of living for a shorter work day, it is in part due to the complication and the fatigue caused by modern life. Nevertheless, there has certainly been some net gain. Modern man is able to pass many more hours at home than his grandfather, or even his father.

It is evident that the national product has correspondingly diminished. Whatever the technical conditions may be, production is always positively correlated with the duration of work; although not exactly proportionate to this duration, it is so at least to the point where physical or mental health are threatened.

The great economic facts that can be grouped under the heading of style of life, and to which a growing importance is conceded, are very numerous. They range from extremely subjective elements like the elegance of clothing, the pleasure taken in leisure, sport, promenades, the theatre, the possibility of going to libraries or attending lectures, all the way to such general and classic conditions as the duration of work, the length of schooling, hygiene, and housing.

We cannot possibly enumerate these elements completely, and there can be no question of analyzing them here in any profound way. A whole group of preliminary studies which hardly exist yet are required. Here we can only give some general idea of the problems which present themselves.

The elements of the style of life can be divided into three major groups: (a) occupational elements; (b) individual and familial elements; (c) social or collective elements.

This triple division corresponds to the three principal roles that men take. The way in which a man works is evidently a very important element in his style of life. The novelist, the film star, or the university professor, for example, have a much pleasanter style of life than the miner or the assembly line worker.

However, the individual and familial elements are even more important because they apply to everyone, to the mothers of families and to children as well as to the members of the labor force outside of their employment. These elements include housing, comfort, the household amenities, and everything that goes into the home. They also include personal services, the availability of bathrooms, personal care, and all of the household services. Finally, they include cultural activities and the use of leisure.

Certain social factors overlap slightly with leisure—for example, all cultural and touristic resources, hotels, auditoriums, playing fields, skating rinks, ski-lifts, libraries, broadcasting stations. These things are both social and individual.

Other social elements are fundamental, such as those of hygiene and of health. All of us need to have clean and safe public places; hospitals, clinics and dispensaries as well-equipped and designed as possible.

Another social element consists of the material organization of secondary schools and universities.

The style of life must not be considered solely from the

point of view of the healthy adult. We must also examine the style of life of children, of invalids, of the handicapped, of the sick, of madmen, convicts, prisoners, and recluses. We must observe to what degree economic development promotes or diminishes the comfort and security of invalids or children. The social factors lead to very general problems, somewhat outside the scope of this book, concerning culture, social morality, individual initiative and freedom. Here stands the boundary between welfare and happiness.

It would be interesting and useful to know in what measure contemporary economic evolution, with its industrialization and technical progress, has been favorable or unfavorable to individual freedom, to the traditional or religious conceptions of life, and to the equilibrium of human existence. All we can do here is to prepare the way for such studies of these topics that would be so advantageous for humanity and that have not been successfully undertaken as yet, except in a limited way by novelists.

Thus described, the problem of style of life is almost limitless. It includes existing disciplines like hygiene and public health, sciences in the course of development like city planning and pedagogy, and almost non-existent bodies of knowledge like the science of housekeeping.

There can be no question, as we have already said, of studying all of these problems here. Like a walker in the night, we can only distinguish a few confused lines in a vast landscape. More precisely, we shall limit our examination to certain aspects of the problem that, perhaps wrongly and certainly by guesswork, have seemed to us to be fundamental: the duration of work, the education of the young, the human habitat, and the domestic skills.

Chapter V

OCCUPATIONAL FACTORS, DURATION OF WORK, EDUCATION

TECHNICAL PROGRESS has tended steadily toward the increase of human occupations. Without going back to that distant age when hunting was perhaps the only occupation, it is evident that the specialization of work has not ceased to develop throughout history. For example, in the sixteenth century the cabinet makers split off from the carpenters, and shortly afterward, the furniture builders separated from both.

The industrial revolution accelerated this tendency considerably, to the point where the classic economists attributed the results of *machinisme* to the division of labor. In reality, the division of labor is not a cause of increased productivity. It is only one of the means, although extremely efficacious. Thus we find often but not always an association between technical progress and an increase in the number of occupations.

It is worthwhile to consider the changes that have taken place in the past century and a half in the nature of occupational life and some of the consequences for the geographic distribution of the population and for the duration of work.

OCCUPATIONAL LIFE

Our object here is not to study men at work. Nevertheless, the attitudes engendered by an occupation little by little become part of the worker's personality. We cannot understand

twentieth century man without understanding the twentieth
century worker. This area has been studied by Professor Friedmann and no brief discussion can take the place of his great
work *Machinisme et Humanisme*.[1] All that we can do here is
to recall the influence of the conditions of work on the style
of life. We shall try to do it by isolating three series of important facts from the stream of recent development.

1) *Machinisme and automatism*. The machine of 1955 is
very different, for the man who operates or who serves it, from
the machine of 1900. We may sum up the change by saying
that the machine of 1900 had to be fed by a man. It was a
semi-automatic machine. The machine of 1950 may be entirely
automatic, which is to say that its alimentation is also automatic.

I suppose that all of my readers have seen in factories how
man is the victim of the machine. To serve the 1900 model
machine—which is still found throughout French industry—
it is necessary to make a fixed gesture, always the same, and
this must be done as regularly as the period of the machine's
operating cycle. For example, the operator must take little
pieces of copper out of a box and put them in a definite position on a table. The machine drills the holes and usually
ejects the piece, but it does not position the new fragment of
copper that it must handle. The man must constantly repeat
the same movement to feed the machine. This is the type of
semi-automatic machine that was considered advanced in 1900.

By contrast, the totally automatic machine that is coming
into general use feeds itself. The difference for the man at
work is that with this type of machine he tends to become a
supervisor or a controller. He intervenes only to renew the
supply of material upon which the machine works, for example,
to insert a new ten-meter spool when the previous one has
been consumed. Replacement of the ten-meter spool may take
place, for example, once each half hour or each quarter hour.
The replacement of the spool is a less purely mechanical task
than the placement of the metal piece described above, for at
the same time that he feeds it, the workman must check the
machine that has been left to its own devices and is about to
be left again.

The second phase in modern labor, then, is to control and schedule the work of the machine, intervening only when the machine jams, or breaks down, or produces defective pieces.

2) *Machinisme and aesthetics.* We cannot say that factory work has been transformed to a truly human calling, promoting intellectual and moral progress for the individual, but there is certainly a favorable tendency. The machine of 1955 is less frightening, less brutalizing, less exhausting than the machine of 1900. This can be seen even in its external appearance. The machine of 1900 was a monster, hideous to see. We need only compare a locomotive of 1900 with a locomotive of 1955, or a motorbus of 1955 with its predecessor of 1920.

Similarly, household machinery has assumed a more pleasing appearance. The modern washing machine, enclosed in a shell of white enamel, and fitting very prettily into the laundry or the bathroom, hardly resembles the primitive model of 1925.

In fact, we can generally identify the date of a machine by its general appearance. The pre-1910 machine was covered with bristling projections; it was blackish, slimy, oily. It spit oil and fumes. It made a frightful noise for a relatively feeble output of power. By contrast, the modern machine gives an impression of force, of equilibrium, of sobriety, and of precision. It awakes sentiments of admiration and confidence.

The 1900 machine did not seem pretty to the men of 1900. Why then does a modern machine look beautiful to us? In my opinion, it is better adapted to man, and man understands it better, considering it almost as a friend. The impression of beauty is, in good measure, the intuition of a harmony between man and nature. What we call a lovely countryside is essentially a human countryside, a landscape in which men feel that it is possible to live, or feel that other men have been able to live, to act, and to develop their personalities. In order to find a machine lovely, it must give somewhat the impression of being a faithful assistant whose employment, far from debasing the man who uses it, can even exalt him.

3) *Machinisme, Productivity, and Individuality.* The evolution of the machine has certain consequences that are even more important.

Not only may we hope that with the passage of time the machine will become less brutal and easier for the workman and more beautiful and intellectually stimulating for the user, but as economic development proceeds, we may hope that the number of men engaged in serving machines in the servile industrial occupations will no longer tend to increase.

In the course of the long period of contemporary economic development, it was often thought that the future would bring the complete triumph of the machine. As technical progress proceeded, the countryside would be depopulated and the factories more densely crowded. Occupational evolution would transform every man into a factory worker and make all of us slaves of the machine. It is hardly possible to grasp the dolorous effect of this notion among the novelists and the writers of science fiction.

We know today that the real tendency of the world is very different. We note that, beyond a certain point, there is a tendency for the "secondary" population to level off and that this leveling should normally be followed, given the nature of technical progress, by a decrease. We realize that the sector which finally benefits from occupational evolution is not the secondary but the tertiary. This occurs because the machine increases productivity and is finally able to satisfy consumption needs with a reduced number of workmen.

Thus the labor force leaves the secondary sector, leaves the factory, and moves into the tertiary occupations that by definition are those of individual initiative, unaffected by the determinism of the machine.

So technical progress gradually transforms the occupational structure. It moves men from agriculture towards the non-mechanical occupations.

In these occupations, which by definition are technically unprogressive, the assembly line has no efficacy. As a matter of fact, when a new discovery in a tertiary activity permits assembly line production, there has been technical progress, and the occupation becomes secondary. In a field which has become secondary and involves mass production, the needs of consumption can be satisfied after a certain lapse of time with a smaller and smaller number of workers.

By contrast, wherever there is no mass production, wherever mechanical energy cannot be used on a large scale, the productivity of labor is hardly greater than it was a hundred years ago and a growing demand can only be satisfied by a larger number of workers.

The typical activity of the man of our future civilization (like the present 50 per cent of the citizens of the United States or 30 per cent of the French—which is by no means negligible—or 45 per cent of the English or 20 per cent of the Russians) will be an occupation not much affected by technical progress. The general conditions of labor will not be very different from those prevailing in the world before the industrial revolution. They will differ, obviously, by the fact that the work place is no longer rural. But the *methods of work* will not be very different, because individual initiative will be required.

The barber will work 50 years from now much as he worked 200 years ago. The substitution of the electric clipper for the scissors will not change the intellectual climate of his work. In the same way, the lawyer, the notary, the teacher, the pupil —for being a pupil is also an occupation—will work, at least in the near future, as they do now and as they did in the past.

Of course, this is only a general tendency. We cannot say that the general conditions of work in the year 2050 will be identical with those of 1700, but I am sure that they will not be as different as they are usually described and as might have plausibly been supposed when the civilization of the future seemed destined to be a secondary civilization. The fact that it will be a tertiary civilization confers new importance on the methods of individual work and on human relations, which have been familiar since time immemorial. What may take place in remoter centuries of the future is still impossible to describe.

THE DURATION OF WORK OF THE ADULT

Another very important factor in a comparison of the modern style of life with an earlier style of life is the duration of work. Even very strenuous and inhuman labor becomes supportable if it does not exceed a few hours a day.

It is obvious that our progress in this regard is already notable. I have presented some information on the traditional duration of work and on recent developments in *La Civilisation de 1975*. This is an extremely important topic that, so far as I know, is not thoroughly treated in any book. Meanwhile, most of us have lost all memory of the traditional duration of work.

The traditional duration of work. Annual work schedules of the order of 3,500 to 4,000 hours were common until the end of the nineteenth century. These work schedules were first established in agriculture. They were simply transposed into industry. Originally, working time in industry was based upon the customary duration of work in agriculture.[2]

However, there was an important difference. In the country, the schedule of 3,500 to 4,000 hours per years was accomplished to a very special rhythm. They worked, in fact, much more during the summer than the winter. There was a peak period in the summer at the time of the harvests, and a considerable slowdown in the winter. In sum, the 4,000 hours were actually worked, but at a rhythm that suited the human animal. The human animal—like other animals, incidentally— is better suited to work intensively at certain times with long rests in between, than to work regularly 12 hours a day for 300 days the whole length of the year. The traditional rhythm, regulated by the seasons, was better adapted to man than any mathematical regularity.

Moreover, agricultural work is the work of a free man, and this was even more so formerly than now. The worker is master of his own rhythm. He can chat with his neighbors, drink when he is thirsty, approach the road when a pretty girl passes —nothing of the assembly line, nothing of the automatic and coercive character of modern labor.

Thus the rhythm of 3,500 to 4,000 hours per year probably could not have been permanently sustained by humanity in the great industrial centers. Nevertheless, it was adopted and remained in use in Europe until about 1900.

This harsh era, in spite of being so close to us, is almost forgotten. I cite here a text which I cannot read without a painful reaction. These are the first pages of a popular text, much used in the elementary grades until 1914. The edition cited is of 1898. It shows the spirit of classical social literature only little more than a half century ago.[3]

Francinet enters his apprenticeship. One Friday, early in the morning, young Francinet, in the company of his godfather Jacques, made his entrance as apprentice in the great textile factory directed by M. Clertan.

The gate was located just opposite Francinet's home. There was only the street to cross. Often before this day, Francinet and his little brother Eugene, seated on a fence near their house, amused themselves by watching M. Clertan's mansion. When a servant opened the double gate to let the master's carriage pass, the two urchins were able to inspect the great sandy court, planted with trees. In the middle a pretty lawn described an oval with a bank of flowers at each end. At the end, the high walls covered with climbing plants made a green horizon which satisfied the eye. More than once the two children had wished for a closer view of these pretty things as well as the interior of the factory from which the sound of work and machinery could be heard all day.

On that day, Francinet followed Father Jacques nervously along the path which surrounded the lawn. After having crossed the court, they entered a rather dark corridor which led to the dyeing shops where Francinet was going to be employed. His work would consist of turning the indigo mill.

The room where the mill was located was a sort of dark cave. A single small window admitted light from the entry court, but it was masked by a curtain of ivy. However, the curtain was not thick enough to prevent a view of what went on in the court.

Certainly Francinet's work place was not gay or pleasant, but the child, already used to a dark, poor and sad house, hardly noticed this at first. Following the instructions of Father Jacques, he sat himself down on a small plank at the back of the cave and began to turn the mill courageously. It was not so difficult and it required more patience than force. Once started, the mill ran without great effort.

Father Jacques let Francinet alone and went to attend to something else. Our little worker did not remain unsupervised, however. Just above his mill there was a large square opening giving onto the next room where there were other workers. From time to time, the foremen came to see what the child was doing.

The first half hour did not seem very long to Francinet. He thought of his dead father; he remembered the words which his mother had spoken more than once:

"You are the oldest of the boys, you must behave, because you will later be the head of the family."

Francinet, who had a good heart, felt proud to be helping his mother to earn their daily bread; and he had reason to be so, for it is a great and fine thing to work for your family and so to return to your parents part of what they have given you.

... *At 8:oo,* the owner of the establishment, M. Clertan, appeared.

He was a tall, old man—dry, lively, alert, with an eye on everything. He carried out a sort of inspection of the factory from high to low, encouraging some, scolding others, noticing the smallest omissions, just as a good master should do.

Finally, he entered the cave where Francinet was. Father Jacques was also there.

"Come here, little one," said M. Clertan in a sharp tone.

The child approached, hat in hand.

"How old are you?"

"Nine years old, sir."

"Can you read?"

"Not much, sir."

"You would be better off at school than here, my boy."

Francinet bowed his head.

"The mother is a widow, M. Clertan," said Father Jacques, "she has three children and before teaching them to read she must keep them alive."

"That's true," said the old man.

"What is your name, my little man?"

"Francinet, sir, at your service."

"Very well François, Francinet, you must work courageously. If we are satisfied with you, your pay will be raised, but if you are a lazy one, we shall send you away."

Francinet had not been used to sustained work, because his mother never had the time to supervise him. The widow Roullin left for her work at 7:00 in the morning. She did not return until evening, sometimes very late. Francinet and his little brother, always alone, wandered in the street outside of class hours.

One can see how difficult steady work must have been for Francinet. Nothing, truly, is more difficult than to escape from a settled habit, and it is for that reason that we must form only good ones. It did no good for Francinet to resist the desire to leave his work. He finished by forgetting the task which was assigned to him, left his mill, and consoled himself for not being able to play by at least watching M. Clertan's daughter play a few paces away.

Francinet had been there for only five minutes when a harsh voice shouted at him.

"So now, lazy bones, this is the way that you earn the day's pay that you'll get tomorrow?" The shame-faced boy returned to his mill, hardly daring to look at the severe expression of the foreman who had just scolded him . . .

When 9:00 sounded, all of the workers stopped work and removed their aprons. They washed their faces and hands in the river which ran alongside the factory, then they crossed the fine sanded court of M. Clertan and went home for lunch . . .

When the workers were gone, Aimée, the daughter of M. Clertan, picked up her book again. She read with close attention because she had a lesson to learn by heart. The book which she studied was the Bible . . .

However, it was getting later in the evening. Aimée would have liked to return because she was anxious for a reconciliation with Francinet. But M. Clertan, who had important business at his farm, had ordered the farmer's wife to prepare dinner for them, so that it was *8:00 in the evening* when the carriage of M. Clertan brought him home. *The workers had just left.*

. . . *9:00 sounded.* The silence was so complete in M. Clertan's house that Aimée could count each stroke of the great clock. Then the clock itself fell silent and Aimée heard nothing more.

But a moment later, a small dull noise caught her attention. It was like a steady ticking coming up out of the ground.

Aimée thought suddenly of Francinet, because this sound

resembled that of his mill. As the little girl's room was above his cellar, it was not surprising that she heard it.

"But," said Aimée to herself, "Francinet is still up? Grandfather does not usually let the children stay up. The work must be very pressing. Poor Francinet . . ."

And little Aimée, joining her hands together, began to repeat in a sweet voice the beautiful prayer of Our Father. Francinet responded in his turn. They were there, both of them, on their knees next to one another on the sand of the cave: The one, poor, dressed in rags; the other, rich, dressed in silk muslin; but their two equally young little voices, equally pure, united fraternally to address God by the same name, Our Father.

When the prayer was finished, Aimée rose, "Goodnight Francinet," she said, "Now I can sleep without remorse. Until tomorrow." *One hour later,* the overtime was finished, the doors shut, and all the world asleep in M. Clertan's house.

THE REDUCTION IN THE DURATION OF WORK

The reduction in the duration of work began in the United States because of the weakness of traditions there and the very strong pressure created by the intensity of industrial effort. The 60 hour week was quite usual in the United States after 1860; it did not become so in Europe until 1900.

At the beginning of the movement, the reduction of the duration of work was determined by the agreeableness of the occupation. In the industries which were least fatiguing and closest to agricultural labor, the long working day was preserved longer. There were many examples on the railroads, where the work of a section hand or the station agent at a little country station takes place virtually under traditional conditions. By contrast, the work of locomotive engineers, mechanics and so forth is quite different and the reduction in the duration of work began with them.

However, after a time, the reduction in the hours of work came to be considered in political rather than economic terms. The working classes, without understanding very well that they were sacrificing the level of living to the style of life, and the length of schooling for children to adult leisure, demanded a *general* reduction of the duration of work. From the standpoint of most militant workers, the reduction of the duration of work appeared as a victory of the working class over the managerial class, as if it had involved a curtailment of profits or rents. On the contrary, the general reduction in the duration of work, by reducing the total national product, necessarily diminished the quantity of goods disposable, and increased the incidence of scarcity and, consequently, the profits and privileges of acquired wealth. Whatever the economic system of a country, whether collectivist or capitalist, a reduction in the duration of work has the same effect upon consumption as a reduction of productivity. If the average productivity of a nation is p, and the level of living is L, and the duration of work is reduced from 2,000 to 1,800 hours per year, the level of living then becomes:

$$L' = \frac{1800}{2000} \times L$$

The same value which would be obtained if p were reduced by ten percent. In fact, in both cases, the national product is reduced by ten per cent. We see, therefore, that there were childish and dangerous elements in the policy promoted, albeit in good faith, by the International Labor Office between 1920 and 1939. This policy aimed at obtaining, by legislative enactment, the same duration of work in all the countries of the world. In political and social terms, this equalization appeared

Table XXXI—Time Budget of an Adult Worker (in hours)

	TRADITIONAL EPOCH		1950	
	Daily	Annual	Daily	Annual
Sleep and meals (365 days)	11	4,015	11	4,015
Leisure:				
Sundays and holidays (60 days)	—	780	—	780
Paid vacation (19 days)	—	—	—	182
Daily leisure time	—	—	3	873
Recesses in daily work	1	305	1	291
Journey to and from work	—	—	1	291
Work	12	3,660	8	2,328
Total hours	24	8,760	24	8,760
Leisure hours		780		1,835

necessary and easy. The I.L.O. did not realize that it was impossible or harmful because of existing differences of productivity among the nations. Equalization involved invisible sacrifices for the working classes of those countries with low productivity, which were much greater than the visible advantages obtained by the increase of leisure. Thus, by adopting the same standards as the United States, after 1920, France held down the level of living of its inhabitants, and also *ceased to modernize its industry*. It is obvious that if the length of the work week in France had been maintained at 50 hours from 1920 to 1939, as it was from 1900 to 1920, World War II would have been avoided, because French industrial power would have been sufficient to discourage the Nazis' ideas of revenge. Moreover, this working effort would soon have given the people of France an industrial machine whose productivity, instead of stagnating, would have doubled in twenty years. By working as much as, but not more than, the generation before it, the past generation could have increased its level of living, avoided a war, and left to the present generation a standard of productivity such that it would now be possible to reduce the duration of work to 40 hours while maintaining a level of living worthy of a civilized people—a level of living that we do not yet have, and that, in spite of the current speed of scientific progress, we shall need twenty years to attain.

This example shows very clearly the importance of *time* in the modern economic scheme. To try to gain time at the wrong time is to lose it, for economic efficiency is closely bound to *investments* and any premature reduction of the duration of work is made first and foremost at the expense of human and industrial investments. The erring country, badly equipped, leaves the normal route of progress to linger in a backwater of mediocrity.

Duration of work and level of living. Let us sum up in scientific terms: The man who wishes to reduce the duration of his work must realize that this improvement in his style of life can only be realized at the expense of his level of living. He must realize, above all, that if the reduction is premature to the point of interfering with technical modernization, progress will be stopped and the future compromised.[4]

Another aspect of the political reduction of the duration of work is that it is accomplished almost uniformly in all the sectors of economic life.

From a strictly economic point of view, it would be normal to reduce the duration of work in those industrial occupations in which the work itself is very hard and exhausting. Moreover, this particular reduction would be relatively easy because the productivity of such labor tends to increase. However, working time has been reduced simultaneously in tertiary occupations, those in which there has been practically no change for a hundred and fifty years. We have reduced, for example, the duration of work of office messengers, museum guards, lawyers, and clerks, although practically all of these employees do their jobs under the same conditions as a hundred and fifty years ago. This is not to say that the duration of work should have been kept at 3,000 hours per year for clerks and notaries, but simply to note the economic and social consequences of the practically uniform reduction in the duration of work in occupations subject to very different rates of technical progress.

In those callings that were much affected by technical progress, and where the productivity of labor had increased, the reduction of labor time was achieved without hiring supplementary workers. A part of the gain from technical progress was absorbed in this operation, but the social structure of the occupations involved was not changed. However, in the tertiary occupations, reductions in the duration of work immediately involved either a reduction of output or an increase of personnel. Thus the reduction in the duration of work retarded the depopulation of the secondary sector, and by contrast, increased and hastened the crowding of the tertiary. Consequently, a reduction in the duration of work without a change in technology, involves not only a reduction in the level of living, but also a redistribution of the labor force. As a further result, it accentuated the disproportionate increase of tertiary prices in relation to secondary prices.

The reduction in the duration of work in the tertiary sector accentuated the natural rise in tertiary prices. This much is easy to understand. Let us suppose, for example, that the duration of work was reduced from 3,000 to 2,000 hours per year in an insurance company. If 300 employees were sufficient with the former working schedule, 450 are probably required now. To house those 450 employees will obviously require larger offices, more desks, more inkwells, more typewriters, more telephones. To service this larger working force, more people will be needed in the payroll department and other services. In consequence, *tertiary expenses are appreciably increased whenever the duration of work is reduced.*

This phenomenon shows itself in the "overhead" of every enterprise. Since "overhead" is predominantly tertiary, it increases continuously in proportion to direct expense. The reduction in the duration of work hastens this process.

It may appear necessary in the future, if new reductions in the duration of work are desired, *not* to make them uniform in all occupations. For example, we may be led (as is sometimes done now), to make special reductions in the duration of work in those occupations which remain "servile," in the special sense which, following Marc Bloch, I give to that word: those occupations based on muscular strength and involving strenuous physical labor. Such occupations, like coal mining, have difficulty maintaining their necessary rate of recruitment.

Two important observations should be made concerning the reduction of the duration of work by general political action. The first is that the laws and decrees limiting working hours have, by custom and the force of circumstances, been badly and belatedly applied to agriculture. We are thus led to the economic paradox that the reduction in the duration of work has been more noticeable in the tertiary than in the primary. The level of living of the cities has increased to the detriment of that of the countryside. The economic crisis of agriculture has been aggravated.

The duration of intellectual work. The second result of statutory limitations on the duration of work has been to equalize the working hours of intellectuals and those of manual workers. The traditional assumption was that intellectual work could not exceed seven or eight hours per day if it was to be efficient. The length of vacations in the courts, the ministries, and administrative agencies, was much the same in the traditional epoch as it is today. Working time was limited in the winter by the absence of efficient lighting and heating, in the summer by the motive of allowing the intellectual worker "vacations for reflection." Thus, in England, high functionaries still have two months of vacation per year. In France, only judges and professors have preserved certain remnants of these customs. The present situation is that the director of a ministry in France works 3,000 to 3,500 hours per year, and his office messenger 2,500. (The situation was reversed in 1800.) This arises from the fact that the high functionary always works more than the required schedule. Eventually, it is felt that a director who doesn't pass 60 hours a week in his office is not doing his duty. The situation is almost the same in private business. As a result, the effectiveness of public and private administration in France cannot compare to what it was at the beginning of the nineteenth century. Top executives, absorbed in bothersome minor tasks, are no longer in control of their affairs. We have arrived at that disastrous situation described by Sauvy in *Le Pouvoir Et L'Opinion,* where the high official no longer has *time to think.* The machinery collapses and futile chores accumulate around the wreckage. We have forgotten that the essential function of the executive is to plan and organize for the long run, and that to do this well, he must have the same conditions for reflective thought as the man of science reviewing his experiments.

In giving our major administrators the tasks of bureaucrats, we have paralyzed the progress of administration. Here as everywhere, an hour of creative work may save hundreds or thousands of hours of application. If the labor of creation is suppressed, it is certain that the efficiency of the labor of application will suffer.

It is very likely that the near future will see the great hope implicit in the reduction of the duration of work better utilized than in the past. Those laborers whose physical or intellectual work is the most unpleasant will be relieved. Special care will be taken to provide time for thought, by giving sufficient leisure for reflection to the rare workers who are capable of new ideas.

I have discussed in *Le Grand Espoir du XX° Siècle* the reasons why it is probable that the era of great general reduction in the duration of work is now finished in Europe and in our generation. Only a few countries, by the way, would dare any large scale experimentation today.

The scarcity of tertiary services is making itself felt in the most advanced countries—services demanded by the population in the form of commerce, transportation, housing, medical treatment, instruction, personal care and so forth—services that are required by civilization itself. The more complicated civilization becomes, the more the effects of technical progress are felt, the more need there is for coordination and interconnection among enterprises and collectivities of all kinds. Technical, political, or economic action increasingly involves great numbers of men and can only be effective through their rational collaboration in a common effort. This implies good communication, a continuous process of integration, and scientific research, all of which involve an inevitable complexity of public and private administration.

This growing complexity—cause and consequence, price and reward—of technical progress, may be observed everywhere in the world, as well in the United States as in the Soviet Union. In spite of automation and cybernetics, it marks a limit or at least sets a brake to the improvement of the productivity of labor and, in consequence, to the improvement of the level of living and of social conditions. It is not possible to resolve these administrative problems rapidly. The solutions must be found and put into operation gradually. The *scarcity* of tertiary services will long maintain the concomitant restraints of labor and scarcity that have traditionally framed human life —the work necessary for production, the earnings necessary for distribution.[5]

EDUCATION AND JUVENILE LEISURE[6]

The trend to the reduction of the duration of work has doubled the leisure time of adults in Europe and tripled it in the United States. To understand this phenomenon clearly, we must remember that the rhythm of the seasons gave leisure in the traditional epoch a very different character than it has today. The absence of light and the inadequacy of heating, the excessive labor of the spring and summer, gave to the life of the average worker a vegetative quality which can still be observed in the poorest rural areas.

This is not to say that the 1,800 to 2,300 annual hours of leisure now at the disposal of the city worker are used to the best of his capacities and possibilities. We shall have a word to say in the following chapter about the utilization of leisure for intellectual, artistic, moral, and religious development. Yet it cannot be denied that the average man is almost permanently molded at the age of twenty-five. After that age it is difficult for him to adapt himself to new ways of seeing, feeling, or understanding. This is why a man's leisure can only serve to deepen what he has already acquired, and if he has acquired nothing his leisure remains sterile.

Hence it is only the leisure of the young that can be the source of a true civilization. Happily, technical progress has not limited itself to the reduction of the working time of adults. It also reduces the number of years during which a man must deliver himself over to a job. And so the problem of national education is posed in every modern nation.

The educational consequences of these powerful economic movements are obviously very numerous and very important. Just as it was not possible to treat the problems previously raised in detail, so we cannot here consider this fundamental problem in any profound way. Nevertheless, it is possible to array the facts that appear essential by grouping them into two categories: the increase in the school population on the one hand; the separation that has developed between the French educational system and the real needs of youth, on the other.

The increase in the school population appears, as previously suggested, not as the result of fashion or of transitory impulses, but as a structural phenomenon related to the whole of contemporary economic evolution. This increase results directly from the rise in the average level of living and from the reduction of the duration of work necessary for a given national production. It is thus a direct consequence of technical progress, and will continue as long. Since it is certain that technical progress is still going on, the educational boom is nowhere near its peak. It shows no signs of exhaustion in the United States even though four out of five adolescents receive secondary instruction there, as against one out of five in France.[7]

We must suppose that economic conditions will lead, within the next 15 to 20 years, to the quadrupling of the school population of the French *lycées* and a quadrupling of the population of the universities. However, this movement will lead France no further than the *present* position of the United States.

The number of students reaching the baccalaureate in Sweden was 434 in 1866. This is a low number. The baccalaureate is more difficult in Sweden than in France. It is usually attained at about the age of twenty there, and at about seventeen in France. Our object is not to make comparisons between the Swedish and the French systems, but to follow the evolution of each country separately. In 1866 then, there were 434 graduates; in 1939 there were 3,713, ten times as many. The school-age population had not varied in the same proportion. There were 377,000 persons between 15 and 20 years of age in 1870, and only 550,000 in 1939. The size of the school population had increased from 1 to 1.4, while the number achieving the baccalaureate had jumped in the ratio 1 to 9.

The same general rule applies to the universities: more people attended school and they remained at school a longer time, since the number of students in higher education increased by a factor of 5.5.

Sweden has been taken only as an example. It is common knowledge that the same sort of development has occurred in all of the industrialized countries.

France does not make a very favorable showing. Since 1900, the teaching professions in the United States have seen their numbers more than doubled. They have remained unchanged in France. Moreover, the average age for the termination of schooling is approximately 17 years in the United States against 14 years and 9 months in France. The number of young people in active attendance in higher education, which was 10 to 15 per thousand of the adolescent population in 1880, now reaches 160 in the United States, 50 in France.

The only obstacles which might oppose this movement would be a sudden arrest of technical progress, which is unlikely, or grave political disasters such as wars, revolutions, the isolation or blockade of continents.

It would be criminal to retard this evolution, either by deliberately sacrificing our children to the premature reduction of the annual duration of work of adults, or, as is actually done today, by examinations which debar children of eleven from secondary and higher education. The real problem is not how to select the elite and to reject the others. It is rather to welcome and to educate, each according to his capacity, the hundreds of thousands of children and young people whom technical progress has liberated from physical labor. It must be recognized that the civilization of 1975 will include the opportunity of secondary education for the entire population. Either technical progress will be erased, or the average age of beinning work, which was nine years in 1830 and which is 14.9 years now, will be advanced to 17 by normal economic determinism.

It is already possible to note the appearance, happily still inconspicuous, of an idle adolescent population whose parents cannot send them to the *lycée* but do not yet wish to send them to work. A quota policy in education would increase these bitter fruits.

Although the civilization of tomorrow will have 25 per cent of its young people reaching the level of higher education and profiting from its advantages, this does not mean that they will all become ambassadors or university professors. Most of them will be farmers, merchants, garagists, construction superintendents, barbers, photographers. People with degrees will be found in every modest employment. Nonetheless, they will be cultivated and civilized men.

Such is the problem to be resolved—not to deform young people by disciplines which are inappropriate for the life which most of them will lead, not to consider education as a kind of machine which selects recruits for a ruling group and rejects the great majority to outer darkness, but on the contrary, to construct an educational system that welcomes all young people, however modest their capacities and ambitions may be, and urges each one as far as he can go without discouragement.

This program implies a great extension of the material resources of today's educational system. More schools, more teachers, more money will be needed. It is not a question of making education obligatory, but of creating sufficient means to satisfy the natural demand. *Two hours more of weekly work in industry and commerce is an extra year of schooling for each of our children.*

This program also implies a change in the *spirit* of education. A greater and greater gap appears between what one learns at school and what one must do in life, between what the teacher talks about and what the father talks about. The classic French education is the heritage of our great seventeenth century. It is largely oriented to the shaping of the *gentleman,* for whom work is less important than talking of Euripides or Racine in the parlors of beautiful women. To this core, there has been hastily and reluctantly added some hasty summaries of what people like Descartes, Napoleon, Ampère, Newton and Einstein were or did. We are thus led, more or less consciously, to that self-image that the gentleman develops by accumulating a large store of miscellaneous information. From insufficiency and mediocrity, we expect a fruitful synthesis. Our average secondary school graduate, poor or mediocre in geometry, in arithmetic, in algebra, in ancient history and modern history, in geography, in physics and chemistry, in Latin verse, in English, in Greek, in French grammar, in literature, in the history of art, in geology, in natural science, in cosmography, has neither the scientific spirit nor the literary spirit. He has not grasped any of the fundamental ideas that make up human progress and dominate daily life—the scientific method and the moral tradition. Hence, this nervous, unquiet and skeptical generation. Who can resist the fragmentary and proliferative education that requires so much money and so little initiative? Each year I see the best minds nearly overwhelmed by it.

It would be better to give our children an education that is not general in the sense of involving familiarity with a great number of facts, but general in the sense of facilitating the knowledge of those facts which they will meet again and again in the course of their lives. It is not a question of learning a little bit of everything, but of preparing to live by making the acquaintance of the fundamental facts of the contemporary world.

In this contemporary world, economic facts take on increasing importance. They are at the base of many political and social movements. They constitute the essential material of the working life of executives and many other tertiary workers. It is inconceivable under these conditions that economics can rest entirely outside the curriculum. Nonetheless, in most countries, and especially in France and the other Latin countries, the essential facts of labor force distribution, of the business cycle, of unemployment, of the level of living and the purchasing power of wages, of technical progress—all of the facts discussed in the present work—are overlooked in primary and secondary education and just barely mentioned in a few centers of higher education.

Still, if technical progress is a cause of the increase of the school population, it must be recognized that it is also a result. Technical progress permits popular education, but popular education is necessary for the pursuit of progress. Not only does the gradual abolition of physical work permit the increasing utilization of intellectual talent, but more specifically, the development of the tertiary sector requires that an increasing number of workers be introduced to the essential mechanisms of economic life.

Contemporary economic civilization, by freeing youth from the servile labor formerly necessary to insure subsistence, opens to increasing masses of men and women the *material possibility* of receiving secondary and advanced education. This essential fact is the hope of future civilization.

The duty of our generation is to wait, before electing any new reductions in the length of the adult work day, until the terminal age of schooling for our children has been raised to eighteen or twenty.[8]

Notes to Chapter V

1. *Machinisme et Humanisme*: Vol. I., *La crise du progrès*; Vol. II., *Problèmes humains du machinisme industriel* (American edition, *Industrial Society* [Glencoe, Illinois: The Free Press, 1955]).

2. For numerical and statistical data on the duration of work, see the corresponding chapter of *La civilisation de 1975*. Intellectual work (administration, teaching, etc.) formerly benefited from special privileges.

The working day of 13 to 15 hours, with 1.5 to 2 hours off for lunch (therefore 11.5 to 13 hours of actual work) was common before 1860 in the factories of the north and east of France. More detailed information on this important subject can be found in Villermé, *Tableau de l'état physique et moral des ouvriers, 1840*, Vol. I, Reybaud, *Les populations ouvrières et les industries de la France* (1860); and Audiganne, *La condition des ouvriers en soie* (1859). The latter gives the hours of work at the unbelievable figure of 17 hours a day. Paul Louis (*Histoire de la classe ouvrière en France*), in a perfectly matter-of-fact manner, describes the situation before 1860 thus:

At Mulhouse, the shop opens at five in the morning and closes at eight or nine in the evening. The day is thus 15 hours long, with a break of an hour and a half for lunch. At Thann and Wesserling, the conditions are identical; at Bischwiller, the working day is 16 hours.

At Sainte-Marie-aux-Mines, the day is 14 hours with a break of an hour and a half.

At St. Quentin, the working day is from 14 to 15 hours, without counting travel time to work.

At Rouen, 15 to 15½ hours constitutes the normal day, with an hour and a half for lunch. The weavers put in 17 hours.

At Tarare, they have a 13 to 14 hours working day, with 12 hours of actual work. (This is the minimum for this era.)

At Reims, the workers are held under orders for 14 hours, the actual work day being 12½ hours. At Sedan the clothing workers, work up to 14 hours a day.

3. G. Bruno, *Principes élémentaires de morale, d'économie politique* . . . *Francinet* (Paris: Librairie classique Eugène Belin, 1898), p. 1 ff.

4. The C.I.O. has undertaken a campaign for the 30 hour week. But what is good for the United States is not necessarily good for other countries. In my opinion, in a country where schooling stops at the age of 14, the work week can not and should not be reduced.

5. I cannot sketch here a theory of the relationship between wage differentials and the productivity of work. From the purely economic point of view, a salary appears as a ration ticket which gives the right in periods of scarcity, to a part of the total production, proportionally equivalent to the individual salary. As early as 1925, Reboud proposed a remarkable theory of wages which should have opened the way to larger developments. As long as scarcity exists, that is, as long as production remains insufficient to satisfy potential demand, a

system of rationing must be maintained. The wage level has resisted control, no matter what the political regime.

6. Cf. my articles in *l'Education Nationale*, Dec. 8, 1949, and in the *Cahiers pédagogiques pour l'enseignement du second degré*, Jan. 1, 1950.

7. *La Civilisation de 1975*, p. 22. The ratio increases each year.

8. The superior intellectual development and manners of the aristocracy of the seventeenth and eighteenth century were due to their education and that of their predecessors. It is reasonable to think that if a majority of the young received a university education, the artistic and intellectual life of a society would greatly improve. In contrast to the eighteenth century, when 2 per cent of the population was educated, true civilization would be extended to a larger and larger proportion of the people. However, it would be necessary to know more than we do now about the distribution of talent. In the poor societies of the past, economic inequalities have been preponderant; in the society of the future the risk will be that of intellectual inequalities.

Chapter VI

INDIVIDUAL AND
FAMILY FACTORS

THE INFLUENCE of *machinisme* and of technical progress on individual and family life is obviously considerable. This problem, which forms the very center of the study of style of life, is still practically untouched. It is curious to note that the subject was first approached through the study of prehistoric man. As in the previous chapters, we cannot hope to treat so large a subject profoundly.

Our sole object is to call attention to the problem and to give a few suggestions for a simple study that the reader himself may undertake by observing the life around him.

The technical factors of individual life are all more or less connected with housing: first, housing per se, the general features of the house and its geographic location; then the household equipment—furniture, appliances, utilities; finally the household arts, the questions of household work, of rest, of leisure time activities, and of what may be generally described as comfort.

It is the evolution of these diverse elements of the style of life during the past 150 years in the technically advanced countries that we must try to trace in broad outline.

HOUSING

From earliest times until the last century the home was essentially a shelter—against the rain, against the cold, and against wild beasts and human marauders. The traditional house is fundamentally a fort. It is not active but passive. It protects, it does not serve.

The notion of the defensive habitation that comes to us out of the distant ages of the past is still very much alive in France, in a fashion that hardly strikes the French themselves unless they have traveled abroad. The protective character which the house in countries of old civilization has for its inhabitants, and the hostile aspect which it presents to the passerby, make a lively impression on anyone who knows the newer countries. Nothing appears more natural to a Frenchman than an enclosing wall. The wall of the court and the garden is part of the house. It seems quite natural that people should shut themselves in to escape unwelcome observation, and at 8:00 in the evening in October, one may walk down the main street of a city like Étampes without seeing more light in the windows than if the houses were uninhabited.

By contrast, one of the things that most surprises the French when they travel in highly industrialized countries, like the United States or Canada or Sweden or Norway, is that the houses in those countries have practically no provision for protection against outsiders.

The home in the new countries has no enclosure. Certainly it has walls and a roof for protection against cold and rain, but it has no exterior barriers. When there is a garden, the garden is not enclosed. The very windows generally lack exterior shutters. The defensive equipment of the doorway is rudimentary. Most of the time it is not used.

This shows that in the new countries, almost as soon as they were populated, such general conditions of security prevailed (whether because of policing or because morality followed the upward trend of the level of living) that man did not need to fear the assault of other men.

The house in the tertiary civilization is a machine. In France, tradition has conserved a certain air of "my home is my castle"—attitudes of distrust and even of hostility towards the trespasser, the passerby, and often the neighbor. This is the tradition of the domestic stronghold which furnishes protection against nature and against men.

On the contrary, in the modern house (or, as far as France

is concerned, the future house), this role of shelter is only secondary to the active and dynamic role of rendering services to the inhabitant. This would have been inconceivable before 1820 or 1830. But little by little, mechanical energy, water under pressure, then gas, and finally electricity have permitted the incorporation into the home of machines, motors, and tools that render services to the occupants.

Little by little a whole series of instruments and devices that were formerly portable have been incorporated into the dwelling. Heating provides the perfect example. Originally there was no stove. At first the firewood was placed on the ground anywhere, later in a given spot with a chimney above. There were no material instruments except a few flat stones and later some andirons. With more advanced techniques, which hardly appeared in France until 1750, came the stoves, items of furniture. Then, with the industrial era, the central heating equipment was finally incorporated into construction of the building.

This is the case not only for central heating but also for the plumbing complex—sinks, washbasins, toilets, bathtubs, and showers. Similarly, lighting, which had formerly been accomplished with oil or kerosene lamps, became incorporated into the house because well-designed conduits and electric circuits must be installed at the time the house is built. It is possible, of course, to add them to an old house in the same way that a bathroom may be added to an ancient building, but this is only a temporary and makeshift solution, justified by the need of using the leftovers of the past.

The modern house becomes truly a machine. It was once passive, it becomes active.

It is necessary to study the fundamental features of this radical development by dividing them into two parts: the building itself, and the furniture and appliances.

The geography of habitation. It is easy to visualize the general problem of habitation in contemporary civilization. Economic development has permitted and has required considerable migrations of population. Until about 1830, most men were bound to the soil by agriculture and could not find a livelihood except by dispersing themselves over the territory in relation to the supply of arable land.

The increase in agricultural productivity, by reducing the number of workers necessary to produce food and raw materials, has broken the age-old ties of man and the soil. Primary labor is bound to the land. Secondary labor is much less fixed. It depends more upon means of communication and upon the concentration of goods and materials than upon the surface features of the earth. Finally, tertiary labor is essentially dependent upon the distribution of the population for whom the tertiary services are to be performed. Thus the diminution of the primary sphere and the expansion of the secondary and the tertiary spheres have created urban concentration.

This transfer of man from the rustic setting of Virgil to the urban setting of New York is the most conspicuous and most serious phenomenon of the transitory period.

As a matter of fact, it has been a grave problem for the Occidental countries to find lodging for all of their people who migrated from the countryside and it is still a problem for those nations in the course of rapid industrialization, like the Soviet Union and Japan. In the abandoned villages of Quercy or the Aveyron, the ancestral houses fall into ruins, while in the cities, the population crowds into tenements.

From the primary habitation to the secondary city. The traditional dwelling was the result of a very slow development. The richest land had been occupied first, and little by little the forest had been cleared, always by a choice of the best lands. Thus, the dwelling site was determined by natural factors— the best exposure to the sun, protection from floods, and so forth.

By contrast, in the chaos of the transition period, for no other reason than the construction of a factory at a certain place and of a freight yard at another, tens of thousands of men and women poured in within a few years. Houses were built hastily to satisfy the immediate demand for a rental profit.

In this way urban centers were created and multiplied during the past century in almost all of the countries of the world. The movement was produced under the pressure of economic determinism in the period of transition; the men affected by it were unable to see its direction or to control its effects. The contemporary city was constructed to absorb a demographic inundation, without thought of the future or of the whole pattern. This was one of the typical symptoms of spiritual disorder during the period of industrialization. A continuous stream of people came to seek lodging in the cities. Large profits were offered to the builders and proprietors of houses. The long term social problem was resolved any which way, from day to day, under the impulses of profiteering and speculation.

For example, in the suburbs of Paris, construction was undertaken on land that had been agricultural until about 1830 or 1870 or 1900. The tracts were bought up by promoters or speculators, then they were subdivided and sold off bit by bit so as to obtain the maximum monetary return. The idea of private property was victorious over any concept of the public interest. The plan of great cities was designed by the desire to make money out of real estate. City planning was sacrificed to the anarchy of individual interests.

So grew those cities that have no general pattern, no traffic plan, no center, no organic unity. Rows of apartment houses are ranged along unending corridor streets. Traffic, work, commerce, housing are inextricably mixed and mutually interfering. These secondary cities (born in the secondary phase of the period of transition) are the least human which humanity has built, with the exception of Rome under the Caesars.

Since Haussmann who, by the way, was inspired by typical principles of his era, Paris has not had any general plan of improvement and extension. The royal tradition of Paris has been lost without the substitution of any democratic or social tradition. From the sixteenth through the eighteenth centuries, the Place des Vosges, the Avenue de Breteuil, the Invalides, the Étoile were designed. By contrast, with no plan at all, with no intervention of governmental authority, the bourgeois governments have left the field to individuals. At most, they take the precaution, in America, to require the laying out of a gridiron of streets in a new subdivision of vacant land. But the fundamental fact is that individuals build according to their holdings. The typical pattern is a restricted facade fronting on a narrow and noisy street, with a rear exposure on a dark court giving practically no air or sun because it is too small and too narrow. The typical modern city presents itself as an interminable collection of ugly little cubes, jammed against each other the whole length of narrow, noisy, and dusty trenches.

The secondary city in which most of us are condemned to live is at once irrational, uneconomic, unwholesome, and ugly; in a word, anti-human, because problems which required planning and foresight have been settled piecemeal. The men of the nineteenth century who built these great cities were not aware of the phenomenon and had no clear idea of its scope. They built badly, they built cheaply, they built quickly to satisfy an immediate need. No one thought of the future. Today the serious consequences of this kind of housing are all too evident. The nineteenth-century tenement houses fewer members of the population on a given amount of land than modern housing; above all, it houses them much worse. Restlessness, anxiety, the moral disequilibrium of the current generation is largely attributable to the defects of their dwellings. If Hitler and the workers of Munich, if Mussolini and the workers of Turin, had lived in a more human environment, would the fascist movements have arisen and led to the war of 1939? It is essential to see that this question has its scientific side.

The problems of city planning are only beginning to be understood. We are just beginning to suspect the influence of daily conditions and surroundings on the character and mentality of the people. Until about 1920 no one had realized that the problem of city building was a national problem. More exactly, it had been forgotten in the confusion that attended the beginning of the industrial revolution. The men of an earlier civilization knew that city building is public policy. Under the *ancien régime* in France, the construction of a city was always regarded as a matter for the royal administration.

Happily, contemporary city planners are slowly rediscovering this conception. They now know that all new building of any scale presents problems that involve the public interest and that must be treated not only in terms of immediate needs, but also in terms of the future and the probabilities of development that exist for the region, the city, and the neighborhood.

One gets a fairly clear idea of the tertiary city by visiting certain foreign countries such as Sweden. But it is in the United States that the transition from the secondary to the tertiary city can best be observed.

The city of New York is typically secondary. Impressive in its size, inspiring in the human achievement that it evokes, it is really uninhabitable. All of the defects of the interminable secondary city are concentrated there at a maximum intensity. It is crowded, confused, dirty, without green spaces. For the adult, it is a painful environment. For the old and the very young it is completely "unlivable." But this city, the perfect image of the flooding of population into a limited space, is increasingly abandoned to the functions of production while twenty or thirty kilometers from New York, the tertiary habitat develops.

What are the fundamental features of what I call the tertiary city, or rather the tertiary suburb and even countryside?

First of all, dwellings are dispersed. The cities which are built today no longer give that impression of density and complexity, characteristic of secondary cities and suburbs. In fact, the first impression is of very few buildings. This is sometimes an erroneous impression, for it may be that the population per unit of area is actually greater than in the older cities. This is because the houses are higher, the innumerable little courts are lacking and the open spaces are rationally combined, but most of all because factories, industrial buildings, warehouses, stores, and so forth have been rigorously segregated.

The tertiary city is thus dispersed. Moreover, it allows nature to flourish around it, and this is extremely important. There are trees, plants, flowers, grass. The water remains, the birds and squirrels are welcome. There has been a kind of adjustment by which nature becomes an organic element of the home.

Further out still, beyond these new cities which are still urban by the criteria of density, we find little strings of houses, really individual this time, which extend over hundreds of kilometers. The observer who leaves New York is struck by the fact that over the whole extent of the surrounding area one finds independent houses every fifty, one hundred, two hundred, five hundred, or eight hundred meters. The group village of the Ile-de-France or Beauce type, is rare. There are practically no villages or spaces between villages. The houses are found anywhere where someone has thought that he might find pleasure and live in tranquility. Here and there certain clusters, hardly more dense, grow up around a railroad station, a church or a school.

It is not difficult to find the major causes that lead to the transformation of the secondary habitat into the tertiary habitat. The first is the better utilization of local means of production, leading to the decentralization of industry. The second is the preference of evolved and civilized man for a calm and natural setting. Finally, it is easy to see how this new dispersion of the tertiary habitat, which reproduces para-doxically, but quite exactly, the primary dispersion of pop-ulation in well-watered countries, is dependent on ease of transportation (transportation of persons, transportation of goods, transportation of mechanical and heat energy).

The inhabitants of these new country houses have auto-mobiles, often one which the father takes to work and another for the use of his wife and children. These suburbanites are no longer bound to a railroad or bus station, as we are still in France. They depend only on themselves. On second thought, however, it is obvious that this new type of dwelling requires not only individualized means of transportation, but also all of the other elements of tertiary civilization. There is a whole organization of economic and social life, which includes the telephone and the television set, the forty-hour week and the country club, automatic heating and the refrigerator. Without stressing too much all of the elements that are bound together by the determinisms of productivity and that con-stitute the civilization of 1975, it is important to show that two conditions are essential for the development of the tertiary habitat. These are home deliveries, and certain school and social services.

The tradesmen pass daily with their delivery trucks. They sell not only salad, milk, and beefsteak, they also deliver the essential element of the modern home, mechanical energy. In many of these little houses there is a tank for butane gas, filled every three or four months, which supplies the furnace, the kitchen stove, and many household machines.

There are other special systems for education, sanitation, medical services, and religious observance.

The school problem is solved by the school bus. A motor-bus comes on schedule every morning, serving all of the houses where there are children, or at least coming to the foot of a private road. The child is taken to school by the bus, he eats there at noon, and is taken home in the evening. Sunday, the same vehicle serves the churches. In many localities it also provides a postal service.

This solution of educational problems obviously has significant effects on the basic organization of the school.

In France a solution has been sought by the creation of schools in the smallest villages. In certain places the results are truly astonishing, for example, where the school has been built halfway between two hamlets which are four or five kilometers apart. The school is thus located two kilometers from any inhabited house, and the unfortunate teacher sees no one all week but the few children between 7 and 13 who are confided to his charge. It is hardly necessary to add that in winter half of his pupils, on the average, do not answer the school bell.

The French solution is disastrous compared to the American solution, as far as the cost of instruction, the education of the pupils, or the situation of the teacher is concerned. From the budgetary point of view, it is necessary to construct and maintain miserable buildings for a teacher who often has less than ten pupils. From the point of view of the children, these schools are far away and hard to reach on small legs. The pupil is often the only one of his age. He finds no beneficial, or even attractive, social climate. The teacher, embittered by his isolation, often loses interest in his small heterogeneous troupe. The dispersion and isolation of our country schools is one of the reasons for the present crisis in the recruitment of teachers.

In the United States there are hardly any one-class schools, or any with less than four or five teachers. There will be 20 children in a class, and at least 80 to 100 in all. The sons of farmers mingle with the sons of factory and office workers. Friendships are formed, ideas are exchanged. The school has its own life. I confess not being able to understand the reasons why so attractive a solution, so well tested by the experience of other modern countries, has not yet been tried in the French countryside. It is sometimes explained by the fear that the departure of the schoolmaster would mean the administrative collapse of many rural communes.

It follows from this brief analysis of the facts that the new pattern of tertiary countryside is based upon a high level of living and cannot be abruptly introduced into a country like France with a middle level of living. This explains the total failure of the subdivisions of the 1920-30 type. A great mistake of these French subdivisions was that they required a dispersion, less great perhaps than that of the American suburb, but distinctly excessive considering the means of transportation, the public services, and the income of the population housed. The "villas" stretch out in Indian file at great length. The proper organization of shops, schools, churches, bus stations, athletic fields, and even the open country is made impossible by these distances. The housewife every morning must travel miles to find a marginal grocer or butcher who cheerfully exploits her.

The solution that would correspond to the contemporary economic situation of France must resemble the Swedish type of urban housing projects, planned in such a way that in less than five minutes, protected from traffic, the children may walk to school, the housewife to market, and the commuter to the station.

In this matter of housing, the industrial revolution began its course in a direction which, as we now see, was essentially anti-human and quite temporary. Perhaps the solution to the housing problem that has begun to emerge today will be no more permanent than the previous one, although it is certainly better adapted to the essential needs of the human body and mind. At any rate, it is certain that the 1900 type of dwelling is completely obsolete. In this respect, as in many others, the period of transition was characterized by instability, by a break in homogeneity between the short-term measures that were taken and the long-term realities that eventually made themselves felt.

Having shown the general tendency of contemporary civilization with respect to housing, we must describe the French situation more exactly. The proportion of Frenchmen occupying modern homes, in the sense just described, is hardly one out of ten thousand. It is a smaller proportion than in any other major country. A comparison of the present situation of France with that of the United States shows clearly that the reason for the poor condition of French housing is the lack of new construction from 1935 to 1939, and again from 1946 to 1949, plus the destruction of the war.

The rate of three new dwellings per one thousand of the population annually, which prevailed at the beginning of this period, was adequate, but after 1935 there was hardly any construction and immediately after the war there was no construction at all. Throughout the entire year of 1948, France produced 20,000 dwelling units. In the single month of March, 1949, England produced the same number.

If we compare the small volume of housing constructed annually with the one million units destroyed during the war, we see it will require many years more merely to replace the losses of the last war. The total for the period 1935 to 1952 is minus 320,000 dwelling units, or seven units less per 1,000 inhabitants in 1952 than in 1935, while the calculation for the United States shows about 80 units added per 1,000 inhabitants. The effect of the war is evident, but the real problem that must be resolved in France is not so much to reconstruct what was destroyed during the war, but to develop housing worthy of the modern age. The task is incomparably greater than that of reconstruction alone.

How can we explain the inadequacy of construction in France? It is impossible to answer this question here in any thorough way. Obviously, the freezing of rent is one of the major factors. The result of this freeze has been that from 1944 to 1950, many Frenchmen spent less on rent than on tobacco. This deprived new construction of all profitability. Here again, we find an opposition between long-term and short-term mechanisms. We see the grave disadvantages for the people of measures which, at the time they are voted, appear to promote the general welfare. New construction cannot now become profitable except through a long and difficult process of rent revaluation.

At the present time, serious efforts have begun to produce results in this area. The housing "reconstruction" of France got under way in 1949 and the situation has been much improved since that time. The situation for the future looks moderately hopeful.

There is still another aspect of the problem that is less familiar and that nevertheless is more important than what has been mentioned; in the long run it must necessarily determine the level of housing of a population.

The productivity of labor in construction. When we see that France builds 20,000 units of housing in a year when England builds 240,000, we are led to suppose that the number of our construction workers is 10 to 12 times less than that of the English. This is not so at all. There are 700,000 French construction workers. The English number is 1,500,000, or a little over twice as many. The United States has 4,000,000 construction workers.

In 1948, with these labor forces, 20,000 units were constructed in France, 220,000 in England, 800,000 in the United States.

By dividing the number of units constructed by the number of workmen, we obtain the following crude productivities: 3 units per 100 workers in France, 13 units per 100 workers in England, 20 units per 100 workers in the United States. Thus, our construction workers build only three new homes while the same number of American workers are building twenty and the English workers are building thirteen.

How can we interpret these very different figures? Of course, no one will suppose that the variation is a result of the work-

er's personal effort. On the contrary, we know that in general
the higher the productivity, the less physical labor is demanded.
The enormous difference between 3 and 13 or 20 is obviously
due to the level of technique and the general organization of
the economy.

The problem of the general organization of the economy
is the principal one here. It may be summarized in a very
simple phrase—France repairs instead of building. Our construction labor force is engaged in making repairs. They patch
up old houses. They remodel the interior of bars and cafés in
Paris and the provincial cities. They dig and fill in, pave and
tear up. They install bathrooms in old houses as best they can.
They prop up crumbling walls and replace the roof over
rotted rafters. This is what two-thirds or three-quarters of our
700,000 building workers do. Only a small number of them
actually build houses. Thus it is not surprising that the total
number of new houses is laughably small.

Nevertheless, it must be understood that we pay much
more money for housing than we suppose. When the workman
is paid to repair, he repairs. When he is paid to construct, he
constructs. In any event he is paid. To estimate the level of
expenditure for housing in France, it is legitimate to use
the number of workers employed in construction.

This poses squarely the problem of productivity for the
nation as a whole. Individually, we may each find it to our
private interest to have a country house repaired or to remodel
a room in our Paris apartment. Collectively, the outcome of
these operations is deplorable, because when old buildings are
"improved," we conserve obsolete structures a little longer.
The operation is comparable to that of prolonging the life of
a twenty year old automobile by care and repair. Each year
it costs a third the price of a new car, and it will never render
the same service. We save the wages of a metallurgist and
pay a garage mechanic instead. It is not by adding ten years
to the life of a collapsing building or by installing a toilet in
an old apartment that we get air, light, calm, and a beautiful
view. All that is done is to prolong the existence of the secondary city, a little more dilapidated, a little shabbier, in-

creasing troublesome to maintain. We do not thus prepare the tertiary city.

Beyond a certain point, the expense of maintaining the old car or the old city becomes so high that the desirability of having replaced them at an earlier time becomes quite obvious. By that time, however, finding the resources necessary for replacement may have become impossible because of the very scale of current expenses. This is the classic situation of the poor country, poor because it has no industrial equipment and too poor to equip itself. It is the typical problem of the first phase of industrialization which can appear anew in a developed country as a result of an interruption in its development. To repeat, the same men can be employed either at repairing the old or at building the new, but the costs of repair must be perpetually continued and increased. *Only expenditures for new products lead to real improvement in the style of life.*

These examples show that the problems of productivity are not only problems of the technique of labor at the work place, but are also problems of general organization. To obtain high productivity, it is not sufficient to study the methods of production, but also what is produced. *The labor of repair is always tertiary in relation to the labor of production.*

At the same time, there is a technical problem of productivity in the French construction industry. In this sense also, productivity is lower in France than in the United States and in England. The studies which have been made permit us to estimate that this technical productivity is 20 to 30 per cent less in France than in England, whose productivity in turn is less than the American standard. These discrepancies arise specifically from the lack of collaboration between the architect and contractor, the rarity of long-range planning, and the weakness of production scheduling on the work site. The improvement of productivity, relatively easy to arrange in this sector, should in the normal course of events permit a reduction of about 25 per cent in the selling price of new houses, which at the present time in France is equivalent to about 20,000 hours of unskilled labor, for a single four room bungalow of simple modern type.

The first result of the deficit of new construction in France is the housing shortage. A similar shortage has been felt recently in almost all the countries of the world, and even in those countries where there is considerable construction, like the United States and Sweden. It is particularly serious in France.

COMFORT AND DOMESTIC SERVICES

The problems of domestic life are slowly entering the perspective of scientific analysis and observation. The vulgar patterns of housekeeping and dishwashing are coming, little by little, to seem worthy of rational consideration. The demanding labor of keeping house is being lightened by investigations that are described at first as ingenious (with a kind of sneer), but which really belong to the great domain of experimental science.

The scientific spirit thus invades the kitchen and the household, and it transforms the domestic scene as much as the occupational scene. There is as much difference between the kitchen of former times in the country, where the housewife crouched on the hearth to prepare a meal, and the modern kitchen, rationally designed and equipped with a variety of labor saving devices, as there is between an ox cart and a late model car. However, the average housekeeping equipment in France today lags conspicuously behind industrial and agricultural equipment. In the country, the average farmer uses machines and tractors while his wife must usually struggle with her firewood and her open well.

Public opinion inquiries in France and in the United States have recorded considerable differences in the time required for the execution of certain household tasks. While a French housewife needs five hours for her daily chores, some American housewives can manage them in an hour and a half. As a matter of fact, from the point of view of comfort, we live in France, especially in rural areas, very much as our grandparents lived. The period of transition has hardly begun in matters of housing and household equipment. Nevertheless, the possibilities of improvement are impressive, and there is an increasingly conspicuous gap between what exists and what might exist.

The Plan and Shape of the House

In ninety per cent of traditional French apartments, the housewife is the victim of poor construction design. Her daily work is annoyingly and fruitlessly prolonged by two or three hours by the faults of the construction plan, the poor arrangement and dimensions of rooms, the length of corridors, the staircases, the waste spaces, the absence of closets, and so forth. There are plans whose sole purpose was to use up a given piece of land or to satisfy an unrealistic building code. Unheated rooms, haphazardly lighted, walls covered with inconvenient and uncleanable ornamentation, waxed floors, loose joints, badly fitting doors—this is the general character of traditional houses, including the castles and the palaces. The apartments of traditional palaces were a succession of rooms without logical order, distinguished only by their interior decoration and furniture. When the mason finished his work and left the house, there would be no visible difference between the future bedroom and the future dining room. Only the chimney and the drain might identify the kitchen. Even in luxurious houses, the rooms were in line; each one was entered through another. Luxury consisted only in the size of the rooms and their decoration. The Château of Blois gives the modern visitor a good idea of what traditional housing was like in France. The drawing rooms and dining rooms are immense dark halls —because the cost of glass was so high—and, of course, they are unheatable. No partitions, no intimate corners, except perhaps for the secret stairway which suggests assignation and intrigue rather than freedom of movement for the residents. Even Kings and Queens could hardly claim a room of their own. The crowding of the Court was determined by the hazards of arrival and departure. At best, there were three or four persons per bed. When more visitors arrived, as Brantôme tells us, they slept on straw in the great halls.

Versailles marks a considerable progress over Blois. Not only was a civilized life possible there, but the general character of the place stimulated intellectual activity in an extraordinary way and encouraged a sense of political responsibility. Versailles was a model community that ennobled its inhabitants, but everything there was for the King, nothing for the man. The plan is as crude as at Blois. The rooms lead into each other interminably. In the seventeenth century plan there were no toilets, no access corridors, no centers for family life. In fact, the very idea of private life had not yet developed.

The earliest château, to our best knowledge, where the architect thought to reserve facilities for private family life, was the admirable Château of Champs, on the Marne, very close to Paris. Built toward the end of the reign of Louis XIV, this château shows by its bathrooms, its small studios and work-rooms, its flexibility, a new development of civilization—individualism with its correlary needs for solitude, relaxation, and intimacy. It is too often said that *machinisme* kills individuality. On the contrary, it might be better said that man cannot achieve intellectual and moral individuality except after a long initiation to an advanced style of life that gives him enough leisure and an adequate level of living.

The early stages of the industrial revolution were marked by ugly adaptation of the classic architectural norms to the cramped and irregular building lots which capitalism offered in the great cities. There was already a certain sense of independence, but ideas of respectability and ostentation remained uppermost. With gradual adaptations, this gave cities like Paris and London the lugubrious structures in which practically all of us live—interminable corridors, dark corners, uninhabitable living rooms, obsolete kitchens, sonorous walls and ceilings. These are the unfortunate vestiges of obsolete situations. What was an intelligent design in a former era has become completely absurd in our time.

The optimum design changes from one period to the next, with the increasing adaptation of man to the realities of the tangible world. At the present stage of development, a rational plan must include a central plumbing stack which serves the kitchen, the bathroom, and the toilets at the same time. The architect treats this stack like a closet whose place in the plan is easily changed. He does not encumber the apartment with ugly and useless mazes of pipe.

The rooms are of modest size, designed with the intention of limiting the floor area to be maintained and heated. Keeping the unit on a single level also simplifies the housewife's work.

The bedrooms have an area of at least 12 square meters— the kitchen, for a family of five persons, should have an area of 6 to 8 meters. There is a bedroom for the parents, for the girls, one for the boys, and, if the level of living is sufficiently high, rooms of their own for the children who have passed the age of eight or ten. Each bedroom has toilet facilities, a dressing room, and a closet. The family also has a bathroom or shower. The unit includes storage space, the dimensions depending upon family type and size.

The room in common use, often called the living room, includes facilities for meals, for work, and for leisure. Due to lack of space, the duality of salon and dining room tends to disappear. Instead, activity centers are organized in the general-purpose room. Movable partitions are sometimes used. Either rolling or folding partitions permit the isolation of part of a room or make it possible to join several rooms together.

The bad plan, bearing the lasting imprint of the bad architect, is a lifelong burden to the housewife who exhausts herself in innumerable domestic journeys. There is also another source of sterile servitude—the wrong materials. Most of the traditional materials and most of the current forms are checks on the productivity of the mistress of the house. The problem was totally ignored until recent years and no one noticed its familiar harmfulness.

The hereditary enemies are the oxidizable materials, particularly copper. Copper doorknobs, faucets, electric switches, require around 50 hours of polishing per year in a four room apartment, without providing either comfort or, for most people, the least pleasure. Similarly, wood surfaces which require waxing and polishing are undesirable in a modern home. They require a large fraction of the time and energy of anyone who must take care of them. There is an evident conflict between outworn aesthetic preferences and modern practices. The prestige of sparkling copper and waxed parquet floors dates from the time when palaces had such floors and copper was the symbol of luxury. There was then no other choice but planking, stone, or beaten earth.

We need to do away with the multiplicity of angles, of moldings, of plinths in relief, of cornices, milled edges, sculptured detail, exposed piping, and in general, all of the projecting surfaces which retain and accumulate dust. There are materials, in rounded and graceful forms, that facilitate woman's work, like stainless steel, glass, ceramic, enameled surfaces.

The role of science in the arts of the decorator and the architect will become increasingly important. It will enable them to avoid the serious errors which now burden our physical and mental life without our being aware of the precise source of the burden. The new methods, far from imposing uniform regulations, will give a surer base for the extension of individual tastes and preferences. Far from imposing the same rules on all human beings, science has begun to give the means of more complete satisfaction to various human desires. It has begun to give to the urbanite, brusquely deprived of the great spectacle of nature, some element of the conditions necessary for equilibrium.

Thus the house of the future will be able to give its inhabitants some approximation of the harmony which the most fortunate men were formerly able to enjoy in the infinitely varied spectacle of the countryside. The house will stimulate or calm, according to need, at the same time that it protects one from noise, from heat, and from cold.

Isolation and Protection against the External Environment

Throughout history, man has required of his house that it protect him against the rain, against the excessive heat of the summer, against the cold of the winter. The house must create an interior environment favorable to human life, and thus isolate itself from the exterior environment that is often hostile or unfavorable.

But man, as the machine permitted him to enlarge his requirements, has become more and more demanding with respect to the interior environment. Until about 1800, he was usually satisfied with a climate which permitted the minimum essentials of physical life—eating, drinking, and sleeping, and in the winter, some hours of heat in front of a wood fire. The high cost of light and heat meant that 99 per cent of the population dined in winter at 5:00 in the evening and went to bed at 6:00. The rhythm of life was implacably controlled by the rhythm of the seasons. There are abundant proofs of the lethargy that seized hold of the most civilized society after the middle of autumn, as still happens today in a significant but decreasing proportion of peasant communities in Europe.

In our time, however, man seeks in his home an interior environment that not only permits him to indulge a similar rhythm of physical life in winter and in summer, but also allows a constant level of intellectual activity. Glass windows, artificial lighting, heating and air conditioning, and sound-proofing give or promise such facilities to the average city and village dweller as Descartes would have envied. This obviously does not create a swarm of Descartes, but the possibilities of intellectual life open more widely for the mass of people today than they did for the elite of past centuries.

Windows and window glass. The first great achievement of *machinisme,* practically indispensable to the development of intellectual life in our climate, was that of window glass. Without artificial light it is impossible north of the river Loire, in an average year, to read or to write steadily between November and April. This is why the intellectual civilization of traditional times was so invariably associated with Mediterranean and tropical climates. For a history of civilization in the countries situated to the north of the forty-fifth parallel of latitude, the technique of window glass is as important as the technique of the revolving belt in the history of work.

A brief review of the history of glass was given in a previous chapter. As far as the closure of the house is concerned, the essential stages were the following:

From the year 1000 to about 1500, flat colored panes of glass, no bigger than two inches square, were manufactured at great cost. The high price is shown by an occasional view of a window in paintings. Glass was so costly that even in the richest mansions only the upper part of the windows were ordinarily glazed. The lower part remained, as formerly, covered by a shutter of plain wood, or in summer, by a wooden lattice. The window openings were small and few.

After the Renaissance, the dimensions of glass panes increased. The windows of wealthy houses were completely furnished with glass. The size of the window openings increased considerably.

In 1800, as we have noted above, peasant houses often still lacked glass, but by 1900, the poorest French houses had their glass windows.

At the present time we have arrived at a new phase in the closure of the house. The windows may now, because of the low price of glass resulting from modern manufacturing procedures, be of large size with panes up to 10 square meters and more, in place of the small glass squares of former times which were so difficult to clean. Balconies and terraces permit the city dweller to live in the open air when the weather permits.

One may summarize in this way the history of lighting in the home. The man of our climate—traditionally obliged to choose between light and insulation—could only sacrifice the light. Hence, the fortress and Romanesque effects, with narrow casement openings. Only the technique of window glass has been able to resolve this dilemma and to open ordinary homes to the light, as a literate civilization requires.

With respect to noise, the effect of *machinisme* has not been as clearly beneficial as with light. On the contrary, one might say that real noise first appeared with the industrial revolution. Before that, there were only sounds. Today, factories, trains and trams, motors, the radios of neighbors, are among the horrors of the transitional period.

As far as permeability to sound is concerned, the house of today is really inferior to that of former times, because of thinner walls and the use of sonorous materials. It should be much better, because the noises have been multiplied. Given the density of population of the great cities, the number of neighbors disturbed in their sleep or at their work by a single inconsiderate radio listener may be as high as 300. The locomotives and the trains, mechanical music, and street sounds do away with peace and quiet. An automatic bus ticket distributor placed next to an apartment house can disturb the lives of many people to an appreciable extent.

Some buildings are so permeable to noise that one can hear through the walls and the floors the sounds of footsteps, of dishwashing, and even the voices of neighbors.

Meanwhile, sound insulation has become a science, at once a branch of physics and one of the human sciences.

A *phone* is the variation of sound intensity necessary for the human ear to note a change. One phone is about equal to one decibel for a sound of frequency 1,000. Above 120 phones, noise is painful for the normal man (motors on the testing bench, steam hammers). Noisy radios emit as much as 80 phones, auto horns 60, normal radio volume 40, a conversation 30. Below 20, we have tranquility. The "silence of the country-side" gives about 2 to 5. Below one, the average ear perceives nothing.

The art of sound insulation is already well developed. The usual soundproofing materials can be ranked this way, in ascending order of efficiency: concrete, brick wall, stone, wood paneling, and cork. Concrete is a very poor insulator in houses of modern construction; sound is suppressed by layers of material whose nature varies with the length of the sound wave to be absorbed—factory noises, the sounds of speech or street noise, for example. Glass wool is usually very satisfactory. Sound insulation is accomplished at the same time as thermal insulation. The most effective measures can only be taken at the time of original construction. A number of materials which are excellent thermal and phonic insulators are currently available. These materials sometimes permit a reduction of half or more in the heating expense of a winter season. They favor the well-being of the occupant to an unimaginable degree by the quiet of the evening and the coolness of the summers.

Heating. Heating permits us to obtain more easily than by means of food a physiological equilibrium between the heat lost and that retained. Taking variations in climate into account, artificial heat is a necessity, even for a strictly vegetative life, as soon as the daily average temperature falls below about 50 degrees.

This is why, since the most distant times, heating and housing have been closely associated. In the most primitive houses we find a room where a fire may be laid. This fire is usually used at the same time for cooking, so that the room with the fire, if it is the only one, is always a kitchen. This does not prevent it from serving as a common living room, and often as a bedroom, too.

As the level of living rises, there is a demand for more continuous heating which gives a temperature somewhat adapted to individual preference, to the activity which takes place in the room, and to the humidity of the air.

For any activity, there is an optimum temperature which permits maximum efficiency and well-being. This temperature varies among individuals and according to the activity. It averages about 50 degrees for heavy outdoor work, about 72 degrees for office work, and about 60 degrees for sleep. Theaters should be kept above 70 degrees, operating rooms above 80. Americans generally expect 5 to 10 degrees more heat than the French.

In the same way that poor light fatigues the eyes, some types of heating are physiologically disturbing. The most healthful method of heating is by radiation. The Romans had already developed an altogether remarkable system of radiant wall and floor heating.

There are, of course, a great variety of heating systems, ranging from the primitive wood fire which was still the sole means of heating known to my grandparents in their peasant house at Quercy, to central heating. There are chimneys with controlled drafts and stoves of all sorts and forms (the most curious are probably the gigantic ceramic stoves in Poland and Russia which decorate an entire wall.) It is interesting that the stove, the traditional heating device, invented about 3,000 years ago, has been notably improved only in the last few years. Present day stoves use less coal for an equal amount of heat than those of ten years ago. This progress has been made possible in France by a large-scale research effort inspired by the Foundry Technical Center. Modern *machinisme* has also developed gas and electric radiators and of course central heating.

With large-scale (city central) heating, the economy in labor and fuel is even greater. While the average thermal efficiency of most central heating furnaces is less than 50 per cent because of defects of installation and the limited competence of the operator, the efficiency of a high-powered modern installation can go as high as 85 per cent.

So-called individual central heating is used in isolated houses. It has the important advantage of being entirely controlled by the consumer, who can regulate and adjust it at his pleasure. A central stove, placed between the living room and the kitchen, will heat the house in a convenient fashion. A thermostat regulates the volume of heat without human intervention. Gas or oil stoves can even be started and stopped by the thermostat. Rural American houses often have such systems. Early on a cold September dawn, the surprised French guest feels the heat rise suddenly in the radiator while the whole household is asleep. Two hours later, when the sun comes above the horizon, the furnace turns itself off.

Air conditioning. Every year technical progress makes new regions of the globe habitable for the white race. Before the scientific revolution, an average man of European origin could not live permanently below the thirty-fifth parallel of latitude, or north of the seventieth. Even within this zone there were immense regions of hardship caused by the seasonal variations of the continental climate in Russia, the United States, and to an even greater degree, in Canada and Siberia. Intellectual life was even more limited. Can we imagine the force of character necessary to maintain any civilization at all at Stockholm or at St. Petersburg before the industrial era? It would be interesting to see what would become of our French intellectuals of today who, in unison, express their resentment against *machinisme* and expose the profound decadence of our civilization, who prophesy the end of Christianity and the end of the world, if they were placed for a single year under the conditions in which Peter the Great or Queen Christina lived—six months of ice, four months of darkness. Our Descartes himself could not have stood it.

In fact, in these latitudes, intellectual life was necessarily limited to a tiny minority, privileged in fortune, physique,

and character. It has not been sufficiently understood that even
the United States needed all of the resources of modern *machinisme* to launch its intellectual life. It is sufficient to study the
average January and July temperatures of the principal American cities to become aware of this fact.

Human limitations, already so great with respect to physical
life, are so much more stringent with respect to intellectual
life that before the coming of the machine, European civilization was tied to the Mediterranean climate. It is reasonable
to think that neither Descartes nor Pascal nor Newton could
have equalled Galileo if they had not had window glass in
their houses. Before the glass window, it was difficult for anyone to be a genius outside of the regions where the olive tree
grows. Although window glass was sufficient to open France
and England to intellectual life, much more was needed in
many cases and in many regions. To adjust the temperature
so that it would fall between 55 and 75 degrees, which is most
favorable to the intellectual life of the white man, a new effort
of *machinisme* was required—weather conditioning. The first
effort in this direction does not date from yesterday. It was
the ancestral cave. With the conquest of fire, the conditions
of life became artificial for the first time. Today, air conditioning creates artificial climates by fixing the temperature and
the composition of the air. One of the rules of air conditioning
in summer is to limit the gap between the cool interior temperature and the temperature of the outside air to about 15
degrees. If a greater difference is wanted, then an intermediary
zone is necessary.

Air conditioning installations purify the air as much as possible by removing dust. They also control the water content
and even the chemical composition to resemble the air of countryside or mountain. The distribution takes place at a determined temperature and with the appropriate humidity for
that temperature.

In our climate in the winter, the air may be circulated at
an average temperature of 110 degrees, at 20 per cent humidity,
so that after compensating for the heat losses of the unit, the
temperature is maintained at 70 degrees and the humidity at

50 per cent. In summer, the air circulates at 70 degrees with 70 per cent humidity.

Air conditioning apparatuses are easier to install in a building at the time of construction than later on. However, small units are manufactured in the United States which contain all the necessary elements for the treatment and circulation of air in a single room.

In general, air conditioning is expensive to install and to maintain. This expense is not essential in our climate, but it is useful in many nations, like the United States, for example, and indispensable for the white man in the tropics. Air conditioning also can provide protection for the fragile moments of existence—certain illnesses, old age, early infancy. Thanks to this, premature infants may now be kept alive after the sixth month. The air conditioning of nurseries in North Africa has saved the lives of many children.

However, air conditioning will never be needed by everyone. On the contrary, too much of it can be harmful to the healthy organism. The human machine needs climatic variations, and the organism should not be deprived of the small struggles and adaptive efforts which are necessary to its normal development and functions.

The purpose of air conditioning—and comfort in general—is not to suppress all variation of environmental conditions, but to assure those variations and contrasts necessary for the normal rhythm of life. The following norm of comfort seems essential to us: the conditions surrounding men should be as close as possible to those prevailing in a healthy, tranquil, and fertile countryside on a beautiful spring day.

In his remarkable work, *Mechanisation Takes Command*, Giedion studies the role of the bath in successive civilizations. He shows that traveling bathtubs preceded fixed bathtubs in western Europe. The water carriers peddled baths through the streets of Paris, delivering both tub and hot water to the customer's home. In 1838, according to Giedion, Paris had 1,015 of these bathtubs for rent, and 2,224 fixed tubs in the public bath-houses. Many of our contemporaries can still remember the water carriers going up the stairs of apartment houses with their copper tubs and their buckets. Many still have in their attics the bathing shirts worn by their great-grandfathers.

A full history of urban water supply would be fascinating. Before 1810, no city in the world had running water fully available for domestic use. Napoleon was responsible for the Parisian system of water mains; the plan was established in 1812. However, it was only after 1850 that the majority of Parisian apartments had a faucet.

In 1869, in a book called *The American Woman's Home*, Catherine Beecher predicted the modern bathroom and published the floor plan of an apartment with bathroom. It was not until 1908 that the first commercial hotel with a bath for each room was built—the Buffalo Statler. It may be remarked in passing that hotels have played, and still play, an important part in educating the masses in matters of hygiene and comfort.

These humble realities of the kitchen, the bath, and the toilet are curiously fascinating when they are studied scientifically. They are an essential element of the social problem. They take up a third of the time of our wives and mothers. They are the necessary foundation of hygiene, and consequently of the reduction of infant mortality and epidemics. Finally, in the great urban centers, there cannot be attractive homes if these essential services are not satisfactorily provided. The fundamental plague of our time and the principal cause of proletarian demoralization in France is the shocking inadequacy of essential services in the working class suburbs, characteristic of the period of transition.

DOMESTIC MACHINES

The availability of power in the home permits the use of domestic machines. The possibility of using such machines would remain purely theoretical if it were not for the trend toward the reduction of their cost when measured in terms of hourly average wages. We have already explained how the increase in the supply of mechanical energy and the increase of the ratio:

$$\frac{\text{wages}}{\text{cost of machine operation}}$$

are inextricably related. Both phenomena express the fundamental tendency for secondary prices to decline in relation to tertiary prices in a period of technical progress. This explains why, in a country like the United States, even poor households can buy, and are motivated to buy, domestic machines, while in countries with little technical progress, like Egypt or India, even high income families who could afford to buy these machines do not have any interest in doing so. We shall return later to this economic law. It helps to explain the present picture of mechanization in the world.

In spite of contrary opinion still prevalent among some authorities, in cooking as in any other kind of work, the problem of equipment is secondary to organization. The machine does not determine organization but organization does produce the machine. Even in previous centuries, it would have been possible and fairly easy to arrange for certain rational improvements in the kitchen, such as better distribution of water, accessible and logically designed furniture, space utilized in relation to a working plan. No one thought of these things any more than they thought of the garbage chute. Even today, many a modern kitchen furnished with an impressive battery of appliances is organized in an absurd fashion and loses most of its efficiency.

In the kitchen of former times, the arrangement of objects was made without any idea of work simplification. The housewife had to draw her water in a well which was far from the kitchen. Many times a day she had to descend into the cellar to put something to cool. She had to go to the woodpile to get wood, and so on. In the kitchens, which were usually very large, objects were arranged either at random or according to family habit. It often happened that necessary objects were kept in the farthest possible place from where they were used or in low cupboards which could not be reached without bending, while ladders were needed to reach other shelves. Furthermore, the actual cooking was done on the hearth in the most inconvenient manner imaginable.

The first principles of household skill are now coming to be known. Courses of technical instruction, varied publications and such magazines as *La Maison Française* and *Good Housekeeping* have had a major influence. Attitudes, the basic essentials of social transformation, are slowly changing. It is especially interesting to observe from this standpoint the developments in a country village where a water system has just been installed by the municipality. During the first year, some of the inhabitants refuse to spend the money, insisting that the well is still sufficient for their needs. Others "take the water" but have only a single faucet installed. This faucet is placed in the barn, above the drinking trough, or even worse, near the cistern or well. The peasants still think it simple enough to carry the water for household needs in pails. We have seen

Table XXXII—Proportion of Residential Buildings with Sewer Connections in 31 French Cities and Suburbs, 1947

	per cent		per cent
Aix-en-Provence	39	Nancy	94
Albi	8	Narbonne	43
Alès	8	Nice	76
Angoulême	1.5	Nîmes	3
Arras	44	Pau	81
Avignon	27	Périgueux	14
Bayonne	69	Perpignan	74
Béziers	51	Poitiers	8
Bordeaux	9	Reims	41
Bourges	6	Rennes	60
Bruay-en-Artois	1.5	Roanne	10
Caen	33	Roubaix	6
Cannes	82	Rouen	12
Carcassonne	80	Saint-Brieuc	45
Châlons-sur-Marne	7	Saint-Etienne	68
Clermont-Ferrand	55	Saint-Quentin	10
Douai	16	Sète	67
Grenoble	78	Tarbes	2
Lens	18	Toulon	53
Lille	10	Toulouse	1.5
Limoges	10	Troyes	44
Lyon	39	Valence	16
Marseille	45	Valenciennes	5
Montauban	9	Versailles	7
Montluçon	29	Paris	94
Montpellier	74	Seine-banlieue	56

people in a village where the water system was two years old installing a new kitchen sink without any thought of adding a second faucet to the first faucet in the barn. It will take several years before these new consumers understand the usefulness of a faucet in the kitchen sink and, in general, it will take a new generation to lead the running water as far as the wash basins and the outhouses.

It is impossible in a book like this to examine in detail the part played by machinery in the home.

However, there are two essential devices that have become so much a part of our habits that we forget to consider them as scientific achievements. These may be taken as typical of the mechanization of the home. They are the radio and the telephone.

The residential telephone provides inestimable services and a saving of locomotion. It simplifies or does away with all kinds of errands. Its function with respect to medical care is fundamental. Its commercial and political importance is considerable.

The radio introduces intellectual and cultural elements into every home. It is the fashion to complain of the mediocrity of the programs. Nevertheless, the musical education of the masses was begun by the radio, and there is no young European who has not heard some fragments of Bach or Mozart. The spoken newscast is of distinctly better quality than the written press. The better programs are such that any man of taste can follow them with profit.

The possibilities of television are currently wasted in sports programs of mediocre interest and tenth-rate vaudeville. It is potentially a marvelous resource for teaching and communication. The material of this book adapted for television, for example, would be both useful and pleasing.

Radio, television, and the telephone play a particularly important part in rural districts. They are, together with automobiles, the necessary conditions for the return to the dispersed habitat whose importance for the future we have previously discussed. They also provide the necessary conditions of safety in travel and transportation.

The increasingly numerous machines—washing machines,

waxers, vacuum cleaners, refrigerators—that surround the mistress of the modern house will slowly develop a scientific mentality in the coming generations. Intuition, flair, chance, and fantasy will be displaced by method, quantitative measurements, concentration and precision. The watch, the scales, the thermometer, become the indispensable instruments. The cartoonists show the cook dressed like a factory foreman and placed in front of as many dials and levers as the pilot of a Flying Fortress. It is not the fault of science if efficiency can only be acquired through exactness, and if awareness is generally unfavorable to romantic myths. On the other hand, humanity must guard its reserves of poetry and its dreams; clearly these are the essential elements of the vital urge. The exaggeratedly mechanical trends introduced in the scientific organization of the home should be balanced by a solid literary and artistic initiation during adolescence, by the use of leisure, and within the home itself, by atmosphere and decoration. I must add that in a country like France, the dangers to be feared from an excess of the scientific spirit among our wives are still extremely remote. This is by no means the case in the United States.

The preceding discussion shows what we are already

Table XXXIII—Estimated Per Capita Consumption of Electricity* (in kilowatt hours)

	1938	1947	1952
Austria	425	586	1,164
Belgium	555	805	1,088
Denmark	290	425	622
United States	1,135	2,130	3,074
France	500	670	956
Greece	40	40	113
Ireland	135	200	391
Iceland	—	—	1,571
Italy	355	460	661
Luxemburg	1,660	1,000	2,754
Norway	3,400	3,900	5,716
Netherlands	400	450	885
Portugal	55	70	156
United Kingdom	485	855	1,272
Sweden	1,300	2,230	2,946
Switzerland	1,670	2,140	—
Turkey	15	30	46

* See French edition for detailed sources

capable of realizing by way of individual welfare. It does not imply that this development of the household arts is already within reach everywhere in the world.

Household appliances consume an enormous quantity of mechanical energy. To guarantee central heating to every Frenchman, two tons of coal per head and per year would be necessary for residental heating alone, or about as much coal as France consumed for all purposes in 1950. To give each French household the average equipment of an American household, it would be necessary to increase three-fold our consumption, and therefore our production of electricity.

The two following tables give some idea of the consumption of electrical energy in the world today. We shall find in the first table the disparity with which the study of the level of living has already familiarized us. The difference between per capita consumption in Turkey and Norway is of the order of 1 to 130. France uses only a third as much electricity per person as Sweden or Switzerland.

The second table shows with what rapidity American consumption of energy has grown. It practically doubled from 1939 to 1949. The development of the household arts is closely linked to general economic progress.

Table XXXIV—Trends in the Production and Consumption of Electrical Energy in the United States (in millions of kilowatt hours)

Year	Total Production	From hydraulic plants	From steam plants	For industrial use	For public use	Population in thousands	Per capita consumption kw-h per year
1939	161,308			33,667	127,642	130,880	1,232
1940	179,907			38,070	141,837	131,970	1,363
1941	208,306			43,519	164,788	133,203	1,564
1942	233,146			47,167	185,979	134,665	1,731
1943	267,540	79,078	183,952	49,781	217,759	136,497	1,960
1944	279,525	78,905	195,664	51,336	228,189	138,083	2,024
1945	271,255	84,747	181,708	48,769	222,486	139,586	1,943
1946	269,361	83,211	181,552	46,184	223,178	141,235	1,907
1947	307,301	83,097	218,625	51,571	255,739	144,024	2,134
1948	336,335	86,941	249,394	53,741	282,594	146,571	2,295
1949	345,066	94,773	250,293	53,966	291,100	148,000	2,330
1950	388,674	100,885	287,789	89,533	329,141	150,600	2,580
1951	435,649	106,640	331,009	64,976	370,673	154,360	2,822
1952	463,056	109,708	353,368	63,432	399,626	156,981	3,584
1953	514,169	106,617	407,552	71,504	442,665	159,630	3,221

More exactly, household equipment is subject to the same economic laws as industrial equipment. Its use depends upon the ratio of secondary to tertiary prices. In the poor countries, the prices of machines and of energy, which are secondary prices, are very high in relation to the price of labor, which is a tertiary price. It is therefore neither feasible for the individual, *nor advantageous for the economy,* to substitute machines for men. By contrast, in the rich countries, the secondary prices are low in relation to the cost of labor, and mechanization leads to further mechanization.

Chapter VII

HEALTH AND
LIFE EXPECTANCY

IT WOULD SEEM DIFFICULT to reject one criterion of human progress: the lengthening of the average span of life. The individual must be alive that he may achieve civilization. Existence is a prerequisite of thought.

The man with forty crowns knew very well that in the eighteenth century in France, one out of two men died before his twentieth year. Admirable conditions to promote an intellectual civilization! In order to be elected to the Academy, it was first necessary to triumph over chickenpox.

The prolongation of life expectancy is the essential phenomenon of modern times—at once a consequence of technical progress and a reason for the acceleration of that progress. This prolongation sums up and synthesizes the improvements that have taken place in both the level of living and the style of life.

The reasons for the prolongation of life expectancy. The lengthening of the average duration of human life proceeds from numerous causes, all of them determined directly or indirectly by scientific progress.

One of the most obvious of the indirect causes is the improvement of the level of living of the great masses. Mortality has been much higher in the poor classes than in the comfortable and rich classes. The fact that mortality is much lower today in the poorest classes of advanced nations than it was in the richest classes around 1750 shows that the essentially medical factor is preponderant.

Here, as in every other field, scientific progress has led to the discovery of causal relationships, permitting men to manipulate and modify a phenomenon and to prevent or to provoke other phenomena that cannot be directly influenced. Here, as everywhere, familiarity with stable or relatively stable causalities leads to predictability, and predictability permits action.

Hence the importance, greater in this respect than in any other, of the speed with which action can be taken to prevent or cure diseases. Physiology describes normal causalities. Pathology describes morbid causalities. Therapy combats morbid developments by trying to release opposed causalities against them. Thus medical and surgical therapy is to biological science what technical progress is to science in general.

The progress of biology in the past fifteen years surpasses the popular imagination. The sulfa drugs (1935), penicillin (1941), streptomycin (1946), chloromycetin (1948), and aureomycin (1949), have conquered practically all of the infectious maladies—typhus, typhoid fever, tuberculosis, cholera, pneumonia, pleurisy. Venereal diseases can be treated with penicillin plus the earlier medications of mercury, arsenic, and bismuth as auxiliaries. They have been definitely curable since 1948.

We have been able to isolate and to obtain from animal glands the hormones that function in the human body as catalysts for the accomplishment of such organic functions as physical growth and mental development.

Furthermore, since 1930, we have known how to manufacture by synthesis a whole series of glandular secretions having regulative or substitutive functions, such as insulin, adrenalin, folliculin, cortisone. These serums permit replacement or supplementation of the products of several glands—the pancreas, the ovaries, the thymus—when they are inadequate.

The use of physical treatments such as radiation therapy, electromagnetic waves, and ultrasonic vibration open other new avenues of progress to medical science.

The science of nutrition and the knowledge of vitamins have led to a reduction in the diseases of malnutrition, such as rickets and scurvy, and have provided remedies for deficiencies in blood production, such as those leading to pernicious anemia.

Surgical therapy has also accomplished almost inconceivable advances since 1950 by the use of new methods of anaesthesia and patient care, as in heart and stomach surgery, and by the use of new operative techniques, often made possible by the antibiotics. Neurosurgery is moving out of a laboratory phase into general use.

Finally, prothesis is in the midst of a revolution. From the pioneer efforts at the end of the eighteenth century when the first wooden legs gave cripples a satanic character, to the artificial limbs of 1955, progress has been decisive. Sight is being more closely corrected, hearing can be improved, and in dental prothesis we see the tendency to a real incorporation of inanimate matter in the human body and the positive correction of anatomical faults and infirmities.

The removal of handicaps leads to aesthetic surgery which may be considered as including beauty care—the permanent wave, the massage, and other cosmetic treatments—and more serious operations ranging from the reduction of varicose veins to plastic remodeling.

All of these techniques reduce the suffering of the sick and improve the lot of millions of human beings. Most of them also contribute to the lengthening of the average life and to an increase in our powers of action.

The lengthening of the average expectation of human life in the course of the past two hundred years is one of the least debatable phenomena of contemporary economic development. As the reader must suspect by now, this evolution in time has produced a disparity in space, so that in the world of today there are some nations whose situation is close to that of 1750; in others the average length of life has more than doubled.

Mortality in the traditional epoch. Reliable data on the mortality of large populations cannot be found earlier than the middle of the eighteenth century. Thus we do not have much real evidence except for the very end of the traditional epoch.

In France, from 1750 to 1800, the mean annual mortality

—the ratio of the total number of deaths in one year to the total population at the mid-point of that year—seems to have been of the order of 30 to 35 per thousand. With the beginning of official statistics, between 1806 and 1810, the rate recorded was 26 per thousand. The Swedish and Finnish demographic statistics, the oldest of the modern world concerning whole nations, go back to 1750 and show for the second half of the eighteenth century an average rate of the order of 25 to 30 per thousand.

If the reader remembers the first part of this book, he will understand why the mortality rates of the traditional epoch were not only very high in comparison to the present rates of advanced countries, which have fallen below ten per thousand in the last 20 years, but also why they varied greatly from one year to another. The extreme instability of the level of living resulted in an extremely fluctuating death rate.

At a time when the average death rate was of the order of 30 per thousand, in the course of the years 1750 to 1800, a rate of 37.2 was recorded in Sweden in 1772 and 52.6 in 1773. In Finland we note a rate of 41 in 1791, 60 in 1808, 59 in 1809, 78 in 1868. These figures give a faint idea of what the mortality must have been in earlier epidemics or famines such as that of 1709 in France.[1]

Excessive death rates are still found in those nations of the contemporary world which have remained closed to technical progress and have only profited from a very trifling improvement in the level of living. From 1931 to 1935 the statistics of India and of Ceylon still showed rates around 25 per thousand. The Egyptian rate was 28 per thousand before 1940. As for China, no general statistics have yet been published, but local investigations carried out between 1929 and 1935 give figures of 30 to 40 per thousand as normal.

These death rates, which are the easiest to obtain from civil registers, do not speak to the imagination until we understand that a rate of 33 per thousand corresponds to an average life span of 30 years and to a median life expectancy of 10 to 20 years.[2]

Life Expectancy Trends Since 1830

We may sum up as follows the trends observed since 1830 in the technically advanced countries:

1) Average and median life expectancies have been greatly increased; the median life expectancy even more than the mean.

2) The variations and fluctuations from one year to another have been much reduced.

3) The poorer classes have made relatively greater gains than the prosperous classes.

In sum, the effective duration of human life has increased and been equalized at the same time.

These facts will appear clearly from inspection of the following tables.

One last time we are happy to cite the name of Villermé, since we regard him, together with Vauban and Levasseur, as founder of this science of the level of living, so necessary to human welfare and so neglected. Villermé wrote in 1835: "To find men suitable for military service, 193 recruits were required from the prosperous classes and 343 from the poorer classes."[3] This simple fact calls attention to the considerable differences of physical conformation produced by the differences in level of living which we noted in the early chapters of this book.

All the statistics of military conscription show the growth of average stature during the past century. For reasonably prosperous districts in the south of France, the increase of average height exceeds five centimeters and sometimes reaches seven or eight.

Even more dramatically, Villermé notes, as part of a remarkable study that he conducted at Mulhouse concerning mortality in the period 1823 to 1834, that the life expectancy at birth was 28 years among the rich, and—one cannot write this without a feeling of revolt—*one year and three months* among the "simple weavers." We should like to be able to say that Villermé had made an error of calculation. Not at all. For every 100 births among these workers whose level of living we previously described, there were 30 deaths in the first six months and 20 deaths in the nine months following. Of the 100 infants, only 27 reached age 10, 17 age 20, 6 age 40, and only one reached the age of 60.

There is still a high mortality among the poor. This has been demonstrated by such studies as those of Huber and Hersch in France, Whitney in the United States, and the official statistical office of Great Britain.[4] But the observed range between the extremes observed after 1920 has been relatively slight and is being rapidly reduced. According to figures furnished by the *Registrar General's Decennial Supplement,* which represents the most serious investigation we have on this subject, the mortality rate of the poorest classes was 48 per cent higher than the most favored classes in 1921-23 and only 24 per cent higher in 1930-32. We are far from the difference of 500 to 1000 per cent implied by the statistics of Villermé. Moreover, this gap of 24 per cent refers to the situation a gen-

Table XXXV—Median Life Expectancy at Mulhouse, 1823-34*

	At birth	At 1 year	At 4 years	At 10 years	At 20 years	At 30 years
Manufacturers, managers, agents, merchants, etc.	28	43	46	42	34	30
Servants	21	37	35	32	23	18
Factory workers, not further classified	18	20	21	28	33	30
Bakers and grocers	12	39	43	40	34	26
Tailors	12	36	39	40	32	28
Day laborers	9	20	33	34	32	26
Masons	4	29	37	35	29	22
Carpenters	4	28	24	30	24	25
Shoemakers	3	31	40	38	31	24
Printers	3	28	39	35	27	21
Cabinet-makers	3	20	39	38	29	25
Factory foremen	2.5	27	35	36	28	23
Simple weavers	1.5	19	28	26	20	17
Simple spinners	1.5	11	18	17	15	13
General population of the city	7.5	30	40	38	32	26.5
General population of the département	13.5	39	46.5	45.5	38	31

* From Villermé, *op. cit.,* Vol. II, p. 251. This table includes those occupational groups from which more than 100 deaths were recorded in the period, with the exception of servants (93) and foremen (80). The median life expectancy at birth for all of France at that time was about 20 years. As may be seen from the table, the mortality in the industrialized department of Haut-Rhin was much higher, and in the factory town of Mulhouse, much higher still.

Table XXXVI—Mortality by Age in the Department of Haut-Rhin for the Total Period 1814 to 1833*

	MALES			FEMALES			TOTAL POPULATION		
	Observed Living	Estimated Life Expectancy years	months	Observed Living	Estimated Life Expectancy years	months	Observed Living	Estimated Life Expectancy years	months
At birth	109,973	7	8	106,122	18	10	216,095	13	5
3 months	88,408	26	9	90,031	33	10	178,439	30	5
6 months	82,430	32	9	85,303	36	6	167,723	34	6
1 year	76,270	37	8	79,859	40	6	156,129	38	11
2 years	68,983	42	8	72,677	42	1	141,660	43	7
3	64,624	45	8	68,355	46	3	132,979	45	9
4	61,747	46	1	65,295	47	1	127,042	46	7
5	59,682	46	7	63,116	47	4	122,798	46	11
10	53,841	45	1	57,210	45	8	111,051	45	5
15	51,671	41	5	54,971	41	11	106,642	41	8
20	49,169	37	11	52,513	38	11	101,682	38	8
25	45,366	35	11	49,817	37	7	95,183	34	10
30	42,542	31	5	46,936	30	11	89,478	31	2
35	39,909	27	8	43,989	27	2	83,898	27	5
40	37,242	24	8	40,693	23	7	77,935	23	9
45	34,330	20	6	37,098	20	4	71,428	20	2
50	30,955	17	1	33,621	16	7	64,572	16	10
55	26,996	14	1	29,228	13	6	56,224	13	9
60	22,734	11	2	24,548	10	7	47,282	10	10
65	17,594	7	9	18,632	8	2	36,226	8	6
70	12,470	6	8	12,925	6	7	25,395	6	7
75	7,545	5	8	7,543	5	2	15,088	5	1
80	3,762	3	11	3,671	4	1	7,433	4	1
85	1,383	3	4	1,366	3	4	2,749	3	4
90	335	3	4	362	3	4	697	3	4
95	72	2	6	86	2	4	158	2	3
100	4	2	6	5	2	4	9	2	3

* From Villermé, op. cit., Vol. II, p. 375.

eration past, before the strengthening of social insurance and the discovery of antibiotics.

While in 1830 the richest groups of the French population had a life expectancy of about 28 years, the poorest groups today have a life expectancy of more than 60 years. The mean life expectancy for the entire French population has a value of approximately 67.

However, as in other matters concerned with the level of living, France does not hold the world record. Holland, Sweden, Norway, Denmark, Switzerland, England, the United States, Canada, and many other countries enjoy life expectancies varying from 68 to 72 years. On the other hand, as we have already mentioned, some rates in the modern world have been, until the last few years, hardly higher than those of the end of the traditional epoch. The median life expectancy for India in the decade 1921-30 was only 26. However, since 1952 or 1955, underdeveloped countries have made extraordinary progress

Table XXXVII—Infant Mortality (Deaths per 1,000 live births in the first year of life)

Dates	France	United States
1806-15	186	190
1856-65	179	180
1866-75	177	
1876-85	167	
1886-95	168	
1896-1900	158	160
1901-05	139	138
1906-13	126	127
1914-19	128	96
1921-25	95	74
1926-30	89	
1931-35	73	59
1936-40	71	51
1940	92	47
1941	73	45
1942	72	40
1943	75	40
1944	78	40
1945	109	38
1946	73	34
1947	67	32
1948	51	31
1949	55	31
1950	52	29
1957	29	26

in this realm. China has published the same infant mortality rates for 1958 as those of France for 1950. The sudden acceleration of progress in reducing mortality has caused predictions of the world population to jump from 3.3 to 6 billion, for the year 2000.

The importance of the struggle against death in the earliest period of life leads us to reproduce here some of the admirable statistics on infant mortality. Humanity itself must have been in a kind of infancy not to have paid any attention until so recently to the fate of its little children. It is only since 1806 that France has known the average number of her newborn who died in the course of their first year. The following table follows this trend and permits comparison with the United States, a comparison which authorizes our hopes for the near future.

Bourgeois-Pichat has calculated the corrected rates of in-

Table XXXVIII—Infant Mortality in Various Countries (Deaths in the first year, per 1,000 live births)

| | STANDARD RATES | | | BOURGEOIS-PICHAT RATES* | |
	1938	1947		1938	1947
New Zealand	25	25	New Zealand	12	6
Sweden	43	25	Sweden	24	8
Netherlands	39	29	United States	30	10
United States	56	32	Netherlands	21	14
Norway	42	35	Switzerland	24	16
Switzerland	47	39	Norway	24	17
Denmark	67	40	England and Wales	36	21
England and Wales	59	41	Denmark	49	22
France	57	61	Scotland	56	30
Northern Ireland	77	53	Northern Ireland	55	31
Scotland	83	56	France	54	37
Finland	66	56	Finland	48	41
Germany (British zone)	66	67	Germany (British zone)	34	42
Eire	74	67	Austria	60	48
Belgium	79	69	Eire	59	52
Austria	93	76	Czechoslovakia	92	52
Italy	100	82	Belgium	57	57
Czechoslovakia	124	84	Italy	78	60
Portugal	140	108	Hungary	107	79
Hungary	139	111	Portugal	109	91
Bulgaria	144	130	Bulgaria	107	93
Rumania	179	169	Rumania	187	153

* Adapted from Jean Bourgeois-Pichat, "De le Mesure de la Mortalité Infantile," *Population*, January-March, 1946 (Paris).

fant mortality, excluding death due to congenital malforma-
tion. These corrected rates show, even better than the crude
rates, the results of social hygiene. Had it nothing to its credit
but this one accomplishment, scientific and technical progress
would deserve the respect of men of feeling.

The above evidence shows the relationship existing between the phenomena of levels of living and styles of life,
studied throughout this work, and the phenomena of mortality.
More generally, the reader may now comprehend the interde-
pendence and intercorrelation of the following apparently
independent factors: the productivity of labor, the duration of
work, the raising of school ages, the intensity of production, the
purchasing power of the working masses, the development of
the structure of consumption, and the related development of
the structure of production; crises of overproduction; divergent price trends and shifts in the labor force; imbalance of
foreign trade. The correlations are so close that it is sufficient
to know one of the characteristics of the system within a more
or less autonomous economic region to know all of the others,
and so to be able to solve problems that a few years ago would
have seemed as impossible as trying to determine the speed of
a ship from the age of the captain or the height of the mast.
For example, we are now really able to deduce from the number of men employed in agriculture the approximate relation
of the price of bread to the hourly wage of the laborer, or the
approximate average school age, or the approximate life expectancy, and so on and so forth. Conversely, each of the factors seems to determine the order of magnitude of the others.
The independent variable of the entire system is technical
progress, measured by the productivity of labor.

More exactly, the relations that exist between the duration
of human life, the level of living and the style of life—again,
we are concerned not with mathematically precise relations but
with trends—can be translated into such facts as the following:

1) Before 1800, the nations of the world were relatively
homogeneous regarding the level of living and the average life
expectancy. Technical progress destroyed that homogeneity. It
released a movement whose speed, very different in different
countries, eventually led to vast differences.

2) In this development, France occupies an average situation. She does not approach the high achievements of progress that might be expected, given her past and present role in the scientific and philosophical domain.

3) The accentuation of inequalities from nation to nation has been accompanied by a reduction of the inequalities recorded within each nation. This is especially true for the most advanced countries. Poor countries are high-rent countries with marked social inequality and a wide dispersion of wages and of average life expectancies.

4) The same forces that tend to lengthen life expectancy lead to the reduction of seasonal and annual fluctuations of mortality. In the traditional era, the first years of life were extremely hazardous, and mortality rates were greatly influenced—as was the level of living—by the seasons and even more by weather. By way of contrast, in technologically advanced nations, the level of living, style of life, and mortality tend to become increasingly independent of natural conditions and free of seasonal and annual fluctuations.

This constitutes a kind of demonstration on a global scale of what Pierre Vendryes[5] has called the autokinetic human tendency: the tendency to achieve more and more autonomy with respect to the external environment.

The consequences of increasing freedom from the environment are obviously innumerable. Some of them are distressing to the humanist, but I cannot believe, myself, that man is increasing his autonomy for no better purpose than to sacrifice the very reason behind his search for freedom—his intellectual and moral individuality.

GENERAL CONCLUSIONS

The seven preceding chapters have clearly shown, I hope, the force of the causal relationships that bind the level of living of any people to the productivity of their labor, and therefore to the scientific quality of their methods of production. We may now write that the productivity of labor is the independent variable of contemporary economic development. Not only is it one of the factors leading to improvement in the level of living, but it is the *preponderant and dominant factor* because it determines or conditions the others: rents, profits, interest rates, the value and income of capital, geographical distribution, labor force, wages and the ladder of wages, social action and social structure.

In this complex machinery of causes and effects, of actions and reactions, there appears a mainspring. This mainspring is important not only because it moves the rest, but also because it is possible for men to act upon it.

Consumption is a result of production. There can be no increase in the level of living without an increase of production.

It is illusory to pursue a short-term improvement in the purchasing power of wages in relation to *all* goods and services consumed. Substantial improvement in the ratio of wages to prices can only be obtained for certain products, those, for example, that show a significant reduction of the profit rate or a significant increase in the productivity of labor in a given period. This is the consequence of the law of value.

However, with increasing output, the pattern of consumption changes, and the improvement of the level of living demands not only an increase of production but a change in the nature of the goods produced, or, in other words, a change in the structure of production.

The structure of production in turn is a result of the distribution of the labor force among different occupations. There is therefore a nearly perfect functional relation between the three following phenomena:

1) the pattern of mass consumption
2) the structure of production, or national income
3) the distribution of the labor force.

If one wishes to modify the first of these structures, and this is necessary to improve the level of living, it is the third that must be manipulated. It alone is directly dependent, in the middle run, on ordinary human initiative.

Economic phenomena are essentially labor force phenomena. Monetary and budgetary facts, like credit, are only a screen between consumption and production. In order to estimate their effects on the level of living, we must estimate their effects on the distribution of the labor force and the volume of production in each occupation. The financial conception of the economic system imposed itself upon the classical economists because it was useful and valid in the traditional epoch, and by the force of tradition, continues to be held today in most countries—for example, in its Keynsian form. This traditional viewpoint reveals itself to be incomplete and less and less useful, because it leads us to think in terms of wealth and capital, of income, of profit, and of interest, when we ought to be thinking in terms of labor.

The productivity of labor is a joint effect of the natural conditions in which the worker finds himself and of the methods which he uses. These two sets of factors are ceaselessly changed and improved, changeable and subject to improvement, by technical progress under the influence of scientific progress. Natural environments not permitting human survival in 1700, like the Canadian plateau or Central Siberia, now contribute greatly to the world's life. The motor of the contemporary economic system is most surely the development of scientific knowledge.

Economic development being thus dominated by the development of technology, and this in turn by the development of science, the areas of economic studies and of the so-called exact sciences, that formerly appeared to be so distant, are now seen to be united; it is impossible to think of an economic system without reference to technology and thus to the whole of experimental science.

Economic history is only a branch of history. It is not possible to make any synthesis unless we study demographic, social and political facts, as well as economic facts. In our time especially, political facts are dominant and tend to orient the world's future.

There has been no question here of attempting such a synthesis. Our object can only be to provide certain source materials for those who may eventually try. Nevertheless, we must raise an objection in advance against certain critical commentators who are likely to propose an erroneous interpretation of the merely economic facts here described. This interpretation would be to attribute to the political regime the credit for economic progress realized during the past century. In reality, it must be said that technical progress has led to economic progress, not so much by means of the political and juridical regime, but in spite of it. By defending property, our law defends its necessary attributes, interest, rent, and profit. The entrepreneur seeks profit. To obtain it, he may seek technical progress, and thus stimulate economic progress. But it is only in this accessory fashion—outside of the initiative and even the awareness of the entrepreneur, and consequently as slightly and slowly as possible—that the search for profit leads to social progress. Larger and larger gaps are thus created between the real and the possible. Here we have studied only the real, but it requires only a little reflection on many of the pages of this book to appreciate what might have been obtained with modern technology if only the political, juridical, and social conditions in France had been less unfavorable to progress.

The improvement of scientific knowledge permits the raising of the level of living of the people. It is still necessary that man, when aware of the causalities imposed upon him by the real world, applies them to the daily realities of the production of consumable goods and services. In other words, it is still necessary that scientific progress be transformed into technical progress. Observation of the modern world shows that there is a considerable lag between scientific progress and technical progress, since scientific knowledge is usually placed at the disposition of the whole of humanity as soon as it is discovered, while technology has progressed at very different rhythms from India and China on the one hand to the Western world on the other, and from the pagan, Hindu, and Moslem civilizations to the Christian countries. The causes that have led a fraction of humanity to secure a lead over the rest, first in science and then in technology, that could not have been predicted by an observer of the previous history of these advanced nations, are still unknown. The study of this question is one of the essential tasks of our generation.[6] It is the study of the sources of human progress.

The confusion of ideas in these matters is so great that the very notion of human progress, in the middle of the twentieth

century, is still questioned by almost all Western philosophers.
Economic and social sciences do not give any place to the
concept of progress. The very word, they say in the schools,
has no scientific sense. The intellectual leaders of our time—
Huxley, Mauriac, Duhamel, Sartre—repeat for the length of
printed columns that humanity has arrived at the threshold
of the Apocalypse or else turns without rest in an infernal
circle. They find it only too easy to illustrate their theses by
some of the frightful adventures into which humanity has
recently been thrown.

No one seems to care at all about long-term trends. No
one seems to notice the passage of the popular masses from a
vegetal life to one that is not so limited. Not a word is said
about the disappearance of famines in the Western world.
No one is congratulated on the development of intellectual
culture, the opportunity of an increasing number of men to
enjoy higher education, or the extraordinary increase in the
means of aesthetic appreciation.

No one seems to suspect the existence of factors favorable
to individuality in the new tertiary civilization. A man who,
two centuries ago, would not even have learned to read, if he
had survived to maturity, profits by his windows, the central
heating of his apartment, and the 300,000 copies of the newspaper for which he writes, to announce that humanity has
arrived at the last stage of barbarism.

We may summarize the effect of technical progress on the
material life of man by saying that technical progress liberates
men from servile labor, increases the length of their life, enlarges their autonomy with respect to physiological needs and
the external environment, permits them to pass from a vegetal
phase to a mobile phase, allows the average man to have advanced education, and opens to him the path of intellectual
civilization.

Doubtless it may be said that if this inventory of the
economist is largely favorable, that of the moralist or sociologist
is not so at all. It is true that contemporary civilization runs
great risks and shows some alarming symptoms. My duty is
to draw attention to the fact that factors favorable to the development of a high intellectual civilization of individualistic

character are numerous in contemporary economic development and that there is no reason to assume that the unfavorable
factors will carry the day.

The maladjustments of the present day arise, in my opinion,
from the natural errors provoked in the human spirit by the
confusions of the transitional period between traditional civilization and the civilization of the future. Nothing is easier—
for us who live so short a time—and nothing is more dangerous
than to take as the direction of history what is only the direction of some few years of history.

Certainly it must be remembered that the area of human
knowledge is not delimited by the scientific method alone, and
that scientific and technical progress do not necessarily imply
human progress, by which I mean the progress of the total man.
It is as dangerous to appreciate technical progress while de-
nouncing the moral stagnation of humanity, as to expect
technical progress to solve all human problems.

More exactly, I believe that the essential evil of our century
arises from the difficulty we have in distinguishing those
elements in our heritage that belong to the scientific field and
must be constantly modified, from those that belong to the
moral and religious domain and that probably ought to be
conserved, or modified only with great prudence.[7]

$\mathcal{N}$otes to $\mathcal{C}$hapter VII

1. Among the most frightful mortalities that local archives reveal are: 300
per thousand in Copenhagen in 1711, 450 per thousand in Danzig in 1709, and
500 per thousand in Toulon in 1720. These three catastrophes were due to
smallpox.

2. Average life expectancy and probable life expectancy. The average life
expectancy is the total number of years lived by a group, divided by the number of people in the group. The probable (or median) life expectancy is the age
achieved by exactly half of the group. Average life expectancy can differ greatly
from probable life expectancy. It is very difficult, but very necessary to be precise when comparing mortality rates for different populations of different ages.

See Adolphe Landry, *Traité de démographie* (2nd ed., Payot, 1949), Ch. IV, by Sauvy, notably p. 203 ff.

3. Villermé, *Tableau de l'état physique et moral* . . . II, p. 245.

4. Jean Daric, *Mortalité, profession et situation sociale,* in *Population,* 1949, p. 671.

5. Pierre Vendryes, *Vie et Probabilité: L'acquisition de la science* (Albin Michel ed., Series, Science d'Aujourd'hui).

6. For a recent and perhaps successful attempt to answer this question, see W. Fred Cottrell, *Energy and Society.*

7. See my *Note sur la philosophie des sciences,* which attempts a solution of this key problem.

APPENDIX

MORE THAN 250,000 copies of Jean Fourastié's books had been issued by 1959. His principal works are the following:

IN ENGLISH (BOOKS AND ARTICLES)

"Economics and the Social Consequences of Technical Progress," *International Social Science Bulletin,* Summer, 1952.

"On the Autonomy of the Living Being," *Diogenes,* Summer, 1956.

"Predicting Economic Changes in Our Time," *Diogenes,* Winter, 1954.

"Productivity and Economics," *Political Science Quarterly,* Vol. LXVI (June, 1951).

Productivity, Prices, and Wages. Paris: OEEC, 1957. Pp. 113.

"The Statistical Measurement of Various Material Aspects of Economic Progress," *Economic Progress.* Papers of a round table held by the International Economic Association, 1955.

"Towards Higher Productivity in the Countries of Western Europe," *International Labour Review,* Vol. LXVII (April, 1953).

IN FRENCH AND OTHER LANGUAGES

La civilisation de 1975. Paris: Presses Universitaires de France. Pp. 130. In Spanish; Barcelona: Salvat. (Published also in Japanese.)

La comptabilité. Paris: Presses Universitaires de France. Pp. 128. (Published also in Portuguese.)

Documents pour l'histoire et la théorie des prix. Paris: Arman Colin, 1959. Pp. 844.

Le grand espoir du XXᵉ siècle. Paris: Presses Universitaires de France. Pp. 275. In German; Köln: Bund-Verlag. In Spanish; Barcelona: Luis Miracle.

Histoire de demain. Paris: Presses Universitaires de France, 1958. Pp. 125. (Published also in Japanese.)

Migration professionnelles: Évolution de la structure de la population active en quinze pays, 1910-55. Paris: Institut National d'Études Démographiques, 1957. Pp. 339.

Pourquoi nous travaillons. Paris: Presses Universitaires de France, 1959. Pp. 127.

La prévision économique. Paris: Presses Universitaires de France. Pp. 151. In Spanish; Barcelona: Bosch.

La productivité. Paris: Presses Universitaires de France. Pp. 128. In Italian; Milan: Garzenti. In Spanish; Barcelona: Editorial Direccion. (Published also in Portuguese and Japanese.)

Révolution à l'ouest. Paris: Presses Universitaires de France, 1957. Pp. 235.

INDEX

A

Academy of Moral and Political Sciences, 54
Accounts of the Château of Versailles, 131-32
Administration, 173-74
Aesthetics, 161
Africa, 101
Agriculture: duration of work in, 164, 172; mechanization of, 76; productivity, 15-16, 68, 85, 139-40, 185; wages in, in France, 29, 30; *see also* Land Usage
Air conditioning, 205-7
American Woman's Home, The (Beecher), 208
Angeville, 76
Asia, 101
Australia, 106, 107, 110
Automatism, 160-61

B

Balkans, 43, 60, 106
Baltic states, 106
Banks, 93
Bathtubs, 207-8
Beecher, Catherine, 208
Bézard, Yvonne, 68
Biology, 216
Bloch, Marc, 61
Bourgeois-Pichat, Jean, 223
Brave New World (Huxley), 14
Bread, 44-46, 59

Brousse, H., 114
Brouwer, Adrien, 64
Budget structure: alterations in, 52-54, 60; and class differences, 53-54; and national production, 140
Bulletin of the General Statistical Office of France, 110
Business expenses, 172

C

Calmette, 66
Caloric needs, 39-40, 41, 44, 50, 101-3
Canada, 106ff, 183, 222
Castro, Josué De, 7
Cattle, 42
Central America, 101
Cereals, 38-46, 59, 63
Ceylon, 218
Chapin, F. Stuart, 7
Château of Blois, 197
Château of Champs, 198
Child labor, 165-67
China, 43, 60, 101, 103, 105, 218, 223
Cities, 185-88, 194-95, 208
Civilisation de 1975, La (Fourastié), 109, 164
Clark, Colin, 7, 19n, 91, 100, 104
Clash of Progress and Security, The (Fisher), 19n
Closed economic systems, 120, 148
Clothing, 46-47, 82, 138

Colbert, Jean Baptiste, 32, 126, 131

Competition, 137

Conditions of Economic Progress (Clark), 7, 91, 100

Consumer goods; *see* Goods

Consumption: and level of living, 115, 116, 122-23, 124; and minimum subsistence, 141-42; and production of goods, 15-16, 120-23, 142, 226; and real wages, 36ff; schedules, 37ff; structure of, 22, 121, 142; *see also* Purchasing Power

Cost of living, 113

Cottrell, Fred, 7, 10

Crises: economic, and level of living, 144-45; of over-production, 79, 122

Currency, 29, 133

Cycles, in Middle Ages, 68

D

Daguin, 32

D'Avenel, 29, 125

Denmark, 222

Depression of 1929, 108

Depressions, 34

Deprez, 66

Dessirier, 112

Duhamel, Georges, 14

Dumontier, Jacques, 90

Dupont de Nemours, Pierre, 27

Duration of work, 164-74, 178

Duvau, 83

E

Earnings; *see* Income

Economic development, 227-30; *see also* Technical progress

Education: curriculum, 178-79; in France, 176, 178-79, 190-91; increase in, 92, 96; school population, 175-78, 179; in suburbs, 190

Egypt, 218

Electricity, 212, 213

Employment, 34ff; *see also* Unemployment

Energy and Society (Cottrell), 7

England, 110-11, 173, 193, 222

Epidemics, 66

Equalization of working hours, 169-70

Equilibrium, 14, 16

F

Famine, 7, 15, 40, 59, 60-62, 65-66, 68-69, 70, 118-19

Febvre, Lucien, 26

Félix, 32-34

Finland, 218

Fisher, Alan B., 19n

Flèche, Augustin, 65

Fleury, André de, 66

Food, 93, 94, 138; described by Young, 72; percentage of budget, 44-46, 52-54, 60, 138; storage of, 61; *see also* Bread; Wheat

Fragonard, Jean Honoré, 64

France, 138, 210; cereal production, 43; depression in, 137; described by Vauban, 26-27;

described by Young, 70-74; duration of work, 170, 173; education in, 176, 178-79, 190-91; eighteenth century, 69-74; housekeeping in, 196-98; housing, 183-84, 186, 192-96, 197-98, 202; life expectancy, 222; Middle Ages, 63-69; mortality in, 217-18; nineteenth century, 75-96; and other nations, 100-16; periods of level of living, 59-96; purchasing power, 36ff, 133; salaries in, 28-36; style of life pre-1800, 154-55

Francis I, 68

Friedmann, Georges, 11, 13, 76, 160

Froment, 90

G

General History (Glotz), 65

General Planning Commission, 90

General Statistical Office of France, 28, 88, 89

Geography of Hunger (De Castro), 7

Germany, 108, 110

Giedion, Siegfried, 207

Glaber, Raoul, 65, 66

Glass, 129-30, 201-2, 206

Glotz, Gustave, 65

Good Housekeeping, 210

Goods and services, 92-94; control of production, 15; prices of, 36, 105; primary, 127, 147; secondary, 127, 147; suburban, 190; tertiary, 127, 147; *see also* Production; Purchasing power; Technical progress

Grand Espoir du XXe Siècle (Fourastié), 173-74

Great Britain, 106, 107, 110

Guerry, 76

H

Hanauer, Father, 29, 63, 125, 126

Hauser, Henri, 125

Haussmann, Georges-Eugène, 186

Haute Autorité de la Communauté Européenne du Charbon et de l'Acier, 55

Health, 93; *see also* Hygiene; Life expectancy

Heating, 184, 203-5

History of Socialism (Jaurès), 38

History of the Middle Ages (Calmette and Deprez), 66-67

Hitler, Adolph, 187

Holland, 222

Homogeneity, 154

Housekeeping, 196-200, 209-12

Housing: air conditioning in, 205-7; in cities, 185-88, 194-95; construction, 193-96; development of, 182-84, 191-92, 197-202; in France, 65, 71, 183-84, 186, 192-96, 197; geography of, 184ff; heating in, 203-5; improvements in, 82-83, 130; kitchens, 209-11;

monetary value, 47; in sub-
urbs, 188-91; *chart, 138*
Hungary, 108
Huxley, Aldous, 14
Hygiene, 71-72, 83, 224

I

Income, 92, 106, 108, 110, 112,
114, 138; in depressions, 34;
determination of, 22, 28; distribution, 139-44; in economic
crisis, 144-45; national, 90,
103-8, 125; nominal, 104; real
per capita, 90ff, 103-8, 113-14;
seventeenth-century   France;
32-34; *see also* Wages
India, 43, 60, 101, 102, 123, 218,
222
Individual initiative, 163
Industrial revolution, 75-76, 84-
85, 159, 185-86, 198
Insulation; *see* Sound insulation
Intellectual work, 172-73, 201,
205-6
International Labor Office, 169-
70
*Inventory of the Physical and
Moral Condition of Workers
Employed in the Manufacture
of Cotton, Wool and Silk* (Villermé), 76
Italy, 60

J

Jaccard, Pierre, 19n

Japan, 185
Jaurès, Jean, 30, 38

K

Kuczynski, J., 88
Kugner, 125
Kuznets, Simon, 104

L

La Bruyère, Jean de, 26
Labor: child, 165-67; distribu-
tion of, 139, 140, 171, 226; di-
vision of, 159; and economic
crises, 145; in housing construction, 193-95; mobility of,
122, 123, 124; and production, 121-22, 139; productivity
of, 225-26, 227; unskilled, in
France, 30-31, 36, 38, 51;
chart, 92
Labrousse, Ernest, 30, 39, 44, 62,
68, 69-70
Laissez-faire, 124
Land: devaluation, 136-37; rents
and profits, 135ff; usage, 42-44
League of Nations, 100
Leisure, 173, 174
Le Nain, Louis, 64
Le Play, Pierre, 54
Lehoulier, 110
Levasseur, Ernest, 21, 34, 44, 76,
219
Level of living, 92-94; average,
70, 87; defined, 17-18, 21; dis-
parity in, between countries,

23, 60, 101-16, 225; duration of work, 170; and economic crises, 144-45; historical evolution, 28-55, 60-96; improvement in, 75ff, 81-83, 124ff, 145, 226; and industrial revolution, 84; and labor force, 121-23; and life span, 215, 224-25; and mortality, 218; periods of, 59-60; and productivity, 121-23; and style of life, 155, 170; yearly variations, 62-63

Life expectancy, 215-25

Life of Workers under the Second Empire, The (Duvau), 83

Lighting, 184

Louis XII, 68

Louis, Paul, 30, 76

Mechanisation Takes Command (Giedion), 207

Medicines, 216-17

Meuvret, M., 39n

Middle Ages, 63-69

Military: conscription, 219; wages, 34

Minimum subsistence, 22, 39, 41; evolution of idea of, 46-54, 58; and per capita consumption, 141-42; standard ration of Villermé, 76

Monopolies, 40

Morogues, Baron de, 45

Mortality, 217-18, 219-20, 221ff, 225; *see also* Life expectancy

Mussolini, Benito, 187

N

National income, 90, 103-8, 112, 125, 141-44

National product, 140, 155, 169; *see also* Production

New York (N.Y.), 188

New Zealand, 102, 106

Noiret, 80

Noise, 202-3

North Africa, 60

Norway, 183, 222

Nutrition, 77-79, 101-3, 216-17; *see also* Food

M

Machines, 160-62; domestic, 208-14; modern home as, 183-84; and progress, 17

Machinisme: and aesthetics, 161; and automatism, 160-61; defined, 13n, 17; and individuality, 161-63; and productivity, 161-63

Machinisme et Humanisme (Friedmann), 160

Maison Française, La, 210

Man with Forty Crowns, The (Voltaire), 142-44

Manpower; *see* Labor

Marchal, Jean, 84

Marx, Karl, 145

O

Occupational life, 159-63

Occupations, increase in, 159

Officials, 33

Overproduction, 79, 122

P

Peasants: in art, 63-64; described by Young, 73-74; in Second Empire, 85

Pirenne, Henri, 67

Plumbing, 184, 198-99

Poland, 204

Political action, 168ff, 172

Politique de l'Emploi et de l'Education (Jaccard), 19n

Population, 92; and famine, 61, 118-19; increase in, 70, 75, 84, 85; optimum, 118; school, 175-78

Pouvoir Et L'Opinion, Le (Sauvy), 173

Prices, 92, 126, 134; determination of, 37; evolution of, 87; and imperfect competition, 137; and productivity, 129-35; and reduction of labor time, 171; stability of, 78; and technical progress, 37, 86-87, 126-28; variations in, 40, 62, 125ff

Production, 140; annual, per employed worker, 107; and consumption, 120-21, 122-23, 139, 142; control of, 15; cost of, 134; national, 140, 155; over-, 79, 122; and purchasing power, 86; real product per capita, 95, 111, 122; structure of, 121, 122, 138, 140, 142, 226

Productivity: in construction, 193-96; defined, 119, 146; increase in, 122; of labor, 225-26, 227; and *machinisme,* 161-63; and purchasing power, 124ff; and rents and profits, 137; and selling price, 129ff; and technical progress, 123-24, 146-47

Profits, 137, 145, 146-47

Projet de Dîme Royale (Vauban), 21, 26-27, 44

Purchasing power, 18, 88, 114; development of, 50-54, 58, 86ff, 127; disparity in, between countries, 104-16; in economic crises, 145; in eighteenth century, 44; and income distribution, 139-44; loss of, 53; and methods of production, 86; and productivity, 124ff; and technical progress, 129-35, 146; of wages, 36ff, 108-14; of working class, 86-96

Puritanism, 8

R

Radio, 211

Real product per capita; *see under* Production

Regressions, 111

Rents: and cost of production, 134; freezing of, in France, 193; in low productivity countries, 120; and technical progress, 135-38

Revue Internationale du Travail, 109

S

Salaries, 28ff, 56; *see also* Wages
Sauvy, Alfred, 118, 173
Savings, 93
Schools, 190-91; *see also* Education
Science, 123, 215ff, 227, 228; *see also* Technical progress
Second empire, 85
Serfdom, 15
Sévigné, Madame de, 154
Sewers, 210
Simiand, François, 28, 109, 125-26
Simon, Jules, 80
Socialism, 141
Sound insulation, 203
South America, 101, 102, 106
Soviet Union, 102, 106, 185, 204
Spain, 60
Spengler, Oswald, 13
Storage; *see under* Food
Stoves, 204
Strikes, 36
Style of life: defined, 18-19; disparities in, 153; education, 175-79; elements of, 156; France pre-1800, 154-55; homogeneity of, 154; housekeeping, 196; housing, 182-96; improvements in, 195; and industrial revolution, 84; and level of living, 155, 170; and life expectancy, 224-25; working conditions, 164-74
Suburbs, 189ff
Sweden, 110-11, 176, 183, 218, 222
Switzerland, 222

T

Teachers, 176
Technical progress: complexity of, 174; and economic progress, 228-33; and improvement in level of living, 129-35, 146-47; as independent variable, 141, 224; machines in, 17; and occupational structure, 162; and price trends, 37, 86-87, 126-28; and productivity, 123-24; and purchasing power, 129-35; and reduction of labor time, 171; and rents and profits, 137-38; and school population, 175, 179
Telephones, 211
Television, 211
Time: and economic efficiency, 170; and production, 121, 122
Toynbee, Arnold, 13
Transportation, 93, 189
Tristan, Flora, 80
Turgot, Anne Robert, 46

U

Unemployment, 34, 75, 79, 145

Uniformity of work reduction, 171

United Nations, 101, 102

United States: construction in, 193; education in, 176, 191; electricity in, 213; housing in, 183, 187; housekeeping in, 196; life expectancy in, 222; purchasing power in, 105-6, 133; work week, 168

Unskilled labor, 30-31, 36, 38, 51, 92; *see also* Working class

Urbanization, 75-76, 79-80, 184-86

V

Valéry, Paul, 14

Vauban, Sébastien, 26-27, 34, 44, 46, 47, 63

Velocity of production; *see* Productivity

Vendryes, Pierre, 225

Versailles, 197-98

Villeneuve-Bargemont, 76

Villermé, 21, 45, 47, 76-78, 80-81, 82, 219

Vincent de Paul, St., 63

Voltaire, 142

Voyage in France (Young), 70-74

W

Wages, 31, 33, 35, 89, 92; aver-

ages, in France, 28ff; in economic crisis, 144-45; eighteenth-century France, 70; evolution of, 89; and prices, 126, 128; and purchasing power, 36ff, 108-16, 128; real, 36, 86ff, 108; of unskilled labor, 30-31; variations in, 22, 62

Water supply, 208

Welfare, 17

Wheat, 38ff, 85, 92

"White Negroes," 81

Windows, 201-2, 206

Wolfe, Martin, 19n

Women, 29ff

Work week, 86, 91, 168

Working class: food budget, 44-46; nutrition of, 76-79; purchasing power of, 41, 86-89; real per capita income, 90ff; style of life, 168ff; working conditions, 80-81

Working day, 86, 155

World Population and Production, Trends and Outlook (Woytinsky), 110

World War I, 76, 85, 90

World War II, 76, 108, 170, 192

Woytinsky, W. S. and E. S., 110

Y

Young, Arthur, 21, 46, 70-74